The Tales We Tell

Recent Titles in
Contributions to the Study of World Literature

The Tales We Tell

Perspectives on the Short Story

Edited by
Barbara Lounsberry, Susan Lohafer,
Mary Rohrberger, Stephen Pett, and
R. C. Feddersen

Under the Auspices of the Society
for the Study of the Short Story

Contributions to the Study of World Literature, Number 88

Greenwood Press
Westport, Connecticut • London

Library of Congress Cataloging-in-Publication Data

The tales we tell : perspectives on the short story / edited by
Barbara Lounsberry . . . [et al.] ; under the auspices of the Society
for the Study of the Short Story.
p.   cm.—(Contributions to the study of world literature,
ISSN 0738–9345 ; no. 88)
Includes bibliographical references and index.
ISBN 0–313–30396–7 (alk. paper)
1. Short story.   I. Lounsberry, Barbara.   II. Series.
PN3373.T44   1998
808.3′1—DC21   97–13712

British Library Cataloguing in Publication Data is available.

Library of Congress Catalog Card Number: 97–13712
ISBN: 0–313–30396–7
ISSN: 0738–9345

First published in 1998

Greenwood Press, 88 Post Road West, Westport, CT 06881
An imprint of Greenwood Publishing Group, Inc.

Printed in the United States of America

The paper used in this book complies with the
Permanent Paper Standard issued by the National
Information Standards Organization (Z39.48–1984).

10 9 8 7 6 5 4 3

Contents

Introduction

Susan Lohafer

This volume has its origins in the story of short fiction theory. Without that often lonely history of a field-in-the-making, we might never have had the outpouring of scholarship, dialogue, criticism, and sheer delight in the short story captured in these pages.

As everyone knows, the first theorist of the short story was Edgar Allan Poe. He gave us our primary emphases in discussions of the form: style; brevity; status. He identified what he called the short prose tale, and told us it could be read in one sitting. He placed it once and for all between the lyric poem, with its power to concentrate effect, and prose forms like the novel and the sketch, with their power to represent the world. He was a writer of the very form he defined, and he gave short story theory a practitioner bias it has to this day.

For Poe, the short story was nearly at the top of the pantheon of genres. It was, after all, the form he and Nathaniel Hawthorne reimagined, turning the stuff of tales and sketches into poetically crafted, resonant short fiction. However, Poe's theories and practice were co-opted by the hacks of later decades when the short story was too often seen as a formula-driven genre for slick magazines. Long inaccurate, the stigma lingered in the air of condescension with which stories were viewed as apprenticeship for the novel.

Then, in the first quarter of the twentieth-century, writers of the short story found a dominant image—the organic form so lyrically described by, among others, Sherwood Anderson, Katherine Anne Porter, and Elizabeth Bowen. Stories grew from seeds, these writers said. The intensity of the form came from subjective points of view, pervasive imagery, controlled tone, ellipsis—in short, the techniques of impressionism. Porter was a practicing argument for the highbrow status of this nuanced art in the Joyced world of High Modernism. In the decades following her famous little jibe—"No Plot, My Dear, No Story"—the short story became the favorite "demo" narrative for New Criticism and the cult of close reading.

Although today we have waded free of *explications de texte*, most short story theorists, no matter what their ideology or method, continue to care about the aesthetics of language, the layering of meaning. You will see that concern frequently in this volume, quite strikingly, for instance, in the work on graphic analogues: filmed versions of famous passages in well-known stories (as discussed by H. R. Stoneback and Brenda O. Daly), or visual imagery (as in Susan Jaret McKinstry's look at the use of photographs in Anne Beattie's stories).

The plot of short fiction theory heated up in the 1960s with pioneering work in two areas that later drifted apart: the history and aesthetics of the form, and the social dynamics of genre. Mary Rohrberger turned Hawthorne's art into modernist theory, and quite fittingly, she'll have the penultimate word in *this* volume. Frank O'Connor, the famous Irish practitioner-critic, linked the short story with the angst and rebellion of excluded peoples, whom he called "submerged populations." It is a phrase that has haunted short story criticism ever since. Recent work on fiction by and about persons marginalized by region, gender, politics, or disease owes much to O'Connor's perception, and is candidly discussed in the pages ahead.

Later theorists, including myself, were influenced by other developments in the 1960s: by the newly translated Russian Formalists who targeted the form, and by the anthropo-linguistic Structuralists, whose work led not only to narratology, but eventually to discourse analysis. The definition of story seemed to lie in the origins of culture, the morphology of folktales, the oral tradition, the circuits of the brain. Brevity was understood as an abbreviated narrative grammar—a notion psychologists are now updating, as you will see in the rare glimpse here into the work of cognitive scientists who study literature.

The 1970s brought the second wave of academic genre criticism, or really a lone whitecap—Charles May's *Short Story Theories*, a collection of writings—some famous, some little known—about the form itself. (In *The Tales We Tell*, by the way, he's in the vanguard again, with his studies of short fiction pedagogy and computer technology.) Finally, in the 1980s, reception theory filtered in. The short story was defined in terms of the reading experience it generates, and that meant a return to Poe's emphasis on the imminence of endings. A number of books appeared in that decade, including John Gerlach's *Toward the End*, my own *Coming to Terms with the Short Story*, and, with a rather different set of emphases, Valerie Shaw's *A Short Story: A Critical Introduction*.

In 1989, Jo Ellyn Clarey and I put together a collection of essays intended to map the field of short fiction studies up to that point. It was by no means exhaustive. Other contributions have come from Ross Chambers, from the British critics Clare Hanson and Dominic Head, and from a host of people who have studied the short stories of a particular era or culture. It seems clear that a third wave of academic interest has begun, expressed not only in print but also in the international conferences on the short story held in Paris and Iowa and in the formation of The Society for the Study of Short Stories.

We are seeing the end of the romance of the short story critic and theorist as "outsider," fitting as that label may have been for devotees of the "lonely voice" genre. Students of the form are looking askance now at the very boundaries that brought the field into existence (tale versus sketch, novel versus story, oral versus written . . .). We're losing our defensiveness about genre; we're bored by taxonomies. Indeed, discussions of the short story tend now to be genre-bending and interdisciplinary, as many chapters in this volume suggest. Take, for example, the musings of Gay Talese on relations between fiction's art and artful nonfiction or Mary Swander's account of turning journalistic interviews into storied essays.

John Barth, invited to discuss the short story, avers a preference for novels, spinning, all the while, a witty tale that illuminates both genres. Robert Coover's lively essay is, among other things, an imbrication of history and story, text and hypertext, that teases and instructs. In short, this book is a rich and varied introduction to the opinions, theories, and research of people who take stories seriously, but often tell tales on themselves. The storytellers who speak at greatest length here (Barth, Coover, Joyce Carol Oates, Barry Hannah, Leslie Marmon Silko, and W. P. Kinsella) offer a range of tonalities—whimsical, poignant, polemical, or brash. Their voices, distributed throughout the volume, bracket the critical discussions of new and old issues in the study of short stories.

The traditional view of the form as compressed, unified, "stripped down," is humorously tweaked by Barth, and, in the process, underlined. However, writers of story cycles reveal that narratives may grow and re-form, defying the logic of genre categories. Gerald Lynch, in contrast, systematically applies classic genre theory to the history of Canadian story cycles.

Today's ongoing debate over "minimalism" shows up here, too, with Ewing Campbell offering an appropriately lean and telling definition for this much-abused term. We can also see how revisionist concerns can be solidly grounded in short story aesthetics, as in Hilary Siebert's essay on one of our best-known minimalists, Raymond Carver. Tensions between author and editor come to life in discussions of the publishing scene. We see this tension in high relief in the dual roles of writer/editors like Joyce Carol Oates and Claire Larriere, and in the challenges faced by short story anthologists like Ann Charters.

For me, one of the most exciting revelations of this volume is the survival, in so many new forms, of the old duality in the short story's life: its connection with primary ways of knowing the world, yet its easy adjustment to—or, indeed, its prefiguring of—the newest themes and techniques in literary representation. Barry Sanders finds the short story twinned with the joke, and traces both back to Chaucer—and the instinct for play. Silko describes the short story in terms of "fractals," elemental hints of a shape-in-the-making, and Ian Reid explores the fundamental ways in which stories "frame" experience. From four psychologists—Steven R. Yussen, William F. Brewer, Paul E. Jose, and Erwin M. Segal—we learn that story processing entails cognitive strategies that are certainly "learned," but rely, perhaps, on "hard-wiring" as well.

All of these suggestions point to the primal nature of storying as a human activity, a powerful simplicity beneath the trickiest text. The very primacy of that appeal, taken with the peculiar alignment of the short story with the marginalized speaker, gives the form high visibility in today's debates over cultural diversity and social concern versus literary hegemony. Barbara C. Ewell talks about the short story's role in creating a space in the South for two side-lined groups, women and African Americans. Roger Berger and Reid, speaking of the story in Africa and Australia respectively, place the story in colonial and postcolonial literatures. Feminist perspectives are in the foreground of what Ewell and Silko have to say, as well as Daly's discussion of a story by Oates, but similar issues play, for example, through the essay on Raymond Carver. AIDS, the most timely of topics, both "in" and "out" as a subject for short stories, is brought to our attention by Sharon Oard Warner. The oldest form and the newest themes have, as we see in this volume, a mutual attraction.

In an era when "literary" study is under review, when the profession is divided by splintering interests, the contributors to this book offer spirited testimony to the enduring value of one form in particular. Along with the confessions and the criticism, you will find here a knowing and vivid appreciation of narratives that deal with the eternally particular in human experience.

The Tales We Tell

A Novel Perspective:
"It's a Short Story"

John Barth

The title of this essay is something like "It's a Short Story," for it concerns this writer's love affair with that literary genre, and although my regard for it is long standing and ongoing, our actual affair was brief. An early-middlescent fling is all it was, really, in the tumultuous 1960s, when the form was a-hundred-and-thirtysomething and pretty well domesticated, but I was thirty-plus and restless; an unprecedented (and unsuccedented) infidelity, it was, to my true love and helpmeet, the novel—whereto my steadfast commitment had produced four robust offspring already by the time I tell of, and has produced another four since, and bids to produce at least one more yet. For a season, however (a maxi-novelist's season: about six years), I strayed. It was a sweet and productive *liaison dangereuse*, the fruits of which were one volume of short stories in 1968 and a trio of novellas in 1972: resonant dates (the first especially) in our nation's political-cultural history, with a special poignancy in my personal scriptorial history.

You hear in what terms I recollect that interlude, no doubt pumping up the recollection a bit in its retelling. That is because I am by temperament monogamous; it was a relief to put that memorable aberration behind me and come back to husbanding the genre of the novel. And I have gone straight ever since—twenty years clean now! Though I still remember. . . . Well: It *is* a short story, even though it commences with a digression. I shall retell it discreetly, as such stories should be told. I'll even drop, to everyone's relief including mine, the sexual metaphor: *Auf Wiedersehen*, sexual metaphor.

*

"A yacht race! A yacht race!"
Is that exclamation familiar to all of you? (To any of you? To some of you?) The story goes, no doubt apocryphally, that in 1872, just after *War and Peace*

had been published, Count Tolstoy woke from a nightmare with that exclamation (in Russian, it goes something like "*Parusnaya regatta!*"), realizing
that he had neglected to include a yacht race in his vast novel; his only omission from the whole panorama of nineteenth-century human activity. (For that
reason, I made certain to incorporate, in one of my own novels, both a yacht
race and this Tolstoy anecdote, so that when unfriendly critics like Tom Wolfe
charge me with insufficient social realism, I can reply that I have touched bases
overlooked even by Leo Tolstoy.)

Whatever the truth of the yacht-race story, it certainly sounds to me like the
bad dream of a novelist, not a short story writer. That the genre of the novel
tends toward inclusion, that of the short story toward exclusion, goes without
saying, once one has allowed for plenty of exceptional instances on both sides
—minimalist novels, maximalist not-so-short stories. Those exceptions granted, we may safely generalize that short story writers as a class, from Poe to
Paley, incline to see how much they can leave out, and novelists as a class, from
Petronius to Pynchon, how much they can leave in. Many a fictionist of the last
century and this has moved with apparent ease between the modes, not only at
some point in her or his career, but right through it: Joyce Carol Oates, John
Updike, Robert Coover, who have you. Plenty more work the short form abun-
dantly in the earlier part of their careers and then, for one reason or another,
practice it seldom or never thereafter: James Joyce, Ernest Hemingway, William Faulkner, Philip Roth, Kurt Vonnegut—the list is long. Do we know of
any writers, I wonder, who abandoned the novel form in mid or late career and
devoted their literary energies exclusively thereafter to the short story?

In any case, more populous than any of those three categories are the categories (a) of congenital short story writers who seldom, perhaps never, publish a
novel (Chekhov, Borges, Alice Munro, Raymond Carver, Mike Martone) and
(b) of congenital novelists who never or seldom publish a short story (Ralph
Ellison, William Styron, most of the big Victorians, not to mention Richardson,
Fielding, Smollett, Jane Austen, and the other pre-Poe novelists—this category
is the most populous of all). It seems reasonable to infer that despite numerous
exceptions, by and large there is a temperamental, even a metabolical, difference between devout practitioners of the two modes, as between sprinters and
marathoners. To such dispositions as Poe's, Maupassant's, Chekhov's, or
Donald Barthelme's, the prospect of addressing a single, discrete narrative
project for three, four, five years (perhaps for seventeen or twenty-two) would
be appalling—*atrocious*, I imagine, would have been Borges's adjective, not to
mention aesthetically unseemly, perhaps presumptuous, at this advanced hour
of the print medium. Such novels as such writers perpetrate, if any (I think of
Barthelme's four, of Maupassant's four also, I believe), are slender, econom-
ical: They are the hors d'oeuvres or side dishes, paradoxically, to the chef
d'oeuvre of their short stories. (Knowing that Barthelme's novels did not come
to him as naturally as his short stories, I once very tentatively asked him, in the
period of his wrestling with *The Dead Father* how that project was coming

along. "Oh, it's finished," he replied. "Now all I have to do is *write* the damn thing.") Conversely, to many of us the prospect of inventing every few weeks a whole new ground-conceit, situation, cast of characters, plot, perhaps even voice, is as dismaying as would be the prospect of improvising at that same interval a whole new identity. Indeed, for some of us that analogy is so rigorous as to be more an identity itself than an analogy. Like hermit crabs (up to a point), we comfortably *live* in the shell of our project-in-progress, and do not shed it until we must, and feel naked and uncomfortable until we've found another to inhabit. Once every few years is quite often enough for that.

I say "we" because, except for the six-year lapse aforecited, I am willy-nilly of the camp of the congenital novelists. This circumstance is nowise an aesthetic principle (congenitality doesn't operate by aesthetic principle; it cobbles up a suitable aesthetics ex post facto); it's a metabolical donnée. I didn't plan or presuppose it; congenitality doesn't make such plans and presuppositions. Like everybody else in post-World War II America, I started out writing short stories in an entry-level creative writing workshop. More particularly, I happened to stumble into virtual charter membership in the second oldest creative writing program in our republic, although not the second oldest creative writing *course*. This was 1947; the Johns Hopkins program had been established just the year before, and the only other such operation in existence then (so we at Hopkins believe, anyhow) was Paul Engle's in Iowa, already by that time of some dozen years' standing (up at Harvard, Albert Guerard was coaching the likes of John Hawkes and Robert Creeley, but his was an isolated workshop, not a degree-granting program—of which we now have, God help us, above 400 in the USA). The poetry workshops at Johns Hopkins in those maiden years were respectably professional, presided over by Elliott Coleman and by Karl Shapiro (who had just won a Pulitzer prize), with the distinguished Spanish poet Pedro Salinas standing by in a neighboring department. But the fiction operation was unavoidably makeshift; one would have had to look far to find a career fiction writer of any stature employed by an American university in the 1940s (Robert Penn Warren is about the only one whose name comes to mind—and he was at least one-third poet and one-third critic).

I myself had signed up as a journalism major, an even more makeshift curriculum—though it doesn't seem to have damaged Russell Baker, who was one year ahead of me. Our journalistic requirements, interestingly, included the entry-level fiction writing course, and so it came to pass that my first creative writing coach was a veteran Marine Corps combat officer and fledgling literary scholar pressed into service by our short-handed department while he finished his dissertation on Edgar Poe. The departmental reasoning must have been that inasmuch as Poe first codified the modern short story, a Poe scholar could run the workshop. I have written of this chap elsewhere: a gentle Mississippian who encouraged us raw recruits to call him Bob; whose deep-Dixie accent charmed *writing* into *rotting*; who urged upon our attention such exemplary rotters as William Faulkner, Eudora Welty, and R. P. Warren (one discerns a certain principle of selection there); who, because he had no creative-rotting aspirations himself, was oddly respectful, even a touch deferential, to those of us who callowly so presumed. Bob's seminar—we seem not to call them *workshops* at Johns Hopkins—was a whole academic year long and could be repeated for credit, as the department had not many course offerings in those days. Bob's gentle requirement of apprentice aspirants to the craft of rotting fiction was a story every two weeks—and these, mind you, were the byegone days of honest fifteen-week semesters, before the campus riots of the 1960s frightened administrators into shortening the U.S. college semester to thirteen weeks, a whole story's worth of time (*two* stories' worth per academic year; *four* stories' worth over two years.) So: fifteen weeks times two times two divided by two gives thirty stories minimum that I must have written for Bob in my first two years' apprenticeship. Nowadays the number would be a piddling twenty-six stories, if any workshop in the land still requires a story every fortnight, no excuses or late papers accepted (Bob was gentle; Bob was respectful and soft-spoken; but Bob was a veteran Marine combat officer, whose deadlines one tended not to diddle with).

It is well for me that all this was the case, for I had been ill-educated in general, had next to no familiarity with the vast corpus of literature and no prior experience of or interest in the art of writing fiction. I was a disappointed musician, a Juilliard dropout scrabbling around for some other vocation, and I had squandered my high school reading budget mainly on the likes of Ellery Queen and Agatha Christie in mass-market paperbacks, which had just been invented. What I turned out for Bob and my fellow novices in those two years was unrelievedly abysmal in every particular except grammar, spelling, and punctuation, at all of which I was reasonably competent. Those manuscripts were letter-graded: Mine scored C's, mainly; the odd D, the occasional B, for two full years, and this from the most considerate of coaches—who, however, had his standards. It was rotten rotting; altogether talentless twaddle. No false modesty here; the stuff was unredeemed garbage, for although I was in that same period taking unto myself a freight of literature—not just the canonical classics plus Bob's Southerners plus the monumental European and expatriate American high Modernists, Pound/Eliot/Joyce/Proust/Mann/Kafka (whom the literature departments back then wouldn't touch, but our maverick writing department did), but also, and extracurricularly, the likes of Rabelais and Boccaccio and Scheherazade and Somadeva—although, as I say, I was on-loading the literary corpus in straight shifts, it was going unsystematically into an all-but-empty cargo hold, and so it took some stevedoring indeed before the vessel ballasted into even rudimentary stability.

No more of this; I'm sure it's a story with analogues in the experience of many, and it is not what this present story means to be about. I don't want, either, to give the impression that *literature* is the main thing one needs to learn about if one aspires to write it, although I certainly do believe it to be *one* of the main things. I can't help wondering, though, how it would have gone

with my apprenticeship if semesters in those days had been of their present ab-
breviation, for it was not until Story no. 30—more particularly, it was not until
the *closing passage* of that final item of my two-year stretch of random Bob-
bing on the ocean of story—that I had what amounted, by my then standards, to
a "breakthrough." Number 30 itself was little better than its twenty-nine predecessors: a presumptuous bit of bogus realism about the postwar adjustment
problems of . . . *a Marine combat veteran*, of all imaginable human categories—the whole thing largely derivative from Hemingway's "Soldier's Home"
without Hemingway's authentic knowledge of his material, not to mention
Hemingway's literary skills. But the story's denouement contrived to soar from
wretchedness up to mediocrity with a most un-Hemingwayish purple stream-of-
consciousness passage that, while also bogus, derivative, and overwritten to
boot, was nonetheless not without a certain rhetorical force. It was duly praised
therefore by Bob and my fellow seminarians, and published in an ephemeral
undergraduate lit mag (a tautology, I suppose).

It took no more than that to persuade me of my vocation, though by no means
yet of my talent for that vocation. Still a junior undergraduate, two years shy of
voting age, I immediately married the woman I was living with and com-
menced churning out children and fiction with equal facility and no thought for
the morrow. "The Fifties," John Updike somewhere sighs, "when everybody
was pregnant." The babies survived and thrived; the short stories (for that is
what I was writing: stories, stories, stories) suffered a 100 percent infant mor-
tality rate. Their constituent prose sentences, it may be, slowly improved in
grace and efficiency—the case could scarcely be otherwise, given the number of
them that I was generating and the stacks of good literature—literal library
stacks of it—that I was unsystematically running through. But my plots were
gimmicky and my characterizations inauthentic; my psychological penetration
was barely subcutaneous and my texture of rendered sensory detail unimpres-
sive. Moreover, like many American undergraduate writing apprentices, I had
not anything to say nor, had I had, any *Weltanschauung* to afford me a handle
on it. (Which of those two is logically prior doesn't matter here; to para-
phrase Beckett, having neither chicken nor egg, I had neither egg nor chicken.)
What I did have were an all but reality-proof sense of calling, an unstoppable
narrativity, and, I believe, a not bad ear for English. I have coached many an
apprentice since who manifested something like that mix of strengths and
shortcomings, and relatively few of the opposite sort—young aspiring writers
with a strong sense of who they are and what their material and their handle
on it is, but little sense of either story or language. I regard that latter syn-
drome as by far the less promising, although I would be reluctant to tell the
patient so. Experience may confer narrative focus and authority, perhaps even
a world view, but essential imaginativeness and articulateness, not to say elo-
quence, are surely much more of a gift.

My other problem—as I came to understand in retrospect but could not then,
nor could any just routinely knowledgeable coach have told me—was the *form*

that we all were working, and that nearly every fiction-workshopper cuts his/her teeth on, with good pedagogical reason: I mean the *form* of the modern short story, as articulated by Edgar Poe, developed by Maupassant and Chekhov and the rest, and celebrated in this volume. Its aesthetics were simply not my cup of tea; but in those days (and in many more fiction workshops than not to *this* day) it was the only aesthetic on the menu. *Compression*, it turns out, was not my strong suit; *showing instead of telling* was not my strong suit; neither were implicativeness, singleness of effect, epiphanic peripety, psychological realism, or for that matter realism in general. But those suits were regarded almost unquestioningly as the indispensable, indeed the only, ones for a properly modern writer, which I certainly aspired to be. It would have taken an extraordinarily large-viewed coach in the American academic 1940s to have seen that a subtle and inhibitory conflation was operating there, of the terms *modern* and *Modernist*. What a few of us really needed to do (I see now but could scarcely have seen then) was to invent or be invented by Postmodernism, as I understand that term in its best literary-aesthetic application—but that's another story, to which I'll presently return.

Meanwhile, back in the seminar room, there one was, fretting away at that artistically splendid and pedagogically effective but, for some of us, hyperconstrictive, more or less constipative form, the modern short story. Surely it's a truism by now that the admirable efflorescence of the American short story in recent decades is owing to the proliferation of our college creative writing programs: not simply the raw number of young writers being spawned therein like blue-crab larvae in Chesapeake Bay (and confronting a similar statistical fate), but the prevailing pedagogical assumption, anyhow belief, that the most suitable vehicle for their training is the "classical" modern short story as aforedescribed. Understand, please, that I have no serious quarrel with that prevailing belief; indeed, I rather share it. Novels, to name one alternative vehicle, are more cumbersome and time intensive to deal with in fiction workshops—more cumbersome to write in timely instalments, more cumbersome to revise, to reproduce, to read, to critique, to respond to useful criticism of. The academic year runs out before the dramaturgical bills have been paid; or a whole season of apprenticeship gets invested in what at best is likely to be a single narrative conceit, voice, point of view, cast of characters, and plot, and what at worst may prove to have been a large mistake, without coaching time left to try something else. A conventional short story, on the other hand, we can hold in the mind's eye of the seminar; in the allotted hour or so we can attend with some critical efficiency both to representative details and to overall matters of pace and plot and narrative viewpoint. What's more, as the season wears on we can come to know the author's *characteristic* strengths and weaknesses and idiosyncrasies of imagination, and can assess a new effort in the light of its predecessors, a sort of mini-oeuvre. These are undeniable pedagogical assets. The associated aesthetic values, too—compression, implicativeness, rendition as against mere assertion, precise observation, subtlety of effect—are undeniable literary values (though not the only ones); undeniable especially for apprentices, most of whom will not in fact turn out to be working fiction writers, but a fair fraction of whom will turn out to be teachers, editors, writers of other sorts of documents, and—the chief and worthy product of those 400-plus U.S. creative writing programs—*readers*, more sensitive and knowledgeable in the art of reading literature than they would likely be if they hadn't practiced writing it.

I assert again, however, that those literary values are not the only ones. In the very best workshops (and by definition there can never be a great many of those), the pedagogical virtues of the conventional modern short story will not be conflated with its aesthetic values, and its aesthetic values will not be assumed to hold for all times, places, temperaments, and talents. There is a narrative metabolism, equally honorable and with at least as long a pedigree, that valorizes expansiveness, even extravagance, complication, nonlinearity, even telling instead of showing (telling, after all, is one of the things that language can do better than a camera), and perhaps fabulation or some other admixture of irrealism over unadulterated realism. Such a narrative metabolism may find the now-classical short story form claustrophobic: Rabelais and Laurence Sterne oughtn't to have to walk in Maupassant's moccasins, or Scheherazade in Chekhov's, and vice-versa.

When I first set about, at age twenty, to write a novel, I approached the prospect with due trepidation. It seemed a presumptuous undertaking, as indeed it was, in a number of ways. True, Thomas Mann had been only twenty when he wrote *Buddenbrooks*—but Mann at age twenty was forty already, and what's more, he was Thomas Mann. I went ahead and perpetrated my maiden novel, and it was an unpublishable travesty—turgid tidewater ersatz Faulkner, without Faulkner's moral-historical vision and deep acquaintance with his subject—but I felt immediately at home in the form, as if my hands and feet had been unshackled. "The novel, the novel!" I exulted to myself at the time. "Room to swing a cat in!" "The novel, the novel!" I exulted in some novel many novels later, "with its great galumphing grace, amazing as a whale!" I doubted that I would ever go back to the short story.

And by puristic standards, I never quite did. My very next apprentice project (the last, in fact, of my apprenticeship) involved short fictions again, but with at least two differences from my earlier Bob-Bob-Bobbing that it pleases me to find significant in retrospect. Having imbibed Boccaccio and Scheherazade and company along with the big Modernists, what I projected was a cycle of 100 tales about my native tidewater county—my saltmarsh Yoknapatawpha—at all periods of history, but not in chronological order. In other words, the thing was to be a *book*; a narrative whole like the *Decameron*, larger than the sum of its parts, not every one of which would need to be freestanding; and those parts, many of them anyhow, would be in the nature of *tales* or even anecdotes, not post-Poe short stories. They would *tell*, here and there, instead of show: *He was a jealous and miserly old oysterman; she was a wanton young crab-picker;*

whatever. They would ramble and digress; they would deploy narrative effects from the eighteenth and earlier centuries, tongue half in cheek and one foot always in the here and now.

This project, too, was a failure (I aborted it round about Tale 50), but it proved a valuable learning experience, as they say, and in the event I was able to recycle a number of those Dorchester Tales into *The Sot-Weed Factor* (1967), three novels later. What I had in place, although I didn't know it yet (this was the front end of the 1950s), were some of the field-identification marks that I now associate with Postmodernist art, at least by my definition: notably, the ironized recycling of premodern forms and devices for modern readers with upper-case Modernism under their belts.

There is, of course, more to the making of fiction than a geographical predilection and the deployment of forms and devices, ironized or otherwise. There is, for example, the little matter of what one aspires to narrate by means of those predilections and forms and devices. Once the material, the craftsmanly means, and the aesthetic objective have somehow reciprocally clarified one another and jiggered themselves into synergy, with luck a career of "professional" literary production may ensue. In my fortunate case, once I had discovered by trial, error, and serendipity my narrative space and pace, I was not of a mind to do other than vigorously continue exploring it for a couple thousand pages' worth of novels over the next dozen years: short novels, midsize novels, long novels, but novels all. Now that I was not committed to and therefore not straitjacketed by the short story, I was free to admire it uncovetously and its masters unenviously. This I did, and taught their works with respectful pleasure to my literature students and the form with profit to my fiction writing coachees—until the high 1960s, when three or four factors together led me to give short-storyhood another go.

I happened through the latter 1960s to be living and working in Buffalo, New York, and while many young Americans were crossing the Niagara River from that city into Canada for sanctuary from our war in Vietnam (as Americans had done in numerous of our other wars, long before there was a Peace Bridge to facilitate the crossing), there came back across that bridge, from nearby Toronto, the siren song of Marshall McLuhan advising us "print-oriented bastards" that our Gutenberg Galaxy was not only not the whole universe, but a galaxy perhaps petering out in the electronic global village. Self-bound to the medium of the book like Odysseus to the mast of his vessel, I attended this siren song with the same constrained fascination that I lately bring to Robert Coover's and George Landow's serenades to the medium of hypertext (especially Coover's, because he is so gifted and knowledgeable a writer of *text*-texts): About Hypertexties in the Nineties as about Death-of-the-Bookies in the Sixties, I think and thought, "Very possibly they're right, maybe they're wrong, maybe some of each; but most important, maybe there's something here that a writer can make good use of."

I had, as it happened, just published my fourth novel, and the latter pair of those four were baggy monsters indeed (*The Sot-Weed Factor* and *Giles Goat-Boy*); the notion of reattempting brevity, perhaps even terseness, was understandably seductive. Moreover, I had discovered and been duly wowed by the *ficciones* of Jorge Luis Borges, who certainly made maximalist novels seem *demasiado* at that hour of the world. Finally and less creditably (as I have acknowledged in the foreword to the current American edition of *Lost in the Funhouse*), I had by the 1960s been teaching long enough to notice that we congenital novelists do not normally find ourselves included, for obvious reasons, in the standard short story anthologies on which I had cut my own apprentice teeth and which I regularly assigned to the teething apprentices in my charge. (Bill Styron, for example, wasn't in those anthologies either; he doesn't teach school, however, and so perhaps was less aware of his exclusion.) But there were Don Barthelme and Grace Paley and John Updike and Flannery O'Connor and Eudora Welty, not to mention their illustrious predecessors back to Poe and Hawthorne. Along with the more creditable attractions of the short form was admission to that distinguished club, which I unabashedly hankered after. Even today, I confess, when a new anthology comes across my desk, I look first to see how my stock is doing. If I'm included, I check out my new, younger shipmates with benign interest (Aha, Graham Swift; aha, Jane Smiley; ahoy there, Julian Barnes); but if the turkeys leave me out, I toss the thing—unless, as has increasingly become the case, former coachees of mine are represented there, supplanting their erstwhile mentor. Pleasant pain.

Anyhow, for all these reasons I embraced at last the sharp-eyed, relaxless muse of the short story, who, unlike good longwinded Homer, never dozes off, even for a second. Just as wary Odyssues, when romancing formidable Circe, covered his butt (let's say) with a sprig of moly, so I put an anchor out to windward by writing a short story *series*—a book, a book, "for print, tape, and live voice"—in order not to get lost in my own funhouse, excuse the hybrid metaphor. I decided to pay my initiation fee by writing the shortest story in the whole corpus of literature, which however would at the same time be literally endless and a paradigm for the book to boot: a ten-word Moebius-strip narrative called "Frame-Tale" (*Once upon a time there was a story that began* etc. ad inf.). Short on characters, short on plot, short on social realism—but short is the name of the game, right? That done, I spent an invigorating couple of years fabricating tales to be framed by that frame tale, enjoying most the longest and most intricated of them, for that is who I am, but attempting here and there as bonafide an old-fashioned modern short story as I could contrive for future anthologists, and where possible looking to see what other marks I might set in my private Guinness Book of World Literary Records. Some years of casual homework on frame-tale literature, for example, had revealed to me that the maximum degree of *narrative imbeddedness* in the corpus of such literature was about the fifth degree—a tale within a tale within a tale within a tale within a tale—and that the relations among such nested tales was generally at best thematic, seldom functionally dramaturgical. Purely *pour le sport*, therefore, I went for seven degrees (in a story called "Menelaiad"), and saw to it moreover that their concentric plots were rigged for sequential climax triggering from the inmost out. Let me hasten to add, however, that Menelaus's story is about love, not about plot mechanics, for I was in love (love, love, love, love, love, love) with the short story.

And after the short story, with the novella—that sweet, that delicious narrative space, so much neglected in our century. I do hope that there'll be an international conference someday on the novella, and that I won't be too superannuated to attend, for there's another love story altogether. Meanwhile, two cheers minimum for the exhausting muse of the short story—exhausting anyhow to us congenital novelists, who are likely to leave her embraces in the condition of Peleus after Thetis's, or Anchises after Venus's (one notices, by the way, that those old studs aren't complaining in their wheelchairs—and that the issue of their life-altering one-nighter was Achilles, was Aeneas). I romanced the novella form for three or four years in the same sidelong and tracks-covering but truly heartfelt way as I had romanced the short story form, pretending that my trinity of more or less linked novellas was really a unity—a book, a book, a book—and even allowing Random House to market that book (it was called *Chimera*) without any indication whatever on jacket or title page that it's not a novel. This was, after all, exactly twenty years ago, just before the wholesale resurgence of the American short story, when the conventional wisdom among New York trade publishers was that volumes of short fiction don't earn their keep. And the original Chimera, we remember, was neither a managerie nor a congeries nor a colonial organism, but a tripartite, fire-breathing, single-spirited entity, however genetically self-disparate and, well, chimerical.

Then on Yom Kuppur 1973, as you may have noticed, the American 1960s ended. Overnight, women's skirts got longer and men's sideburns shorter; the national economy simultaneously recessed and inflated, and in the general reaction against the 1960s, American fiction swung back to its prevailing aesthetic conservatism and for better or worse has pretty much dwelt there to this hour; nor does it show much sign that I can see of venturing therefrom. At this state of affairs, I shrug my shoulders: Traditionalist excellence is no doubt preferable to innovative mediocrity (but there's not much to be said for conservative mediocrity, and there's a great deal to be said for inspired innovation). This particular congenital novelist went contentedly—nay, happily—back to congenital novelizing; I even made a working rapprochement with social/psychological realism, although not enough of one, evidently, to mollify Tom Wolfe—whom I strongly suspect of having read no American fiction published after the Arab oil embargo, except possibly his own.

*

Ah well, *mes amis, je ne regrette rien*, certainly not my invigorating liaisons with those slender, demanding forms, the short story and the novella. Single-shot dalliances, in their way, but each a novelist's single shot, of several years' concentrated, undivided commitment: quality time. I remain profoundly, satisfyingly wedded to the pace of the novel, most particularly the longish-haul novel. Yet every four years or so, when a new one slides down the waves to whatever postlaunch fate awaits it, I confess to resolving that I will have one more go, this many decades later and this late in the afternoon, at the perennial beautiful possibilities of the short story. At this hour of our cultural history, I ask myself, who needs another large novel—not to say, more particularly, another hefty *Barthbuch*? In no time at all I accumulate project notes toward that end—notes not for a story, never for a story, but a *book* of stories, a book, a book. . . . Next thing I know, the frame has subsumed the picture, the book its constituent stories, and what I'm writing is no longer a book of stories but another book-length story. That mode remains as fitted to my spirit as Homer says Penelope was to Odysseus's, and vice-versa. To that question aforeproposed—Who needs another et cetera?—I sigh and reply, *I* do.

Or rather (as bridegroom says to bride), "I *do*."

Part I:

Form and the Short Story

1

How Minimal Is Minimalism?

Ewing Campbell

How minimal is the fiction we call minimalist? If we spend much time and thought on the question we end up, like it or not, with a theory of minimalism. We also need to define our terms if we are to understand one another. A look at contrasting interpretations of minimalism may help to illustrate the difficulty before we attempt to answer the pertinent questions.

Many individuals familiar with art movements identify *minimalism* with such properties as primary forms, hard edges, precision, and a reaction against the romanticism of abstract expressionism—features, I might add, that we find in most stories by Raymond Carver. And yet Carver associated the expression with smallness of vision and smallness of execution. He was offended when praised as a minimalist. Here are his thoughts on the topic as he talks with Mona Simpson of the *Paris Review*:

In a review of the last book, somebody called me a "minimalist" writer. The reviewer meant it as a compliment. But I didn't like it. There's something about "minimalist" that smacks of smallness of vision and execution that I don't like.

That is as clear as you can put it. At the same time, for me, the word suggests a density that encompasses more than is obvious, the evidence of things present but unseen or things seen but not there, the universe in a grain of sand.

In spite of the differences, most people who think about minimalism have a general notion of what it is because of the family resemblances that overlap and crisscross minimalist fiction. If we call the fiction we are reading minimalist, we do so because it resembles other works going by that name. One of the shared features most often encountered is the "truncated plot" consisting of events and empty spaces that require completion for readers who prefer solidity to voids. In this symmetrizing process, images arranged in certain patterns transform the elliptical shape of the fiction into a more stable form that is the narrative equivalent of what perceptual psychologists call subjective contours.

There is a subliminal match between the structure consisting of missing, but perceived, events and the geometrical figure formed by three pie charts arranged with one centered above a base made of the other two, a wedge removed from each, the empty slots turned toward the center (see Figure 1.1):

Figure 1.1
Subjective Contours

In such a configuration illusory contours are involuntarily extended by the brain and eye, and a stylized triangle comes into view, even though there are no lines, no triangle: only sharp edges, primary forms, and empty spaces.

With other disks you could produce the illusion of a square, rectangle, star, and so on by adding to their number and altering the arrangement. However, because of the family resemblance between this stylized figure and Freytag's Pyramid, perhaps we should stay with it for this discussion. If Freytag's Pryamid represents the traditional plot, the imaginary triangle contains the conditions of stimulation for the minimalist story.

I bring in the phenomenology of visual perception and thought processes because a counterpart can be found in readers' responses to certain literary structures. These artfully fashioned narratives I am calling minimalist fiction present significant details arranged in a way that causes the brain to supply missing information—to extend the lines, so to speak. As a result we perceive information that makes the point, develops character, reveals the theme, justifies the voice.

Size, it should be stressed, is not the determining factor in minimalist fiction, as I am defining it. Two stories out of recent literary journals exemplify the difference: Allen Hibbard's "Crossing to Abbassiya" from the *Cimarron Review* (1992) and Joy Castro's "To Practice the Thing" from *Short Story* (1992).

In "Crossing to Abbassiya," Mostafa Abd el-Salaam begins his day in a state of equilibrium, pleased that he will transport a dozen mentally ill patients across Cairo from the station at Imbaba to the asylum at Abbassiya. When he stops at a coffee house, his charges escape into the city and disequilibrium replaces the initial stability. To redeem himself, Mostafa recruits a dozen gullible villagers from the many unemployed men who travel to Cairo every day looking for work and delivers them to the asylum. This done, the crisis is resolved, equilibrium restored. The story, though brief, is unambiguous, depends on dialectical opposites, and is not minimalist.

"To Practice the Thing" is a different matter. Dense, truncated, elliptical, depending on the juxtaposition of images for its meaning, it is minimalist. Castro's reticent narrator is unwilling to say the crucial word or to present the actual act of her father's suicide. In compensation, Castro devises a narrative tactic of imagistic sequences that—in place of the unspeakable words, the unbearable acts—fashions cosmos from the unrelieved emotional chaos of the narrator. There is no plot. No equilibrium is succeeded here by instability, to be followed by a return to equilibrium. From first to last sentences, instability dominates in a narrative that makes use of sensory devices and groups of juxtaposed images to reveal theme and character without resorting to plot as it is customarily defined and represented by Freytag's Pyramid.

Images of cultural horror, along with the narrator's fantasies of herself in the throes of terrible death, function much like the pie charts in the optical illusion to fashion the cognitive image of the father hanging himself. A childhood bathtub associated by the narrator with the holocaust serves as the vehicle in which she imagines herself transported to the death camp. As an adolescent she creates fantasies of herself as a consumptive heroine experiencing the thrill of a slow terrible death. And at the time of the narrative she imagines herself stepping off, blown up by the hidden killer of Vietnam—the Bouncing Betty—triggered by an unwary step.

The battlefield mine has within it two lines that merge—the explosion itself and the act of stepping off. These merging lines lead to the final images that allow us to answer three important questions: What happens? Who does it? What does it mean?

The explosive is identified with the narrator's daughter (whom she calls her own little heart-bomb, her moon, her rose), and the stepping off is associated with the involuntary image of her father's shoes at the edge of a chair, coming to her as she asks, "Did he imagine me . . . was I his rose, his angel, his moon-flower, before he kicked the chair away?"

This is the kind of story I think of when I think of minimalist fiction. It is dense, suggesting profound and haunting psychological implications, and I should add that, in reading the story as it is composed, no one should feel defensive or apologetic at being challenged. I have barely scratched the surface in my summary, without approaching the sexual elements or dealing with "mother's family intermarried" or addressing the imagination theme, which is the major concern of the work.

Just as the visual system mentioned above requires an internal process between brain and eye to fashion the contours of a triangle that is not in the disks or in the paper, but inside the viewer, so too does the reader's interpretation need a unifying impulse to infer the father's suicide from the available images in "To Practice the Thing." This act of unification within the reader is the goal of Castro's narrative tactics, which assert that, while there are appropriate times and places for amplification, there are certain structures in which amplification reduces the force or destroys the effect altogether. In the context of suicide, a reticent narrator and an indirect method are not merely justified. They are exactly what is needed for the aesthetic effect the story produces.

Although the aesthetic of minimalism is not new—we have had over a century of it—it remains controversial among some critics, writers, editors, and readers. It does so for a number of reasons. To some it suggests the unthinkable, edging too close to acts that should be kept secret, slipping frightfully near to tribal taboos, probing certain barriers that have been erected for purposes of interdiction. Another reason for controversy can be found in readers' hostility to ambiguity and methods of indirection, manifest in a general preference for greater amplification. How many times have you heard—how many times have you registered—complaints about intentionally obscure writers?

While these complaints are typically reserved for the postmodernists, I frequently hear colleagues—professors of literature—say, "Why can't they just come out and say what they mean?" The answer to that question takes many forms depending on the story. Having a psychologically damaged narrator just come out and say what is meant, for example, renders the character unbelievable. Forcing a naïve narrator to explain what is unknown presents the character doing the impossible. So far no one has arrived at the precise number of aesthetic reasons for not doing what is so often recommended, but the controversy continues.

And I suppose there is some controversy in the question that got me started: How minimal is minimalism? So back to definitions and connotations. If by the term under consideration we mean smallness of vision, smallness of execution, then I suggest that this category of fiction is not minimal at all. If, however, we have devised a rubric for narrative tactics that resist amplification or one that brings to mind the universe in a grain of sand, as it does for me, then I believe that it is a metaphor well chosen: vivid, suggestive, and not to be improved upon.

WORK CITED

Carver, Raymond. "Fires." *Fires: Essays, Poems, Stories.* New York: Vintage, 1989. 22-27.

2

Social Critique and Story Technique in the Fiction of Raymond Carver

Hilary Siebert

Raymond Carver has often been described as a "minimalist" writer, one who renders moments of contemporary American life in a language that is spare in expression and bleak in outlook. Implicit in this labeling is the notion that his stories lack any transformative vision, that they present to us tales of alcoholics and losers as though blind, self-destructive behaviors were matters of naturalistic fact and not subject to change through the insight stories can provide to their characters and their readers. Carver's early critics, notably James Atlas in 1981 and Madison Bell in 1986, accused him of what amounts to a flatness, not only in language, but in artistic *vision*; in this view, Carver leaves his characters in lives of quiet desperation (see Saltzman 1988, 178-82).

The assumption here is that, particularly in the most reduced collection, *What We Talk About When We Talk About Love* (1982), Carver had no social conscience as a writer or, as a stylist, he was committed to a technique devoid of social resonance. However, with the publication of *Cathedral* (1984), critical opinion began to register what William L. Stull described in the title of his 1985 article "Beyond Hopelessville: Another Side of Raymond Carver." As Carver began publishing revisions of earlier stories ("The Bath" as transformed into "A Small, Good Thing") and new texts such as "Cathedral," Stull saw a "humanist realism" replacing what had been an "existential realism" (6-7). In these newer texts, Carver made his authorial presence felt, stepping in to offer moments of redemption and insight to his seemingly helpless characters.

My point in this chapter is to question the assumption that Carver's most minimal texts are in fact devoid of social concern and social critique, particularly since the "help" Carver gives his characters in the revised and more expansive texts is, arguably, forced. Ewing Campbell, for instance, suggests that Carver's popular success with "A Small, Good Thing" "testifies to the cultural shift toward sentimentality that characterizes the decade of the eighties" (1992, 49). Carver demonstrates a social conscience in this text only by adding into his earlier story the Christian myths of sacrifice and redemption (56), thereby soothing the pain he had asked his characters and readers to face silently in "The Bath."

To indicate the nature of social critique which I believe is implicit in Carver's harsher, "existentialist," minimalist texts, I will examine the stylistic mediation of meaning in these works. Crucial issues here are both Carver's style of writing and his readers' style of processing the text. Social critique, I will argue, is not far removed from what Carver's stories have to offer, but its presence is a matter of perception. Stull observed that "because what has come to strike most of us as the typical Carver story has been elliptical, understated, and studiously opaque, his influence extends not only to how we write but how we read" (1985, 1). This truth notwithstanding, many readers of Carver's earlier texts do not seem to have understood the kind of processing elliptical prose requires. As Campbell notes, "repetition, parallelism, opposition" are some of the techniques by which Carver patterns meaning into his texts, as Ernest Hemingway did before him (1992, 52). This is a lyrical approach to the story, which Eileen Baldeshwiler has studied in other short story masters such as Anton Chekhov and Sherwood Anderson. It is an approach I will examine here in reference to "Tell the Women We're Going" in order to explain Carver's techniques of structuring meaning and social critique into his stories.

By social critique I am referring to a portrayal of people in situations that allow the social forces acting upon them to become apparent, so that both social causes and the consequences of an individual's behavior can be recognized. Since Carver portrays the sufferings of characters afflicted by poverty, alcohol, job stress, ignorance, and infidelity, it seems important that we scrutinize the implicit authorial understanding of these conditions, lest they appear to be mere facts to which the writer is oblivious.

To a great extent it is not true that Carver fails to attribute causes to his characters' fates. However, he does so more by restrained implication than by direct engagement of the social issues that loom around his characters. The point is that Carver's personal sensibilities and social conscience are inextricable from his aesthetic preferences. Much like Hemingway and Chekhov, he suggests causes and emotion silently or through nuance. These preferences fit the nature of the short story genre especially well. It may be that readers strongly concerned with social oppression feel impatient with the traits of the genre, and with the restraint and patterned subtlety of Carver's style. The novel, by some definitions, deals more overtly and less lyrically with experience, framing it directly in the context of historical reality. Furthermore some short story writers have their characters behave directly as social activists. (Grace Paley is one who comes to mind.) But this is not Carver's approach.

If we first situate Carver's stories in reference to their author's background, we can gain insight into the cultural vantage point from which he speaks. Additionally, we can then look at the aesthetic tradition that grounds his writing to understand better his technical approach. Atlas and others have criticized what Atlas terms a "deterministic handling" of characters and the "enlightened, superior sympathy" (1981, 67) of the implied author. However, in interviews Carver shows himself to be interested both in the lives of the disenfranchised and in the short story traditions that have foregrounded them. Responding to a question concerning his focus on the plight of the "downtrodden," Carver observed: "I do feel more kinship, even today, with those people. They're my people. . . . Half of my family is still living like this. . . . I'm just bearing witness to something I know about" (O'Connell 1990, 137-38).

In another interview, Carver demonstrates the nature of his social conscience in traditional terms, alluding to Frank O'Connor's theory of a "submerged population group" inhabiting the worlds portrayed by James Joyce, Hemingway, and the Russian realists:

It also doesn't seem that, in focusing on this group of people, I have really been doing anything all that different from other writers. Chekhov was writing about a submerged population a hundred years ago. Short story writers have always been doing that. . . . [Chekhov] also gave voice to people who were not so articulate. . . . So in writing about people who aren't so articulate and who are confused and scared, I'm not doing anything radically different. (McCaffery and Gregory 1990, 112)

Like the Hemingway of "Hills Like White Elephants," Carver reveals almost silent moments in the awakening of his characters, while seeming himself to stay out of their affairs. Because the social realities Carver knows are unpleasant, revelations for characters are often moments of honesty: they are moments of awareness—rather than denial—that life has taken a turn for the worse. They are moments of reckoning. In "Chef's House" a recovering alcoholic makes one last attempt to renew his marriage. Told from the wife's perspective, we see, poignantly, that his final attempt will not work. The man cannot try any more and the woman, unable finally to help him try, cooks a last supper knowing that their life together has ended: "I went to start supper. We still had some fish in the icebox. There wasn't much else. We'll clean it up tonight, I thought, and that will be the end of it" (1984, 33).

Sad as it is, the story offers recognition of an ending, rather than continued fantasy by the couple that trying again would be meaningful. In the context of such truth, options that might exist for these characters are matters beyond the scope of Carver's authorial vision. Carver has reminded us that: "Chekhov said you don't have to solve a problem in a story, you just have to present a problem accurately" (Moffet 1990, 242).

While the short story has never been a hopeful place for characters, Carver may seem mean-spirited in his refusal even to send his characters on their way as Chekhov did, for example, concluding "The Lady with the Pet Dog": "And it seemed as though in a little while the solution would be found, and then a new and glorious life would begin; and it was clear to both of them that the end was still far off, and what was to be most complicated and difficult for them was only just beginning" (1974, 433).

For the Carver before and even after *Cathedral* who practices minimalist portrayal, this is too great an authorial intrusion. His apparent coldness, like Hemingway's, silently leaves characters in their plights, yet he shows us vividly as much as they have come to see. Following Flaubert's dictum, Carver seeks to be the writer who is "everywhere *present*, but nowhere *visible*" (Miyamota 1990, 67). Following Pound's dictum—"Fundamental accuracy of statement is the ONE sole morality of writing" (O'Connell 1990, 142)—Carver did not trust himself to say more than what he felt he really knew about people and their situations. Carver might agree with the writer-daughter in Paley's "A Conversation with My Father," who argues that "Everyone, real or invented, deserves the open destiny of life" (1979, 162), but I would argue that Carver's stories are most convincing when they are true to the contours of characters' actual lives. Even in the hopeful ending of "Cathedral," the cognitive blindness of the husband is only filled with a moment of light, as the cognitively insular walls of his house disappear in his mind: "I was in my house. I knew that. But I didn't feel like I was inside anything" (1984, 228). What happens as a result we do not know.

Of the alcoholic husband in "Careful" who leaves his wife and moves to a garret where he eats crumb doughnuts and drinks champagne all day, Carver will only address the immediate problem of the man's ear that is (emblematically) stopped with wax. The wife arrives on the scene and solves Lloyd's ear problem, but Carver will not solve the man's larger problems. Instead, he takes us into the emotional world of an alcoholic, revealing the contours of fear that rule this man's life. If readers react with outright frustration to the reality of such portrayals, perhaps we should credit Carver for affecting his readers powerfully with the social realities in this country; authorial rescues will not alleviate the actual sufferings of men like Lloyd.

On the other hand, some of Carver's most brutal stories go pretty far in ascribing causes to the social malaise he describes. "So Much Water So Close to Home" speaks from a woman's perspective in order to show what type of man would naïvely leave a murdered woman's body for several days where he found it, while he and his buddies enjoy a hunting trip. In "What We Talk about When We Talk about Love," two couples discuss the meaning of love by comparing personal experiences of brutality considered "love" with the story of an old couple who feel grief at being unable to see each other as they lie bandaged in adjacent hospital beds following a car accident. In order to see the implicit critique of amorous behaviors in this text, readers must reflect silently with the story's narrator as the light grows dim and the narrator seems to hear the beating of everyone's heart. In such reflection, we may take stock of the implied author's attitude toward the subject being presented.

I want to examine this matter of reading processing at length in regard to a single text, "Tell the Women We're Going." It is the story of two former school buddies, now married, who go out drinking and murder two female bicyclists. Carver did not include this text in his collection of stories *Where I'm*

Calling From, and it appears to present a brutal rape and murder with little authorial commentary or concern for what takes place. Atlas says of this story, "There is no motive, nothing to explain it [the murder]—yet it seems plausible, a reminder that men are violent, primitive, given to murder" (1981, 96-97). Atlas fails to perceive the exposition of motive Carver *implies*, just as he fails to see the meaning of the silence at the end of "What We Talk About," when reader and narrator take stock reflectively of what has just been said.

As "Tell the Women" concludes, Bill has halfheartedly followed his friend Jerry up the trail to Picture Rock from the highway where the two women parked their bicycles. As Jerry pursues the women, Bill follows Jerry from a distance. The story concludes from Bill's third-person limited perspective:

Bill had just wanted to fuck. Or even to see them naked. On the other hand, it was okay with him if it didn't work out.

He never knew what Jerry wanted. But it started and ended with a rock. Jerry used the same rock on both girls, first on the girl called Sharon and then on the one that was supposed to be Bill's. (1981, 66)

The social value I see in this story derives from its plot design and image structure. An understanding of the possible epiphany for Bill and for the reader depends on following these patterns. Given what Susan Lohafer has termed the "deferred cognitive closure" of short stories, we cannot say we fully understand a story until we have thought through its meaning in light of the ending. For Bill, this story concludes on a note of naïve bewilderment: Why has Jerry done this? For readers, too, there is likely a degree of shock at a story that was intensifying toward a rape scene but not a murder. Because the story does not presume to take Bill beyond the threshold of the final blow, we can only say of this epiphany that he will be compelled to wonder how this has happened— how a buddy he has idolized since high school would end up committing murder and perhaps implicating him. His final awareness may be years in coming, or it may never come. But for readers, Carver lays out a pattern of escalating aggression that makes reasons for the final act clear.

Opening the story is a paragraph of free indirect speech that captures the seemingly innocent ways Bill and Jerry look back on their teenage years:

Bill Jamison had always been best friends with Jerry Roberts. The two grew up in the south area, near the old fairgrounds, went through grade school and junior high together, and then on to Eisenhower, where they took as many of the same teachers as they could manage, wore each other's shirts and sweaters and pegged pants, and dated and banged the same girls—which came up as a matter of course. (57)

This exposition begins to reveal how male bonding behavior in our society contains seeds of the same attitudes toward women that lead to the final scene of murder. Carver develops this further as we see Bill follow Jerry into marriage and eventually into a joy ride. Although Bill notices that Jerry looks disturbed, the men cannot communicate beyond empty phrases that pretend to express identification, such as "You know."

[Bill] said, "Anything wrong, man? I mean, you know."
Jerry finished his beer and then mashed the can. He shrugged.
"You know," he said.
Bill nodded.

A short time later, we hear:

"Guy's got to get out," Jerry said. He looked at Bill. "You know what I mean?"
Bill understood. . . . He knew a guy's got to get out. (60)

In Arthur M. Saltzman's view, Carver is constrained to the same language as his characters, and both Carver and his characters are reduced to "monosyllabic probings" of their subjects (1988, 173). Monosyllabic or not, Saltzman is not accounting here for the role of the reader in making sense of short stories. He also does not account for the role of story language beyond dialogue. Beyond the monosyllables of the characters' speech, Carver uses the language of story plot and story image to show us, authorially, some crucial facts about men like these: how the muteness of male dialogue masks feelings that need to be expressed and how failure at dialogue can lead silently to aggression. Without dialogue to comprehend and address their own feelings, these men act out their frustrations against women, following a particular cultural script—first in seemingly harmless ways known as "banging," then as "getting a little on the side," and finally in murder.

It is reasonable to imagine that Bill will gradually come to see some of this after the story's close. And for us, as readers who can contemplate the action and language as spectators rather than participants, there are clearer patterns to indicate the causes and evolution of a problematic male behavior in our culture. In imagery, one crushed beer can leads to another. In plot, adolescent male behavior sows the seeds of violence toward women. And in register, Jerry's language reveals an attitude that equates women with the targets of male hunters. As they pursue the women by car, images and actions too are of stalking. Jerry says: "Get ready"; "Now find out where they're going"; "It's in the bag." The girls "come into view"; they "go off at a trot"; and finally they are "crouched," like animals being stalked, behind an outcropping of rock. "I'll take the brunette, the little one's yours," Jerry says (62). The sexist language of conquest, applied by men to women, reveals fully now its latent implications.

Finally, Carver's anatomy of this murder is highlighted by a carefully drawn pair of images presented at the threshold to the enactment of the final scene. The external, effaced narrator pauses the action to contextualize this setting before unfolding the story's climax:

The highway forked here at Picture Rock, one road going to Yakima, the other heading for Naches, Enumclaw, the Chinook Pass, Seattle.

A hundred yards off the road was a high, sloping, black mound of rock, part of a low range of hills, honeycombed with footpaths and small caves, Indian sign-painting here and there on the cave walls. The cliff side of the rock faced the highway and all over it there were things like this: NACHES 67—GLEED WILDCATS—JESUS SAVES—BEAT YAKIMA—REPENT NOW. (64)

It is essential to the process of reading a short story, where details are rarely incidental, to analyze the significance of such a passage. The visual name "Picture Rock" at least suggests that we attend to the imagery being presented in this highly descriptive passage which interrupts the rising action. Looking closely at the "pictures" displayed, we see contrasting images of sign painting on cave walls and graffiti on the cliff facade. The ritualized, social behaviors of hunting and religious worship that are likely to have led Indians to this rock for communal activities within the caves pose a striking contrast to the adolescent scrawling of slogans which express competitive sports and religious despera- tion; competition, guilt, and despair are ruling traits of the culture in which Jerry and Bill partake in an *antisocial* communion of hunting women. Given the larger context of Carver's story, these slogans, written at great physical risk by marginal members of society, symbolize extreme acts of behavior which are often rites of passage for American males. Like the violent blows that end many stories by Flannery O'Connor, Jerry's act of murder places readers and characters in a position to examine causes.

The power of Carver's social critique derives from his technique as a story- teller of adding disquieting or reflective notes to lives that are already on the brink. This creates what he once termed the "emotional punches" he expects his stories to deliver (McCaffery and Gregory 1990, 110). Stories that add disquieting notes are those like "Tell the Women," "So Much Water," and "The Bath." Others, in creating silent, reflective moments, present a disturbing need for contemplation, as in "What We Talk About," "Careful," or "Chef's House." In both cases, a problem is posed, and its solution awaits the deferred under- standing, of characters or readers, which might follow.

In the essay "Fires," Carver explained that he cannot write novels because they require that "a writer should be living in a world that makes sense, a world that the writer can believe in, draw a bead on, and then write about accurately" (1989, 35). As Nadine Gordimer puts it in "The Flash of Fireflies," Carver is a writer who believes that "Short story writers see by the light of the flash; theirs is the art of the only thing one can be sure of—the present moment" (1976, 180).

WORKS CITED

Atlas, James. "Less is Less." *Atlantic Monthly* (June 1981): 96-98.
Baldeshwiler, Eileen. "The Lyric Short Story: The Sketch of a History." *Short Story*

Theories. Ed. Charles May. Athens: Ohio UP, 1976. 202-13.

Brown, Suzanne Hunter. "Discourse Analysis and the Short Story." *Short Story Theory at a Crossroads.* Eds. Susan Lohafer and Jo Ellyn Clarey. Baton Rouge: Louisiana State UP, 1989. 217-48.

Campbell, Ewing. *Raymond Carver: A Study of the Short Fiction.* New York: Twayne, 1992.

Carver, Raymond. "Careful." *Cathedral.* New York: Knopf, 1984. 111-26.

—. "Cathedral." *Cathedral.* New York: Knopf, 1984. 209-28.

—. "Chef's House." *Cathedral.* New York: Knopf, 1983. 27-34.

—. "Fires." *Fires: Essays, Poems, Stories.* New York: Vintage, 1989. 22-27.

—. "Tell the Women We're Going." *What We Talk About When We Talk About Love.* New York: Knopf, 1981. 57-66.

Chekhov, Anton. "The Lady with the Pet Dog." *The Portable Chekhov.* Trans. Avrahm Yarmolisnsky. New York: Viking, 1974. 412-33.

Gordimer, Nadine. "The Flash of Fireflies." *Short Story Theories.* Ed. Charles May. Athens: Ohio UP, 1976. 178-81.

Lohafer, Susan. *Coming to Terms with the Short Story.* Baton Rouge: Louisiana State UP, 1983.

McCaffery, Larry, and Sinda Gregory. "An Interview with Raymond Carver." *Conversations with Raymond Carver.* Eds. Marshall Bruce Gentry and William L. Stull. Jackson: UP of Mississippi, 1990. 98-116.

Miyamota, Michiko. "Raymond Carver." *Conversations with Raymond Carver.* Eds. Marshall Bruce Gentry and William L. Stull. Jackson: UP of Mississippi, 1990. 62-67.

Moffet, Penelope. *"PW* Interviews Raymond Carver." *Conversations with Raymond Carver.* Eds. Marshall Bruce Gentry and William L. Stull. Jackson: UP of Mississipi, 1990. 238-42.

O'Connell, Nicholas. "Raymond Carver." *Conversations with Raymond Carver.* Eds. Marshall Bruce Gentry and William L. Stull. Jackson: UP of Mississippi, 1990. 133-50.

Paley, Grace. "A Conversation with My Father." *Enormous Changes at the Last Minute.* New York: Farrar, 1979. 159-67.

Saltzman, Arthur M. *Understanding Raymond Carver.* Columbia: U of South Carolina P, 1988.

Stull, William L. "Beyond Hopelessville: Another Side of Raymond Carver." *Philological Quarterly* 64, No. 1 (1985): 1-15.

3

Picturing Ann Beattie

Susan Jaret McKinstry

The speakers in Ann Beattie's early work often seemed to miss the point of their stories. And so did many readers. Like other so-called minimalist *New Yorker* writers, Beattie contravenes our generic expectations. However, many critics have appreciated Beattie's unconventional fictions. Noting in a 1979 review of *Secrets and Surprises* that "most of Miss Beattie's stories end without a feeling of closure," Anatole Broyard wondered "whether it is unreasonable to expect closure nowadays. . . . Perhaps fiction is being discriminated against when we looked to it to satisfy orderly expectations (C17). Margaret Atwood, reviewing *The Burning House* in 1982, claimed that "these stories are not of suspense but of suspension" (34). Carolyn Porter wrote that Beattie's "mastery of the short story derives from the sensibility of a novelist of manners" whose "most marked talent is for eliminating discrete chunks of exposition" (1985, 11-12). Thomas Griffith, in the *Atlantic Monthly*, praised the "*New Yorker* fiction . . . in its rejection of moralizing and pat endings. . . . Nothing is ever summed up, or brought to an end; a moment passes and is wryly commented upon. It is a fictional approximation of value-free science" (1980, 28).

However, now minimalism is under attack as a dead end, a writerly trick, a failure of authorial imagination, a passed fad. As John Aldridge complains, Beattie may be a "brilliant describer" of details (1992, 58), but those details do not add up to anything, and "if the unexamined life is not worth living, the un-developed character is finally not worth reading about" (70).

In point of fact, minimalism never intended to reduce literature to flatness, to gaps filled only grudgingly by spare-tongued writers. Ernest Hemingway wrote in 1923 that he was discovering "a new theory that you could omit anything if you knew what you omitted, and the omitted part would strengthen the story and make people feel something more than they understood" (Baker 1972, 165). Rather than produce meaningless writing, minimalism is meant to produce meaningful reading, a reader's sense of responsibility for the evocative feel of the text. Thus the act of reading is an act of perceptual imagination, of interpreting the details, as Beattie's speakers and characters recognize.

In the 1983 story "Snow," for example, the narrator says, "One night, giving me a lesson in storytelling, you said, 'Any life will seem dramatic if you omit mention of most of it'" (*Where You'll Find Me* 1986, 22). Beattie, however, goes on to dispel that misunderstanding of minimalism: "This is a story, told the way you say stories should be told: Somebody grew up, fell in love, and spent a winter with her lover in the country. This, of course, is the barest outine, and futile to discuss. . . . Seconds and symbols are left to sum things up" (23). It is not what is omitted, then, but what is included that adds up to meaning. That summing up is imaginative; both the narrator and her readers can, in Hemingway's phrase, "feel more than they under[stand]" because of the evocative nature of metaphor, of linguistic images, so that the smallest sur-vivng details, "left to sum things up," provide rich possibilities of meaning.

Rather than leaving things out, Beattie's more recent writing uses a form of narrative self-reflexivity to emphasize the necessary work of the imagination in interpretation. By combining the artistic image and the interpreting imagina-tion, Beattie celebrates minimalist ordering in a contemporary world that, like the world of her earlier fiction, does not inherently make sense, provide secu-rity, or ensure happy endings.

Beattie's 1984 story "In the White Night" illustrates this juxtaposition of im-age and imagination. Recalling her dead daughter's camera, the central char-acter, Carol, thinks, "There were two images when you looked through the finder, and you had to make the adjustment yourself so that one superimposed itself upon the other and the figure suddenly leaped into clarity" (*Where You'll Find Me* 1986, 15). This struggle to focus separate images describes the tech-nique of the story; the narrative asks "you" as reader to "make the adjustment yourself" to develop the meaning of the characters' actions and words. Like the superimposed images in Sharon's camera, the story finally focuses. In retelling the painful memories of her daughter's death through images of the past, Carol tells herself exactly the present ending she needs to hear: "In the white night world outside, their daughter might be drifting past like an angel, and she would see this tableau, for the second that she hovered, as a necessary small adjustment" (17). Whether Sharon is really a hovering ghost is, of course, ir-relevant; that Carol can imagine her daughter's ghostly presence is the "necessary small adjustment" that can provide meaning in grief. A picture of Sharon's ghost drifts across the cover of *Where You'll Find Me*. For us as read-ers, as viewers, that image indeed becomes real.

Images are a central metaphor in Beattie's imaginative art: images that the characters focus, develop, and interpret through acts of imagination. Most of-ten, not surprisingly, the images are photographs. As the name suggests, *photo-graphs* unite the image and the word. In Beattie's earliest stories, photographs symbolize attempts to fix time, to produce meaning, to create art. In her more recent stories, the photographs can function both to distance the event from the viewer—the character or the reader—and to comment on the composition of the photograph as art. Photographs capture a moment in time, but also demonstrate the interpretive gesture inherent in framing that moment, composing the photograph in order to get selected details into the image and to shut other details outside the photograph: they are not objective slices of reality, but subjective perceptions.

Let me develop that claim. Photographs as images can perform three functions: they can reproduce a moment in history, a personal identity, or cultural iconography. All three functions are linked, in part, by their implied fixity: they stop time at that moment of the image. Distinguishing the photograph as history (photojournalism), as personal identity (a graduation photo), and as cultural icon (a Madonna album cover) helps to clarify the context in which we give meaning to the image. Nevertheless, all three categories finally reveal photography's inability to fix time outside the frame; they are all, in other words, comments on the production of an image whose presentness dissolves at the instant it is taken. Photos become monuments to a lost past. Indeed, they gain power precisely because their recorded present—now past—differs from the viewer's present and requires interpretation. Photographs are not historical documents, then, or simple records of loss, but rather fragmented present images taken out of historical continuity. By juxtaposing the artist's and viewer's imaginative interpretations, we give the subject narrative presence and thus meaning.

In certain of Beattie's early stories, the photographs demand narrative interpretation as images that fail to reproduce history. For example, "Like Glass" begins with a description of an old family photograph of a father, baby, and dog. The baby is "gazing into the distance" and this puzzles the narrator (*Burning House* 1982, 201). When her husband explains the picture to her, she says, "I was amazed that I had made a mystery of something that had such a simple answer. It is a picture of a baby looking at its mother" (205). However, her original intepretation reflects the complex juxtaposition of image and imagination. The photo as history fails to record the meaning of the baby's gaze; the photo as identity shows two lost connections: "The baby grew up to be my husband, and now is no longer married to me" (201). The simple answer is not contained in the photograph, but in the husband's story about the photograph; in the picture the mother is still absent, the baby's gaze still moving outside the image and into the imagination.

In "Shifting," a character told by her husband to inventory possessions for insurance purposes photographs parts of her own body rather than her husband's antiques. She turns herself into a cultural icon, indeed into photographic images of a woman's fragmented body. Such fragmentation of the female body is a traditional way to raise its value, to turn it from image to imaginative object. Thus cultural iconography creates images that do not illustrate historical position or personal identity, but seem to reproduce instead transcendant beauty, ahistorical and impersonal.

The resulting tension between private self and public image (as an individual woman becomes an embodiment of Womanhood, a generic object of desire) is replicated in the photographic images in "Shifting," but ironically, self-reflexively, since it is the woman who photographs herself and studies herself, trying to find her identity in those images as both artist and audience. Looking at the photographs later, "she began to understand why she had taken them. She had photographed parts of her body, fragments of it, to study the pieces" (*Secrets and Surprises* 1978, 68). Recognizing that the image is not sufficiently meaningful, that the fragments she has photographed do not represent her or her story, she tries to see herself more clearly:

She undressed. She looked at her body—whole, not a bad figure—in the mirror. . . . She ran her hands down her sides, wondering if the feel of her skin was anything like the way the sculpture would feel. . . . If she were the piece of sculpture and if she could feel, she would like her sense of isolation. This was in 1972, in Philadelphia. (68-69)

Moving from the image to the object, from photo to sculpture, the narrative still focuses on the imagination: seeing herself in the mirror, she cannot, as Lacan's mirror stage claims, see herself, but only a misrecognized self, a self that becomes an art object, a sculpture. Beattie makes the misrecognition self-reflexive: "if she were the piece of sculpture and if she could feel," she would be both art object and woman. What she is, therefore, is an image of a woman in photographs, in a mirror, and in prose that stops the narrative in 1972, leaving us to interpret her deliberate framing of herself as body, disrupting her husband's inventory of valuable possessions with photographs of herself, and as metaphorical art, as feeling sculpture, and as subject of the third-person narrator's conclusive historicizing: "This was in 1972, in Philadelphia."

In the later works, such as the 1991 collection *What Was Mine*, Beattie's characters construct images even more consciously, more confidently. In the story entitled "Imagine a Day at the End of Your Life," the first-person narrator receives a "Brag book" designed for photographs which he instead fills with leaves, a narrative of images that only he can readily interpret. Delightfully, his narrative process is a response to the complaints about minimalism: he contradicts the minimalist's focus on middles and refusal of closure. Instead he says, "To be truthful, there are a few pages in the book right in the middle that aren't filled. . . . I worked on the front of the book because I had some sense of how I wanted to begin, and then I filled the back of the book, because I found the perfect leaf to end with, but I wasn't sure about the rest" (*What Was Mine*, 1991 7-8).

What is essential to his book is not literal image, but imaginative act: by replacing conventional images with leaves, he creates his own meaning. That imaginative power, as the title notes, can create an identity so powerful that it transcends images, absences, and even death:

Imagine a day at the end of your life. . . . Then imagine that you aren't there any longer, but at a place where you can touch those things that were always too dazzlingly high or too far in the distance—light-years would have been required to get to them—and suddenly you can pluck all the stars from the sky, gather all fallen leaves at once. (9)

That transcendent mystery is precisely the point. In using the photographic image, Beattie's work celebrates the ineffable quality of imaginative products: even the apparently concrete photograph becomes a matter of interpretation—but not limitation. Just as her early characters recognize the complexity of the images they can not fully understand, Beattie's later characters create a world that juxtaposes image and imagination to illustrate the richness of both.

WORKS CITED

Aldridge, John. *Talents and Technicians: Literary Chic and the New Assembly-Line Fiction*. New York: Scribners, 1992.

Atwood, Margaret. "Stories from an American Front." *The New York Times Book Review* (26 Sept. 1982): 34.

Baker, Carlos. *Ernest Hemingway*. Princeton: Princeton UP, 1972.

Beattie, Ann. *The Burning House*. New York: Random House, 1982.

—. *Secrets and Surprises*. New York: Random House, 1978.

—. *What Was Mine*. New York: Random House, 1991.

—. *Where You'll Find Me*. New York: Random House, 1986.

Broyard, Anatole. "Books of the Times: Secrets and Surprises." *The New York Times* (3 Jan. 1979): C17.

Griffith, Thomas. "Rejoice If You Can." *Atlantic Monthly* 246 (Sept. 1980): 28.

Porter, Carolyn. "Ann Beattie: The Art of the Missing." *Contemporary American Women Writers: Narrative Strategies*. Ed. Catherine Rainwater and Will J. Scheick. Lexington: UP of Kentucky, 1985. 9-28.

4

The One and the Many:
Canadian Short Story Cycles

Gerald Lynch

Over the past hundred years the short story cycle has become something of a subgenre within the Canadian short story.[1]   This is not to argue that the story cycle has been ignored by American and British writers (or, for that matter, by the writers of any other national literature)—it has not—only that the form has held a special attraction for Canadian writers. Doubtless there are shared reasons for the story cycle's current popularity internationally and in Canada; for example, publishers often assume readers are more comfortable with the linkages of the cycle than with the discontinuities of the miscellany of stories. But such matters are not within this chapter's literary-historical and theoretical scope. This chapter will sketch the history of the short story cycle in Canada, give an idea of its diversity and continuing popularity, consider some of the fundamental questions about this comparatively new form, and conclude with an illustrative analysis of the function of one important aspect of story cycles, their concluding stories.

Those interested in the Canadian short story cycle can hesitantly claim predecessors in the works of early writers of epistolary novels, collections of letters, and books of loosely linked sketches: Frances Brooke's *A History of Emily Montague* (1769), Thomas McCulloch's *Letters of Mephibosheth Stepsure* (serialized 1821-23), Thomas Chandler Haliburton's *The Clockmaker* (1836), and the writings of Catharine Parr Traill and Susanna Moodie in the mid-nineteenth century. Moreover, much of the serially published and sequentially organized writings of the nineteenth and early twentieth centuries had to have been influenced by Charles Dickens's *Sketches by Boz* (1836) and *Pickwick Papers* (1837). Indeed, Dickens's first books were a seminal influence not only on the Canadian short story cycle—especially on Susanna Moodie and Stephen Leacock—but also on the English story cycle generally. A similar claim can be made for the importance of Ivan Turgenev's *A Sportsman's Sketches* (1852), the book Sherwood Anderson, author of the first modern American story cycle, *Winesburg, Ohio* (1919), considered "one of the great books of the world" (Ingram 1971, 148, n. 2) and which Frank O'Connor described as perhaps "the greatest book of short stories ever written." O'Connor goes further: "Nobody, at the time it was written, knew quite how great it was, or what influence it was to have in the creation of a new art form" (1963, 46).

But earlier writings are too often called upon to perform distorting turns of anticipation and fulfillment, and, intertextual critics to the contrary, it is wise to be wary of committing what Northrop Frye described as a kind of anachronistic fallacy. It is safer to observe that, to the extent these pre-Confederation writings can be said to anticipate the story cycle in Canada—apart from what they are as fictional letters and sketchbooks—the form comes to fruition in Duncan Campbell Scott's story cycle of a town in Western Quebec, *In the Village of Viger* (1896) and, a little later, in Stephen Leacock's classic treatment of small-town Ontario at about the same time, *Sunshine Sketches of a Little Town* (1912). *Viger* and the *Sketches* were the first to weave together for literary purposes the various strands of nineteenth-century short narrative—gothic tale, nature sketch, character sketch, anecdote, tall tale, local color writing, fable, and romantic tale—that formed the modern story cycle. (Scott's *Viger* is a tour de force of nineteenth-century story forms,[2] while Leacock's sketches parody many of these same forms.)

The story cycle continues to be well suited to the concerns of Canadian writers intent on portraying a particular region or community, its history, it characters, its communal concerns—regions and communities as diverse as Viger at the turn of the century, the dust-bowl prairies of Sinclair Ross's *The Lamp at Noon and Other Stories* (1968), the eccentric west coast islanders of Jack Hodgins's *Spit Delaney's Island* (1976), the impoverished Cape Bretoners of Sheldon Currie's *The Glace Bay Miner's Museum* (1979), and the Albertan Pine Mountain Lodge of Edna Alford's *A Sleep Full of Dreams* (1981).[3] Other story cycles, such as Margaret Laurence's *A Bird in the House* (1970), Clark Blaise's *A North American Education* (1973), Alice Munro's *Who Do You Think You Are?* (1978), and Robert Currie's *Night Games* (1983), focus on the growth of a single character in a particular community, thereby illustrating in the story cycle the interest in individual psychology since the rise of modernism.[4]

In addition to providing opportunities for the exploration of place and character, the story cycle offers formal possibilities that allow its practitioners the freedom to challenge, whether intentionally or not, the totalizing impression of the traditional novel of social and psychological realism.[5] Canadian writers who are inspired to compose something more unified than the miscellaneous collection of stories and who do not wish to forego the documentary function of the realistic novel (whose fictional strategies will likely continue to have relevance in a relatively young country), but who are wary of the traditional novel's grander ambitions, often choose the story cycle. It is a form that allows for a new kind of unity in disunity and a more accurate representation of modern sensibility. Even such early cycles as Scott's *Viger* and Leacock's *Sunshine Sketches* portray the struggles of small communities for coherence and survival under contrary pressures from metropolitanism and modernity, and they do so in a form that mirrors the struggle between cohesion and a kind of entropy, or between solidarity and fragmentation, between things holding together and things pulling apart. Later, such writers as Laurence and Munro explore the formation of fictional personality in this form that subverts the impression of completion, of closure and totality, suggesting that psychic coherence is as much an illusion in fiction as it may be in fact.

Forrest L. Ingram, still the foremost theorist of short story cycles,[6] offers a workable definition of the form: it is "a book of short stories so linked to each other by their author that the reader's successive experience on various levels of the pattern of the whole significantly modifies his experience of each of its component parts" (1971, 19). Ingram's definition emphasizes the constitutive dynamic of the short story cycle: its unique balancing of the integrity, or individuality, of each story and the needs of the group, and vice versa—what Ingram calls "the tension between the one and many" (19). Interestingly, Robert Kroetsch has observed of Canadian writing generally a characteristic similar to the distinguishing feature of the story cycle described here—its unique balancing of the one and the many:

In Canadian writing, and perhaps in Canadian life, there is an exceptional pressure placed on the individual and the self by the community or society. The self is not in any way Romantic or privileged. The small town remains the ruling paradigm, with its laws and familiarity and conformity. Self and community almost fight to a draw. (1989, 51)

Kroetsch's observation is based, I suspect, on perceptions familiar to numerous other Canadian writers: in the attempt to find that elusive balance between the one and the many, Canadians, unlike Americans, traditionally have been more willing to sacrifice the gratifications of individualism for the securities of community. Why? The attempt at a complete and convincing answer to that question would require a book. But such an answer would begin with considerations of physical and ideological environment (a geography that isolates, a philosophical tradition of humanism and conservatism) and of broadly historical determinants (the psychic sense of beleaguerment, a feeling of being coerced to choose between opposing positions). Such influences in national character led eventually to various, yet consistent, positions: to the enthronement of compromise as the political ideal, to the positing of the middle way as the best mode of figurative travel, and even to finding in the image of the peacekeeper—the one who literally stands between opposing forces—an international raison d'etre. It was not by chance that Ernest Hemingway declared the first distinctive work of American fiction to be Mark Twain's *Huckleberry Finn*: a first-person episodic novel whose title is the name of its highly individualized hero, a satiric novel from the point of view of an outsider ingenuously castigating his community. The closest Canadian equivalent is Lea-cock's *Sunshine Sketches of a Little Town*, a book whose title focuses attention on the community and whose viewpoint is very much that of the ironic insider, and a book whose form, the story cycle, manages to balance the needs of the one and the many in a manner that may suggest further a geopolitical appro-priateness of this popular subgenre in Canadian writing.

Ingram has also described a system of categorizing story cycles according to the ways in which they were conceived and compiled. He types them as (1) "composed," that is, story cycles that "the author has conceived as a whole from the time he wrote his first story," such as *Sunshine Sketches*; as (2) "arranged," that is, ones that "an author or editor-author has brought together to illuminate or comment upon one another by juxtapositon or association," such as *In the Village of Viger*; and as (3) "completed," that is, "sets of linked stories which are neither strictly composed nor merely arranged," but ones that were com-pleted when their author recognized the links within a group of stories, such as Munro's *Who Do You Think You Are?* (1971, 16-18). This method of catego-rizing has been generally accepted. However, Ingram's landmark study goes only so far in coming to an understanding of this form that occupies the gap between the miscellany of short stories and the novel, between the discontinu-ous and totalizing form.

Perhaps a more useful method of categorizing story cycles is the simpler one of identifying what lends the cycle its coherence. Many story cycles are unified primarily by place. These include such influential classics of the genre as James Joyce's *Dubliners* (1914) and Anderson's *Winesburg, Ohio*; or such Canadian examples as Scott's *Viger*; George Elliott's *The Kissing Man* (1962), which is set in an anonymous town based on Strathroy, Ontario; Hugh Hood's *Around the Mountain* (1967), set in Montreal; Hodgins' *Spit Delaney's Island*; and Sandra Birdsell's *Night Travellers* (1982) and *Ladies of the House* (1984), both of which are set in the fictional community of Agassiz, Manitoba. The other major category would be cycles unified primarily by characters, such as Lau-rence's *A Bird in the House,* Munro's *Who Do You Think You Are?* and Isabel Huggan's *The Elizabeth Stories* (1984).

Although a recurring theme or a consistent style alone cannot be the defining characteristic of a story cycle, it would be a mistake not to consider the role those aspects play in strengthening the coherence of cycles unified primarily by place and/or character. And, it needs to be added, these two major categories overlap. For instance, Hanratty, Rose's hometown, serves also to unify Mun-ro's *Who Do You Think You Are?*, and both the character of Arla Pederson and the setting of an old folks' home help unify Alford's *A Sleep Full of Dreams*.

But even if this alternative system of classifying story cycles according to principles of coherence goes farther than a system based on principles of com-position (Ingram's distinction), it still betrays the spirit of the story cycle be-cause it leads inevitably to the view of story cycles as failed novels. In fact, each genre has a different aesthetic. The traditional novel, from Richardson to

Richler, presents a continuous narrative of character, place, theme, and style—however scrambled the chronology of that narrative. And, of course, the novel coheres most obviously in being an extended narrative: it comprises a plot that unfolds over a comparatively lengthy period of time. Short stories, because they so often describe only climactic actions, are distinguished for their concision. Even in the linked series they will always lack the traditional novel's chief advantage as a unified, continuous, totalizing narrative form. Something essential to stories is decidedly un-novelistic, something, as Edgar Allan Poe realized, that is closer to lyric poetry—the illuminating flash rather than the steadily growing light.[7]   However, reviewers and critics too often persist in approaching story cycles with an inappropriate aesthetic, with the wrong focus. The series of flashes signals a different code altogether from the steady beam.

The success of a story cycle should not be judged, therefore, for its approximation of the achievement of a novel.[8]   Its success should not depend upon the extent to which it is unified by place, character, theme, or style, nor, for that matter, should it be judged finally by any aesthetic grounded in the desire for a continuous and complete unfolding. Although the story cycle accommodates writers who wish to examine particular places and characters, the form is also unique for the way in which it often reflects the *failure* of place and character to unify a work that remains tantalizingly whole yet fundamentally suspicious of completeness. Viger, for instance, does not hold together Scott's *In the Village of Viger*. Place does and does not unify, for place in that story cycle fails to lend coherence.

Viger is about the ways in which the things of Viger are threatening to fall apart before the onslaught of modernity. Perhaps this suspiciously neat paradox can be stated in terms of the outer and inner dynamic of the form, with Viger the setting of the stories, the literal place, representing the outer dynamic that obviously lends coherence to the stories of this cycle, and with Viger the figure of Scott's vision of a communal ideal representing the inner dynamic that is being destabilized and, consequently, destabilizes.

Similarly, Rose does not ultimately unify Munro's *Who Do You Think You Are?* That story cycle is about mistaken notions of coherent personality and character—how they are formed and represented—as whole entities in both life and fiction. Often each story of a cycle raises such questions of essentialism, continuity, and coherence only to defer their desired solutions to the next story in the cycle. Each story's conflict resembles its predecessor's while yet being different, until we reach the final story of the cycle, which now returns us to the preceding stories in the context of the cycle as a whole. The result is something like a formal hermeneutic circle. Story cycles viewed with regard to both their outer and inner dynamic, whether cycles of character or place, seldom achieve a satisfying "presence."

It is understandable, then, that this form came into its own in the late nineteenth century and is in the main a twentieth-century form. (And for once in Canadian literature there is no time lag between its practice elsewhere and its

accomplished handling here, as witness Scott's *Viger* in 1896.) The popularity
of short story cycles coincides with the rise of modernism in literature, when
the revolutionary impact of Darwin, Marx, Freud, and Einstein was cumula-
tively felt and all traditional systems, including the tradition of the realistic
novel, were coming under destabilizing scrutiny (by systems themselves totalizing, of course). Viewed in this context, the short story cycle is a kind of anti-
novel, fragmenting the lengthy continuous narrative's treatment of place, time,
character, and plot.[9]   There were those in Canada at this time, such as Scott
and Leacock, who used the fragmented/fragmenting form paradoxically for
intentionally totalizing purposes. Leacock employs place, Mariposa, to display
ironically his ideal of a tory and humanist community.[10]   Yet repeatedly in
individual stories, the community, portrayed as robbed from within and without
of genuine religious spirit and political leadership, seems always to be resisting
Leacock's unifying vision. Those critics who regret that Leacock did not write,
perhaps could not write, a novel have failed to see just how appropriate his chosen form—the story cycle—was to his lament in the frenetic modern age for an
essentially eighteenth- and nineteenth-century social philosophy of tolerance
and responsibility.[11]

When Scott conceived of Viger, the small town on the periphery of a Quebec
city at the turn of the century, and when his vision showed him, too, that all the
values of the traditional humanist were here under pressure from the forces of
urbanization and modernity, what better form could he have chosen to display
that situation than the short story cycle? Given such visions of threatened dis-
integration, the nineteenth-century novel with its totalizing conventions would
rightly have been considered as (or, more likely, intuitively bypassed as) formally inappropriate to the insights and forebodings authors wished to express.
And what was true of formal appropriateness at the beginning of the century
became only more apparent as the decades passed like fissured beads on a
fraying string.

The story cycle works through a process that Robert Luscher has recently
compared to a musical sequence: "the story sequence repeats and progressively
develops themes and motifs over the course of the work; its unity derives from
perception of both the successive ordering and recurrent patterns, which together provide the continuity of the reader experience" (1989, 149). This process Ingram earlier identified as "the dynamic patterns of recurrence and development" (1971, 20). In such a pattern the first and last stories are of key significance, and the final story of the cycle is the most powerful because there the
patterns of recurrence and development initiated in the opening story come
naturally to fullest expression.

Opening stories in cycles of place usually describe the setting of the ensuing
stories in a way that presents place as one of the cycle's major actors. Cycles
whose primary unity is provided by a central character begin, as might be expected, with a story of the protagonist's childhood, establishing a pattern that is
repeated with variation throughout the cycle. However, it is the concluding sto-

ries of cycles that present the most serious challenges to readers and critics. These stories bring to fulfillment the recurrent patterns of the cycle, frequently reintroducing many of the cycle's major characters and central images, and restating in a refrain-like manner the thematic concerns of the preceding stories. Because of the paramount importance of concluding stories, this chapter will conclude by illustrating their function with specific reference to the final story in a cycle of place, "The way back" of Elliott's *The Kissing Man*, and in a cycle of character, the title story of Munro's *Who Do You Think You Are?*

"The way back" focuses on yet another quirky communal ritual in a cycle replete with public, though mostly private, rituals—all of which ceremonialize the passing on of traditions, personal histories, family memories, both the good and the bad. As the cumulative work of a cycle, "The way back" is stronger, moreover, because it echoes and reintroduces many of the preceding stories' particular symbols, rituals, and characters. Doctor Fletcher delivers Dan; a blown ostrich egg helps illustrate Dan's alienation as a result of his father's not having had the grinderman present at his birth (127); Dan's overly practical father recalls Finn's hard father; Dan avoids the old man who sits by the pond; Dan marries the granddaughter of the community patriarch, Mayhew Salkad; and it is Mayhew who insists that, "there is always hope of return" (Elliott 1962, 132)—all of these details recalling important aspects of preceding stories. By so echoing and paralleling, this concluding story suggests that "the way back" is effected not only by an individual's decision to participate in the life of the community, but also by the cooperation of the entire community, or, to speak literarily, by the whole story cycle.

Dan comes to realize that his father's break with communal tradition is not, as his father contends, "a question of fashion or times changing" (Eliott 1962, 130), though it is also and ominously that. He understands the cultural significance of the grinder man and the reasons for his own alienation: "Things like that, if you don't have a feeling for it, it'll separate you from the kids in school" (1962, 129). Here the concluding story emphasizes the preceding stories' priorizing of feeling over intellectualizing. Dan realizes, too, that his father's attitude is "the difference between the life of [his] father and the life of the heart"—the heart which is presented throughout *The Kissing Man* as the chief sensing organ. Dan resolves: "I want the life of the heart and Mr. Salkald says there is hope, there is a way back. This is the connection" (134). When he is an adult, Dan has the grinder man sharpen some tools, including a scythe that once belonged to Mayhew Salkald, the patriarch who figures centrally in the opening story of the cycle, "An act of piety." Dan's act of concession, which acknowledges symbolically the grinder man's vital role in the life of the community, is simple enough, as simple as tending a grave, blowing an egg, breaking the pendants of a chandelier, or catching a fish (all earlier rituals enabling various individual and communal continuities). The results of the act are complex and profound: the reestablishment of familial harmony, the reaffirmation of the importance of emotion and intuition, the reintegration of Dan's family into the community. Dan's wife places Mayhew's sharpened scythe—temporal symbol of both continuity and necessary disjunction—under the bed of the baby she is weaning, thereby affirming a bond between her family and the community. This is ultimately a cultural bond: "But when I speak of the family, I have in mind a bond which embraces . . . a piety toward the dead, however obscure, and a solicitude for the unborn, however remote." That statement from T. S. Eliot's *Notes Toward a Definition of Culture* provides the epigraph to *The Kissing Man*, and George Elliott has framed his story cycle—whose concern is the family community in T. S. Eliot's sense—with "An act of piety," concerning a piety toward the dead, and the concluding "The way back," with its solicitude for the unborn.

But *The Kissing Man* appears to reach a comforting closure only if its readers forget the earlier stories, which should prove difficult since all of them are figuratively present in this final one. To feel only comforted by the conclusion of "The way back" is willfully to forget those unflattering features of the preceding stories, such as the axe-handle factory that now holds practical sway over the lives of many of the townsfolk, the mysterious pond that has been drained, and the undercurrent of intolerance that also defines this (and perhaps every other) small community. Such a forgetting would be ironic indeed, considering that the stories of *The Kissing Man* focus repeatedly on the importance of memory and ritual in the transference of communal values. Along with its reaffirmation of communal and familial values—through repeated image, incident and character from earlier stories—the concluding story of this cycle simultaneously reminds its readers of the persistence of some old habits of exclusion and the beginning of some new anticommunal tendencies.

Alice Munro's "Who Do You Think You Are?" delivers Rose to a final confrontation with the question of identity and self-possession that, this concluding story reveals, is asked most insistently of oneself by one's origins. Like "The way back," "Who Do You Think You Are?" contains numerous echoes of preceding stories. Both stories focus on eccentric characters, the grinder man and Milton Homer, who embody something essential in their communities. Both characters contain the key to the central characters' search for identity, and, interestingly, both are associated with birth rituals, perhaps because the discovery (or rediscovery) of one's place in the community (for Dan) and self-identity (for Rose) would constitute a rebirth. Epiphany of a kind occurs in the final story of Munro's cycle when Rose recognizes in Ralph Gillespie yet another reflection of herself, recognizes a spiritual affinity with a man who is, like Milton Homer, closely identified with Hanratty. But readers may experience both resolution and a sort of vertigo at Rose's intimation finally *who she is*. With the knowledge that Ralph originally found his identity as an impersonator by imitating Milton Homer—Hanratty's carnivalesque figure—and the revelation that Rose, the actress, the great impersonator, imitates not Milton Homer but Ralph's impersonation of Milton Homer, the possibility of self-possession recedes into a series of reflections of reflections, for Milton Homer is himself a grotesque reflection of Hanratty. This final story with its deceptively illusory resolution actually posits the steady sense of self as something like a series of Chinese boxes. However, literal Chinese boxes do finally end. Perhaps a better analogy would be with those literary Chinese boxes in Flann O'Brien's *The Third Policeman*, the kind that *do* go on into invisibility, pitching readers into the infinite, claustrophic regressus of a hellish *mise en abyme*. That image suggests one tentative answer to this cycle's titular riddle: You may think you possess a stable identity, a steady sense of self, but you are actually an infinitely regressing reflection of every image of yourself that has been reflected back to you by your environment, especially your early environment. Ultimately—and disturbingly nihilistic in a writer often mistakenly considered conventional in her vision—there may well be no grounded "you" from which to launch the self-reflective probe of the book's title.

But I am not as concerned here with exploring the complex issues raised by *The Kissing Man* and *Who Do You Think You Are?* as with showing something of the cumulative function of their typical concluding stories. Both stories depict provisional possibilities respecting the recuperation of community for Dan and of a sense of self and identity for Rose. But those possibilities must remain provisional within both these concluding stories and the preceding stories of the cycle, which the concluding stories ask the reader to reconsider. As much as they tempt with hints of comfortable closure, they also destabilize, resisting closure. This is true also of "Paul Farlotte," the concluding story of Scott's *In the Village of Viger*; of Leacock's *Sunshine Sketches*' "L'Envoi"; of Laurence's "Jericho's Brick Battlements"; and the final stories of numerous other cycles. Such inconclusive concluding stories would appear to be one of the dominant characteristics of the story cycle, and when this conventionalized indeterminacy is worked by writers of Scott's, Leacock's, Elliott's, Laurence's, and Munro's skills, the result is story cycles that return to their origins without ever quite closing the circle.

W. H. New has suggested that the popularity of the short story in Canada results from our status as a marginalized culture and the story's status as a marginalized genre. Stories enable Canadian and New Zealand writers to work, often with subversive irony, in a form that is not the dominant genre in the overwhelming cultures to, respectively, the south and the west.[12]

I would add that the story cycles' tension between the one and the many suits the writers of a country that was, in sociopolitical terms, formed out of the tension between the conservatism of England and the liberalism of France, and subsequently between its own communal conservatism and the liberal individualism of its gigantic neighbor to the south. It may also be that the distinguished Canadian short story in its extension to the story cycle most aptly mirrors in its form the distinctive, yet closely linked regions of Canada: a kind of geopolitical fictional linkage of bonds and gaps *A mari usque ad mare*, as opposed to the continuous totalizing story written *E pluribus unum*.

NOTES

A version of this essay appeared in *Canadian Literature* 130 (Autumn 1991): 91-104.

1. I prefer the term "cycle" to "sequence" because it conveys the form's dynamic of repetition and development, because it describes the cumulative function of the cycles' concluding stories, and because it carries appropriate historical associations with other cyclical forms. For a different view, see Robert M. Luscher, "The Short Story Sequence: An Open Book," in *Short Story Theory at a Crossroads*, eds. Susan Lohafer and Jo Ellyn Clarey (Baton Rouge: Lousiana State UP, 1989): 148-67.

2. See S. L. Dragland, Intro., *In the Village of Viger and Other Stories*, by Duncan Campbell Scott (Toronto: McClelland and Stewart, 1973): 12.

3. Recent evidence of the growing critical interest in Canadian short story cycles can be seen in *Writing Saskatchewan* (Regina: U of Regina, 1989): 155-79.

4. Any survey of the story cycle in Canada must note such unacknowledged experimenters in the form of the linked series as Frederick Philip Grove of *Over Prairie Trails* (1922) and Hugh MacLennan of *Seven Rivers of Canada* (1961), although the scope of this chapter does not permit further consideration of these hybrid forms. See Rudy Wiebe, "Afterword," *Fruits of the Earth*, by Frederick Philip Grove (Toronto: McClelland and Stewart, 1989): 351-59, for a discussion of the cyclical form in Grove's writings.

5. I would emphasize here the adjective "traditional" or "conventional," aware that there are many contemporary novels, such as Julian Barnes's 1989 *The History of the World in 10½ Chapters*, that resemble story cycles, as this chapter describes them, more than novels. According to Luscher, "The form's development has been spurred not only by Joyce and Anderson but also by the possibilities of unity demonstrated in American regional collections and by more recent experimentation with the novel" (1989, 153).

6. Although Luscher disagrees with Ingram's method of categorization (1971, 162), he concedes that Ingram's terminology is the one "critics most commonly use" (1989, 149).

7. See Poe's "The Philosophy of Composition," in *Selected Writings of Edgar Allan Poe: Poems, Tales, Essays, and Reviews*, ed. with an introduction by David Galloway (Harmondsworth, England: Penguin, 1982): 480-92; or Poe's review of Nathaniel Hawthorne's *Twice-Told Tales*, "Twice-Told Tales," in *Selected Writings*, especially 443-46.

8. See Luscher: "These works should be viewed, not as failed novels, but as unique hybrids that combine two distinct reading pleasures: the patterned closure of individual stories and the discovery of larger unifying strategies that transcend the apparent gaps between stories" (1989, 149-50).

9. Again Luscher is worth quoting: "By operating without the major narrative unities of the novel, the writer of the short story sequence courts disunity in order to achieve victory' over it by setting up a new set of narrative ground rules that rely heavily on active pattern-making faculties" (1989, 158).

10. See Gerald Lynch, *Stephen Leacock: Humour and Humanity* (Montreal-Kingston: McGill-Queen's UP, 1988).

11. See, for example, Robertson Davis, *Stephen Leacock* (Toronto: McClelland and Stewart, 1970); and Donald Cameron, *Faces of Leacock* (Toronto: Ryerson, 1967): 138. This view of Leacock is best expressed in the title of Cameron's article, "Stephen Leacock: The Novelist Who Never Was," *Dalhousie Review* 46 (Spring 1966): 15-28.

12. See New, 1987, ix. See also Raymond Knister, Introduction, *Canadian Short Stories* (Freeport, N.Y.: Books for Libraries P, 1928): xi.

WORKS CITED

Anderson, Sherwood. *Winesburg, Ohio*. Ed. Malcolm Cowley. New York: Viking, 1960.

Barth, John. "Tales Within Tales Within Tales," "*The Ocean of Story*," and "Don't Count On It: A Note On The Number Of *The 1001 Nights.*" *The Friday Book: Essays and Other Nonfiction*. New York: G. P. Putnam's Sons, 1984. 218-38, 84-90, 258-81.

Cameron, Donald. *Faces of Leacock*. Toronto: Ryerson, 1967.

—. "Stephen Leacock: The Novelist Who Never Was." *Dalhousie Review* 46 (Spring 1966): 15-28.

Davies, Robertson. *Stephen Leacock*. Toronto: McClelland and Stewart, 1970.

Elliott, George. "The way back," *The Kissing Man*. Toronto: Macmillan, 1962.

Ingram, Forrest L. *Representative Short Story Cycles of the Twentieth Century: Studies in a Literary Genre*. Paris: Mouton, 1971.

Knister, Raymond. Introduction. *Canadian Short Stories*. Freeport, N.Y.: Books for Libraries P, 1928.

Kroetsch, Robert. "No Name Is My Name." *The Lovely Treachery of Words: Essays Selected and New*. Toronto: Oxford UP, 1989. 41-52.

Leacock, Stephen. *Sunshine Sketches of a Little Town*. Toronto: McClelland and Steward, 1989.

Luscher, Robert M. "The Short Story Sequence: An Open Book," *Short Story Theory at a Crossroads*. Eds. Susan Lohafer and Jo Ellyn Clarey. Baton Rouge: Louisiana State UP, 1989. 148-67.

Lynch, Gerald. *Stephen Leacock: Humour and Humanity*. Montreal-Kingston: McGill-Queen's UP, 1988.

New, W. H. *Dreams of Speech and Violence: The Art of the Short Story in Canada and New Zealand*. Toronto: U of Toronto P, 1987.

Poe, Edgar Allan. *Selected Writings of Edgar Allan Poe: Poems, Tales, Essays and Reviews*. Ed. David Galloway. Harmondsworth, England: Penguin, 1982.

Schroeder, Andreas. "Fear of the Novel: The Linked Short Story in Saskatchewan Fiction." *Writing Saskatchewan*. Regina: U of Regina, 1989. 155-79.

Scott, Duncan Campbell. *In the Village of Viger and Other Stories*. Intro. S. L. Dragland. Toronto: McClelland and Stewart, 1973.

Wiebe, Rudy. "Afterword." *Fruits of the Earth* by Frederick Philip Grove. Toronto: McClelland and Stewart, 1989. 351-59.

Beginnings:
"The Origins and Art
of the Short Story"

Joyce Carol Oates

Not that the story need be long, but it will take a long while to make it short.
Henry David Thoreau

Formal definitions of the short story are commonplace, yet there is none quite democratic enough to accommodate an art that includes so much variety and an art that so readily lends itself to experimentation and idiosyncratic voices. Perhaps length alone should be the sole criterion? Whenever critics try to impose other, more subjective strictures on the genre (as on any genre) too much work is excluded.

Yet length itself is problematic. No more than 10,000 words? Why not then 10,500? 11,000? Where, in fact, does a short story end and a novella begin? (Tolstoy's "The Death of Ivan Ilych" can be classified as both.) And there is the reverse problem, for, as short stories condense, they are equally difficult to define. What is the short-short story, precisely? What is that most teasing of prose works, the prose-poem? We can be guided by critical intuition in distinguishing between a newspaper article or an anecdote and a fully realized story, but intuition is notoriously difficult to define (or depend upon). Since the cultivation of the aesthetically subtle, minimally resolved short story by such masters as Chekhov, Lawrence, Joyce, and Hemingway, the definition of the "fully realized" story has become problematic as well.

My personal definition of the form is that it represents a concentration of imagination, and not an expansion; it *is* no more than 10,000 words; and, no matter its mysteries or experimental properties, it achieves closure—meaning that, when it ends, the attentive reader understands why.

That is to say, the short story is a prose piece that is not a mere concatenation of events, as in a news account or an anecdote, but an intensification of meaning by way of events. Its "plot" may be wholly interior, seemingly static, a matter of the progression of a character's thought. Its resolution need not be a formally articulated statement, as in many of Hawthorne's more didactic tales or in William Austin's once-famous cautionary tale, "Peter Rugg, the Missing Man," but it signals a tangible change of some sort; a distinct shift in consciousness; a deepening of insight. In the most elliptical of stories, a characteristic of the modern and contemporary story, the actual resolution frequently occurs in the reader's, and not the fictional characters', consciousness. To read stories as disparate as Katherine Anne Porter's "He," Paul Bowles's "A Distant Episode," Ray Bradbury's "There Will Come Soft Rains," Raymond Carver's "Are These Actual Miles?," and Tobias Wolff's "Hunters in the Snow" is to read stories so structured as to provide the reader, and not the characters themselves, with insight. Because the meaning of the story does not lie on its surface, visible and self-defining, does not mean that meaning does not exist. Indeed, the ambiguity of meaning, its inner, private quality, may well be part of the writer's vision.

In addition to these qualities, most short stories (but hardly all) are restricted in time and place; concentrate upon a very small number of characters; and move toward a single ascending dramatic scene or revelation. And all are generated by conflict.

The artist *is* the focal point of conflict. Lovers of pristine harmony, those who dislike being upset, shocked, made to think and to feel, are not naturally suited to appreciate art, at least not serious art; which, unlike television dramas and situation comedies, for instance, does not evoke conflict merely to solve it within a brief space of time. Rather, conflict is the implicit subject, itself; as conflict, the establishment of disequilibrium, is the impetus for the evolution of life, so is conflict the genesis, the prime mover, the secret heart of all art.

Discord, then, and not harmony, is the subject our writers share in common, although the quelling of discord and the reestablishment of harmony may well be the point of the art.

The "literary" short story, the meticulously constructed short story, descends to us by way of the phenomenon of magazine publication, beginning in the nineteenth century, but has as it ancestor the oral tale.

We must assume that storytelling is as old as mankind, at least as old as spoken language. Reality is not enough for us—we crave the imagination's embellishments upon it. *In the beginning. Once upon a time. A long time ago there lived a princess who.* How the pulse quickens, hearing such beginnings: such promises of something new, strange, unexpected! The epic poem, the ballad, the parable, the beast-fable, sacred narratives, visionary prophecies—the fabulous mythopoetic "histories" of ancient cultures—the "divinely inspired" books of the Old and New Testament: all are forms of storytelling, expressions of the human imagination.

Like a river fed by countless small streams, the modern short story derives from a multiplicity of sources. Historically, the earliest literary documents of which we have knowledge are Egyptian papyri dating from 4000-3000 B.C., containing a work called, most intriguingly, *Tales of the Magicians*. The Middle Ages revered such secular works as fabliaux, ballads, and verse romances; the Arabian *Thousand and One Nights* and the Latin tales and anecdotes of the *Gesta Romanorum*, collected before the end of the thirteenth century, as well as the one hundred tales of Boccaccio's *The Decameron* and Chaucer's *Canterbury Tales*, were enormously popular for centuries. Storytelling as an oral art, like the folk ballad, was, or is, characteristic of nonliterate cultures, for obvious reasons. Even the prolongation of light (by artificial means) had an effect upon the storytelling tradition of our ancestors. The rise in literacy marked the ebbing of interest in old fairy tales and ballads, as did the gradual stabilization of languages and the cessation of local dialects in which the tales and ballads had been told most effectively. (The Brothers Grimm noted this phenomenon: if, in High German, a fairy tale gained in superficial clarity, it "lost in flavor, and no longer had such a firm hold of the kernel of meaning.")

One of the signal accomplishments of American literature, most famously exemplified by the great commercial and critical success of Samuel Clemens, is the reclamation of that "lost" flavor—the use, as style, of dialect, regional, and strongly (often comically) vernacular language. Of course, before Samuel Clemens cultivated the ingenuous-ironic persona of "Mark Twain," there were dialect writers and tale-tellers in America (for instance, Joel Chandler Harris, creator of the popular "Uncle Remus" stories); but Mark Twain was a phenomenon of a kind previously unknown here—our first American writer to be avidly read, coast to coast, by all classes of Americans, from the most highborn to the least cultured and minimally literate. The development of mass-market newspapers and subscription book sales made this success possible, but it was the brilliant reclamation of the vernacular in Twain's work (the early "The Celebrated Jumping Frog of Calaveras County," for instance) that made him into so uniquely *American* a writer, our counterpart to Dickens.

Twain's rapid ascent was by way of popular newspapers, which syndicated features coast to coast, and his crowd-pleasing public performances, but the more typical outlet for a short story writer, particularly of self-consciously "literary" work, was the magazine. Writers from Washington Irving and Nathaniel Hawthorne onward began their careers by publishing short fiction in magazines before moving on to book publication; in the nineteenth century, such highly regarded, and, in some cases, high-paying magazines as *The North American Review, Harper's Monthly, Atlantic Monthly, Scribner's Monthly* (later *The Century*), *The Dial,* and *Graham's Magazine* (briefly edited by Edgar Allan Poe) advanced the careers of writers who would otherwise have had financial difficulties in establishing themselves. In post-World War II America, the majority of short story writers publish in small-circulation "literary" magazines throughout their careers. It is all but unknown for a writer to publish a book of short stories without having published most of them in magazines beforehand.

Edgar Allan Poe's famous review-essay of Hawthorne's *Twice-Told Tales* (*Graham's Magazine*, 1842) is justly celebrated as one of the crucial documents in the establishment of the short story as a distinct literary genre. Poe's aesthetic is a curious admixture of the romantic and the classic: the intention of the artwork is to move the reader's soul deeply, but the means to this intention is coolly, if not chillingly, cerebral. Poe in his philosophy as in his practice is both visionary and manipulator:

A skillful literary artist has constructed his tale. If wise, he has not fashioned his thoughts to accommodate his incidents; but having conceived, with deliberate care, a certain unique or single *effect* to be wrought out, he then invents such incidents—he then combines such events as may best aid him in establishing this preconceived effect.

Magazine publication is the ideal outlet for Poe's hypothesized tale, where works "requiring from a half-hour to one or two hours in [their] perusal" appeared. Indeed, the emphasis in Poe's review-essay is on the reader's experience of the work, and not upon the work itself, as if—can this be genius speaking? in the very language of the hack?—it scarcely matters *what* has been written, only *that* it has been written with a certain preconceived effect. (It should be noted too, and not incidentally, that Poe was a man of vast literary ambitions, and not simply, or not exclusively, a tormented Romantic driven to the composition of uncanny poetry and prose: he wrote for magazines, and he edited magazines, and it was his professional obsession from 1836 to his death in 1849 to found and edit a magazine, to be called *Penn Magazine*.)

As the literary short story derives from the oral tale, so, in Poe's aesthetic, the meticulously constructed short story relates to the poem. While the highest genius, arguably, is best employed in poetry ("not to exceed in length what might be perused in an hour"), the "loftiest talent" may turn to the prose tale, as exemplified by Nathaniel Hawthorne. Poe elevates the prose tale above much of poetry, in fact, and above the novel, for poetry brings the reader to too high a pitch of excitement to be sustained, and the novel is objectionable because of its "undue" length. By contrast, the brief tale enables the writer "to carry out the fullness of his intention. . . . During the hour of perusal the soul of the reader is at the writer's control. There are no external or extrinsic influences—resulting from weariness or interruption."

In Poe's somewhat Aristotelian terms, the secret of the short story's composition is its unity. Yet, within this, as within a well-made play, a multiplicity of modes or inflections of thought and expression—"the ratiocinative, for example, the sarcastic, or the humourous"—are available to the writer, as they are not available, apparently, to the poet. This concept, dogmatic even for its time, relates only incidentally to the stories Poe himself wrote, but it provides an aesthetic anticipating the work of such masters of the genre as Chekhov, Joyce, Henry James, and Hemingway, in which everything is excluded that does not contribute to the general effect, or design, of the story. (Like most critics who are also artists, Poe was formulating an aesthetic to accommodate his own practice and his own limitations. Temperamentally, Poe was probably incapable of the sustained effort of the novelist; this helps to explain his envious disparagement of Charles Dickens, who, for all his apparent flaws in Poe's judgment, enjoyed the enormous popular success denied to Poe during his own lifetime.)

The American short story, however, has had no more thoughtful, visionary, and influential an early critic than Poe; just as the history of the short story itself in America is bound up with the unique work Poe published in 1840, *Tales of the Grotesque and Arabesque.*

A predominant vein connecting many American short stories, from Washington Irving and William Austin through to our contemporaries, is the quest, in some cases a distinctly *American* quest, for one's place in the world—one's cultural and spiritual identity, in terms of self and others.

For ours is the nation, so rare in human history, of self-determination—a theoretical experiment in newness, exploration, discovery. In theory, at least, who our ancestors have been, what languages they have spoken, in what religions they believed—these factors cannot really help to define *us*. And it has been often noted that, in the New World, history itself has moved with extraordinary rapidity. Each generation constitutes a beginning-again, a new discovery, sometimes of language itself.

In our contemporaries, the burden of history and politics as *personal* fate, weighing, at times, almost physically upon the shoulders of survivors and descendants, is dramatized in stories encompassing a wide range of subject matter, style, and vision—from Flannery O'Connor's mordant "A Late Encounter with the Enemy" (an aged Civil War veteran's hallucinatory descent into death, and into his identity) to Bernard Malamud's "My Son the Murderer" (generational conflict in the radicalized, despairing 1960s), Louise Erdrich's "Fleur" (a Native American "witch" resists the fate that would make her a victim), and Bharati Mukherjee's "The Management of Grief" (the surviving member of a Hindu family killed in a terrorist bombing detaches herself, through pain, from the paralysis of grief). The elliptical, poetic tales of Sandra Cisneros and the seemingly forthright, conversational "Two Kinds" by Amy Tan take for granted a dominant Caucasian world outside the family—here, such abstractions as history and politics are realized in the experience of sensitive, yet representative, adolescent girls.

Meticulous chroniclers of lives less dramatically touched by history, though yet distinctly, often disturbingly American, are such writers as John Cheever, John Updike, Alice Adams, Ursula LeGuin, and Raymond Carver, among others, who have taken for their subjects the lives (and what radically differing lives, told in what radically differing voices) of what might be called mainstream Americans of the Caucasian middle class. What these writers share is their artistry, their commitment to the short story, and their faith in the imaginative reconstruction of reality that constitutes literature.

As Tolstoy said, talent is the capacity to direct concentrated attention upon the subject: "the gift of seeing what others have not seen."

Part II

History and Place

5

They All Laughed When I Sat Down to Write: Chaucer, Jokes, and the Short Story

Barry Sanders

I

The great mother of invention gave birth to fraternal twins: storytelling and joking. The ambiguity that jokes and stories share allows both joker and story-teller to get away with murder. The joker pleads, "I'm only kidding. It was only a joke," while the storyteller wriggles off the hook by saying, "Come on; it's only fiction." In writing fiction, the author weaves an intricately beautiful lie—a metaphoric reality—so that the story will be taken seriously. The author plots in order to perpetrate a story on the audience, to hoodwink it into ac-ceptng the fabrication as real. To be successful, the author must take storytel-ling seriously and, at the same time, take delight in playing a practical joke on the audience. This is as true for that trickster Mark Twain as it is for Geoffrey Chaucer, who instructs us in the Prologue to "The Miller's Tale" not to take his brilliant *narratio* seriously. After all, he announces, "I'm only playing a game." This is a tongue-in-cheek bit of instruction, surely, for Chaucer sets the stakes in some of his games fairly high.

Since both joker and author must enjoy being playful, it makes sense that Thoth, the god of writing in the ancient world, is also the inventor of play—the one who puts play into play. The Latin word for "story," *geste*, produces the modern English *jest*, a kinship that surfaced in English as early as the time of King Aelfric, who uses the word *racu* in some places to translate the Latin *his-toria* and in other places to translate *commoedia*. Thus, the word *racu* is de-fined in Anglo-Saxon glossaries both as "narration" and "laughter." Anglo-Saxons refer to their poets as "laughter-smiths" and "minstrels"—singers of stories—and most often as purveyors of laughter, *gleemen*. But a great distance separates funny stories, or even laughter-smiths and gleemen, from actual jok-ing. And it is that elusive creature, the joke, I want to track. It is almost inevi-table that the joke and the short story should emerge at the same moment. That moment occurs in English literature, albeit in embryonic form, in Chaucer's "The Miller's Tale."

II

Medieval England and France developed a rich tradition of jesting and narration, and, of course, laughter, reflected in an almost unbelievable range of traveling performers—an *ordo vagorum* of motley players. If historical record can be trusted, one could barely take a step across the English landscape without bumping into an acrobat or a magician. The medievals have as many names for their entertainers as the Eskimo do for *snow*. *Mimi, scurrae, scenici, Goliards, poetae, parasites, tragoedi, comoedi, comici, joculares, jocistae, corauli, cantatores, joculatores, historiones, cytharistae, thymalici*—all of these vagabonds played, juggled, and with great fanfare and elaboration recited bawdy *iocare* (jests) and *facetiae* (witty stories).

By the thirteenth century, these various entertainers, ultimately all derived from the *mimi* of ancient Greece, were being described by one French word: *jongleur*. The modern English *juggler* derived, in turn, from the same Latin root for joke, *jocare*. Traveling from place to place, these raconteur/jongleurs generated so much hearty laughter that contemporary historians dubbed England a *terra ridentium*—a land of laughter. It is clear from account books of colleges and monasteries, from councils, synods, and the capitularies of Charlemagne that bishops, abbots, and abbesses, forbidden to own hunting dogs, falcons, and hawks, were also denied the company of these bawdy *joculatores*. They were dangerous, tempting the religious to while away their precious time. Certain capitularies, in denouncing the stories being recited by these troops of itinerant players, make clear that their *gesta* are only thinly disguised *jocistae* (jokes). Besides, many are preserved under the name that Cicero gave them, *facetiae*—short, mostly funny, and bawdy vignettes. They resemble the joke in subject but not yet in form.

By the end of the thirteenth century, humanists began collecting and publishing these *facetiae*, putting an end to their circulation by word of mouth. Something more powerful began to take their place, a genre that remains to this day our most unpredictable and playful form of oral entertainment: the joke. Nearly everyone, even those who cannot tell stories, delights in recounting an occasional joke. We owe this extraordinary invention, at least in English, to Chaucer, who brings the history of jesting, narration, and laughter together in one grand literary move.

Chaucer noticed that the physicality of the practical joke could be converted into a verbal punch line, which turned the listener into a target, a butt, no longer subject to a physical blow, but instead made vulnerable, emotionally and psychically, to an image or a word. In "The Miller's Tale," Chaucer has drawn the curtain aside and offered his fourteenth-century audience a glimpse into the literate future: the practical joke domesticated. While the Miller tells a story that revolves around several practical jokes—a fake flood, a misdirected kiss, a perfectly aimed fart, a singed ass—his tale itself constitutes a colossal, nasty joke about gullibility and cuckoldry, fired at another pilgrim character, the Reeve.

Derisive joking in the Classical world was characterized as *aculei*, meaning "barbed" or "arrow-like"; the word *butt* quite appropriately translates as "target," as in archery. These key words reveal something crucial: the punch line cannot hit its mark unless the victims present themselves as fully rounded characters, their vulnerability made fleshly palpable. The Miller must be close enough to the Reeve to know, as we say, where he "lives." A joke misfires unless it finds a personality rife with consciousness and sensibility. Idiots, dolts—*stupidus* of all stripes—will simply miss the point; or the point will miss them—fly by without so much as a glancing blow; or pass over their heads. Corralling the joke into a literate context forced Chaucer into becoming a mature writer, into dropping traditional, flat stereotypes in favor of more rounded characters. At this early stage of storytelling, characters come to life, oddly enough, so they can be murdered, metaphorically speaking, by other characters. This paradox radically affects the storyteller as well, for in writing jokes Chaucer moved to another level of seriousness. In medieval terms, he became an author.

Chaucer understood that the tremendous power and sophistication of this oral form could be harnessed by literacy to realign social status and personal relationships—to produce, that is, the most profound social change. The ultimate effect of Chaucer's accomplishment is staggering. Because of him people still crack aggressive jokes, and for precisely the same reasons, for the history of joking records the outbreak of an uncivil war. Unsuspecting victims keel over, break up, fall apart, double up—all with laughter. They find themselves slayed, murdered, killed. Joking is violent, vicious, deadly stuff. If no one ever stumbled or fell, never slipped or got butted, we would, if jokes provide any evidence, still try to knock them over—either physically (with practical jokes) or verbally (with well-aimed "punch" lines).

III

Since the action of "The Miller's Tale" may not be fresh in mind, let me remind you of it here. By retracing this tale, I also hope to show how the form of the well-made old-fashioned short story follows the form of Chaucer's early joke. The action starts out fast. The Miller announces that he will tell a tale about cuckoldry. No sooner are the words out of his mouth than his pilgrim rival, the Reeve, protests: Tell something more wholesome, less offensive. The Reeve protests too much, of course, revealing *himself* to be a cuckold of the first order, while laying his insecurities wide open for everyone to examine. Every joker begins by asking the question, "Have you heard the one about the . . .?" or, "Stop me if you've heard this one," for laughter thrives on surprise. True, the Reeve has not heard this one—and he does not want to—but he clearly knows what is coming, and that is his problem: He cannot stop the boorish Miller. Chaucer underscores this rivalry graphically. The Miller, bully that he is, outweighs the skinny, choleric Reeve by several hundred pounds. When he punches, it hurts. Miller and Reeve face off in the tradition of fat and lean comic pairs, like Abbott and Costello, Laurel and Hardy, Mutt and Jeff, and Ralph Cramden and Ed Norton. As the Miller unfolds his story, it is clear that he intends to throw his weight around, and the Reeve will undoubtedly get hurt. The Miller goes right for the bull's-eye—the Reeve's jugular—with his opening shot: An old, wealthy man named John, who just happens to be a carpenter, like the Reeve, marries a young, beautiful girl, Alisoun, and because he feels deeply jealous, he keeps her confined. But unfortunately, he is also cheap. And so to make some extra money, the old carpenter rents a room in his attic to a young, handsome university student, Nicholas. And thus we have the "happy incident." The Reeve stomps his foot, but the Miller rolls on.

The young couple, Alisoun and Nicholas, immediately conspire, of course, to keep John at a safe distance so they can, as Chaucer puts it, "rage and pleye." Alisoun hatches a plan; Nicholas carries it out. In a tiny story within the story, Nicholas warns John about a fast-approaching flood so horrendous it will make Noah's flood seem like a summer shower. To escape certain death by drowning, Nicholas counsels, John must hammer together three little tubs and secure them to the roof, high above the waterline. John complies, and with the gullible old man safely tied to the roof and curled up fast asleep inside his tub, Alisoun and Nicholas descend to the ground floor to spend the evening in bed. At this point, the tale has developed an uneasy balance.

But not for long. Just as Alisoun and Nicholas have settled themselves into bed, Chaucer ruins their fun by throwing a new complication their way—an additional yarn he will use to knit up the climax of the story, and to add another flourish to the lovers' triangle. Absalom, a parish priest who earlier had his eye on Alisoun, comes to her bedroom window, in true courtly fashion, to serenade his paramour and charm a juicy kiss from her. After a few minutes of off-key singing, Absalom pops the question and asks for his kiss. Alisoun consents, but by now she is so enamored of practical jokes that she hatches yet one more. Pucker up, she coyly says, as she eases her naked behind out the window. Blinded by the excitement of getting his kiss at long last, Absalom unwittingly kisses her keester, as Chaucer describes, "ful savourly," producing in Alisoun one of the giddiest iambic lines in literature, as well as the first laugh recorded in English: "'Tehee!' quod she, and clapte the window to."

Practical jokes prompt immediate escalation, just as stories inspire competition. "Can you top this?" is implied in every joke and story. As Absalom slowly understands what he has done, he also resolves to get even, which means of course he must raise the ante. He returns to Alisoun's bedroom window and begs for another kiss, just as wonderful as the last, and Alisoun once more agrees. Nicholas now decides he wants to get *his* fair share; this parish fool should kiss *his* behind too. So Nicholas slides his naked arse out the window, "over the buttok, to the haunche-bon" and, because the night has fallen fast, Absalom asks his little turtle dove to let him know where she is: "Spek, swete bryd," he croons, "I noot not where thou art"—triggering a rhyme Chaucer simply cannot resist: "This Nicholas anon leet fle a fart." But Absalom stands ready this time. Taking careful aim, he brands Nicholas smack in the ass with a red-hot poker.

Nicholas has fired off no ordinary fart. No, Chaucer declares, it was "as greet as it had been a thonder-dent." The noise fills the night air. The tale lacks only one element to make it complete: rain. Without knowing it, Nicholas becomes the weather man. Writhing in pain, clutching his smoking behind, he manages a pathetic cry: "Help. Water. Water." That is all John needs to hear. In his dopey sleep, he concludes that Noah's flood has actually arrived and dutifully cuts the rope holding him fast. As Chaucer puts it: "Downe gooth alle." John falls three stories headlong into the street, bringing all the neighbors from their houses alarmed by the great commotion. Nicholas and Alisoun also dash outside, adding to the confusion. All three characters wind up on the street, leveled, finally, by the action of the story.

When the Miller finishes, the pilgrims all howl with laughter—all but the Reeve, who curses and swears at the Miller. He is angry, disgusted, and, what is worse, humiliated. Thanks to the Miller, thirty-three pilgrims now know the awful truth of his life and in embarrassingly graphic detail. The Miller has stepped outside the boundaries of fiction, violating the rules of storytelling by revealing secrets of the Reeve's personal life. He has backed the Reeve into one of society's most feared corners, forcing him to play the butt of a joke.

Ultimately, Chaucer has thrown every character out of his little house of fiction. Indeed, "The Miller's Tale" follows a carefully planned architectural scheme. In the beginning of the tale, the characters are separated by three stories—from attic to ground floor. As the action rises, all three characters climb outside the confines of the house and up to the roof. When the action begins to run down, so do the principal characters. Alisoun and Nicholas climb down from the roof of the house and reenter it at the first story, to the scene of the original sin, the bedroom. The punch line—the climax of the story—comes in the form of a single word, "water," that in good storytelling fashion secures the knot holding subplot to main plot, the inside of the house to the outside, and fiction to practical joke. The story's denouement is a literal untying of the narrative threads that hold all the elements of the story together, a cutting done by the carpenter himself as he comes to groggy consciousness. This architectural pattern prefigures that nineteenth-century template for the well-made short story, the Freytag Triangle. The story's conclusion leaves its readers with a question: Who will now occupy the house? Chaucer answers this question in the very next tale, for the Reeve, dying to retaliate, builds yet another house of intrigue and deception where a miller, his wife, young daughter, and son all reside.

IV

While we play practical jokes for many reasons—to establish our power, to exercise control, or maybe just to engage in plain fun—we tell aggressive jokes at our neighbors' expense out of envy, a connection first pointed out in the earliest analysis of laughter in the West, in Plato's *Philebus*. Usually, we envy that other person's higher social status or better situation. The Miller and the Reeve have been rivals for some time: One rides at the head of the pilgrimage, the other at the hind end. The Miller slowly reveals that he envies the circumstances of the Reeve's marriage—quite specifically, the Reeve's young and pretty wife. He can rectify this inequity in one of two ways: by raising himself or lowering the Reeve. Jokes accomplish both simultaneously. The joke teller elevates himself by displaying, to everyone's delight and amusement, a keen and clever wit, and lowers the other person by exposing him as a dunce before his peers. Try as he may, the jokee rarely ever second-guesses—and thus is unable to defuse—the punch line. Placing himself so diligently on guard, the jokee renders himself even more unstable and precarious, a wobbly target just begging to be knocked over.

Chaucer uses joking as a socially acceptable form of justice, a self-styled peoples' court. While differences in wealth and position can make people feel deeply envious, envious people hardly ever take matters into their own hands. Rather, they act much more indirectly and passively, praying for some catastrophe, some outside event, to come along and wipe out the rival. Jokes provide another way. The Miller can in an instant "get even" by humiliating the Reeve (literally turning him into earth, *humus*). While the joker necessarily satisfies his needs at the victim's expense, the victim too can retrieve at least some of his self-esteem, but only by pulling himself out of his humiliation. If he becomes angry or leaves in a rage, he lowers himself even farther—buries himself—by prompting the audience to laugh *at* him. How small, we say; he cannot even take a joke. The victim can retaliate by telling a joke back on his aggressor, but it had better be a clever one, more clever than the one the joker told, not like the Reeve's feeble escalation. Having gotten there first with a wisecrack, the joker always seizes the upper hand. It is damned near impossible to pay Don Rickles back. One can try, but the risk is great.

The victim can survive socially in one way only, by standing his ground and laughing the joke off, thus demonstrating that he knows how to play the game like a good sport—that he can, like a cat climbing out of its litter box, shake it off. The audience reinforces his magnanimity by laughing along *with* him, applauding his effort at being a "big" person. Through the power of literacy, jokes can rectify social inequities. However, that only describes half their power.

A collection of fifteenth-century sermons titled *Jacob's Well* explains that only mercy can rid our hearts of envy; the sermons direct good Christians to remove the "ooze of envy" from their souls. For a moment, by bringing the pans of justice into balance, the joker has rid himself of envy and thus has gained some satisfaction. And while it may not yet be heartfelt, both teller and victim must at least act as if they have dropped their grudges and inch their way toward forgiveness. They must at least play at being merciful.   This spirit washes the audience clean, too. As Chaucer notes of the pilgrim audience after they hear the Miller's *jape* (joke): "For the moore part they laughe and pleyde." Laughter promotes feelings of community. In this spirit of *communitas*, each person embraces the other as an equal. The temporary effect of joking, then, is to create a feeling that things are even-Stephen; or, to use the Clown's phrase in *Hamlet*, all is "even-Cristen," a state in which everyone under God's gaze stands as an equal.

That same spirit, I think, characterizes a good deal of fiction. I do not mean that stories have to be moral, at least not in the sense John Gardner means, but in reading we come to accept, even to like, the strangest array of characters. We come to forgive them, many times, because we see in them pieces of ourselves.

V

Hermes, the patron trickster for the early Greeks, is superceded in the early Middle Ages by Merlin, the patron saint of letters. This shape-shifter leaves his epigrams on swords, boats, and tombstones, and sends his letters circulating between lovers and enemies, between Arthur and his barons. More than prolific, Merlin is capable of performing the wildest feats of magic, as well as seeing into the future. Legend knows him best of all as a trickster, a riddler— revealing the truth in apparent lies—and a profound practical joker. For Merlin, writing results above all else in laughing matter.

If Merlin serves as the patron saint of playful writing, Chaucer is its incarnation. He is attracted to joking, not because of his keen sense of humor, but because he is in the very marrow of his bones a writer. He delights in what Ezra Pound calls *logopoeia*, "the dance of the intellect among words." To acknowledge Chaucer's wedding of joking and storytelling is to recognize a most remarkable buried fact about the history of literature: Joking is first cousin to medieval *narratio*, fiction.

Play and language, jokes and literature—the connection may seem odd at first. However, play is so basic to animals—human and nonhuman alike—why shouldn't it inform the very foundations of communication itself? Anyone who writes for a time comes to know that truth. Sooner or later every writer naturally falls into punning and joking. Language begs for it. Even before Saussure and Wittgenstein, philosophers have exploited language's elusive nature. The so-called natural language philosophers have broken the implied connection between word and world. We can no longer claim that words hold any necessary or natural correspondence to objective reality; to use them as exact descriptions of reality is to make of language a lie. Every word, then, functions as a tiny joke—on the speaker, on the listener—a practical joke reality continually plays on the observer. Language can only coax and conjole and try to tease meaning out of events and objects.   At the heart of language, playfulness finds a most happy home.

VI

I do not dare venture a definition of the short story; it is as impossible to capture as any other genre.   It would have to be a definition broad enough to hold Poe *and* Chekhov, Hawthorne *and* Carver.   I can only describe where I find Chaucer standing in the fourteenth century, and that is at the delta, on the high ground where the river of narration and joking roils and casts about before separating into two streams.

No one these days deals very much with plot and character, rising action and denouement.   But in Chaucer's day these were fundamental, and he gave them architectural shape.   He triangulated them.   Even if we say nothing much happens in Chekhov's stories, that the reader moves flatly through their action, we still imply that they play off of, react to, a standard shape.

I am interested in rescuing the short story from the clutches of seriousness, and in reuniting it with its twin, the joke.   The world laughed at Christopher Columbus when he said the world was round.   That one was easy.   But after Chaucer, we have to wonder continually: Who has the last laugh *now*?

6

Southern Women Reconstruct the South: Limit as Aesthetic in the Short Story

Barbara C. Ewell

The founding assumption here is rather modest, a commonplace, if you will: It is that place—specifically the American South—is a construction, that the very ground we stand on, the spaces we can or do inhabit, are the products of the stories we tell. The corollary of that assumption, or at least the space I wish to explore, is that places can also be reconstructed, yielding new grounds, new perspectives; and that when "others"—such as Southern women writers of the short story—have confronted one of the most enduring of American places, the patriarchal South, the reconstruction that results has interesting implications for what we have typically regarded as the limits of place, the limits of region-ality, indeed for the notion of limit itself, and what I view as the false equation of limit and insignificance that has plagued not only regionalism, but also the short story, the work of women, and all other "others."

Storytelling is something Southerners are supposed to be good at doing. At least we like to tell that story about ourselves—that part of the birthright is to be aficionados of tales: family stories on the front porch or around the kitchen table, Bible stories from the pulpit and in Sunday School, hunting tales and barroom lies, local legends about Big Foot or Marie Laveau or UFOs, ancient gossip about the relatively rich or the regionally famous or the just plain odd.

But stories construct places as well as lives: Whether we live in Dixie or the Sunbelt (or in the very different Southland of the Pacific Coast), or dwell beside the banks of the Balbahachas, the Fleuve Saint Louis, or the Mississippi[1] de-pends a great deal on the stories we have heard and believed about Mason and Dixon's surveying abilities, or about economic redevelopment, about states' rights, or about the newness of the "New World." Such names, of course, con-solidate histories no less than those we adopt from our fathers. But those names radically affect our behaviors, determining what we think, what we can (or ought) to do, what we can (or cannot) see in the physical landscape around us—food, shelter, beauty, money, ownership, jobs, obstacles, opportunities—where we can go from "here," even where "here" is.

It is the stories that we tell about place, the names that we give to the landscapes about us that give the shapelessness of space its form and significance. European adventurers understood the power of names, and ignorant or careless of the stories of places new to them, they blithely "christened" the landscape, creating in their own image what they thought they had found.[2]

Invoking Heidegger, we might say that naming calls space into the house of being, into language, onto maps. Stories turn the vertigo of wilderness into places where we can stand, perhaps even take a stand, to defend the boundaries, the names, the stories themselves that allow us to make sense of where we are. For when we have conjured a place into being, made a place for ourselves, we can then pause to look around. As the geographer Yi Fu Tuan suggests, that very pausing is the moment when place emerges from undifferentiated space (1977, 6). On newly familiar ground, we have a point from which to view other spaces, other places. We have a perspective.

As Tuan's influential work indicates, the interdependence of place and story and, concomitantly, of perspective, has become increasingly important even in technical definitions of place and of region especially. Geographers, for example, have increasingly reflected the pressures of story on place, defining region not principally through physical or "natural" markers, but as a human construct involving the interaction of groups and social structures with their environment.[3] And at least since George Tindall's studies, the interactions of place and story have been central to historical definitions of the South, a region whose existence is irrefutable but whose physical boundaries have proved remarkably hard to fix.[4] Indeed, in concluding that only the "idea" of the South exists, Michael O'Brien makes explicit the role of the story and perspective in generating those very events and landscapes that make the South—or any region or place—distinctive (1979, xiv).

The fundamental story told about the South is exactly one of difference—of a region so unique that it almost became a separate nation, of a society clinging to its "peculiar institution" of slave labor in a country whose explicit ideal is/was human equality. From that anomaly flowed a powerful stream of stories, whose intent was, especially in the nineteenth century, to explain the South's difference, to engulf in narrative plausibility the persistent obstacles to rationality and democracy that a slave economy and its racism presented. Not just short story writers, but historians, scientists, social scientists, geographers—all constructed stories of the South's differences: its cavalier allegiances, its climatalogical oddities, its yeomanly independence, the inferiority of its black inhabitants, the rightness of its Lost Cause, the wrongness of its Reconstruction.

This story of Southern difference, of the lost utopia, the pastoral ideal of a benevolent patriarchy, was accepted as true by its critics and its apologists alike

(Gray 1986, 62). In fact, that singularity generated a remarkably useful perspective for writers, the very pause that Tuan describes as definitive of place. From that otherness, in that pause, writers found a still point from which to observe with particular clarity the rest of American culture, whose hallmark is mobility. The freedom to move, to pursue the frontier, to immigrate, as Pierce Lewis explains, has operated for Americans as a political and economic touchstone as well as a geographic fact. We have always resisted in principle any limits on movement, refusing to stay "in our places," either socioeconomically or physically (Lewis 1979, 24-26). The South's attachment to place was thus explicitly linked to an anomalous acceptance of limits, to a hierarchical order in which not only African Americans, but women as well, were explicitly denied the ranges of movement at least theoretically available to its white men.

The story of Southern difference thus constructs a perspective in which place dominates, both as locale and as hierarchy. These double dimensions are, moreover, as often transposed and confused as they are linked, so that, for example, when the Agrarians took their stand to valorize the agricultural attachments of Southerners, their perspective as rural Southerners was based on their recollections of very specific—and different—pieces of land (Gray 1986, 142). These places were elided with their shared perspective as privileged white men, a point of view they regarded as universal, but which assumed the "Negro's" subservience as well as the supportive roles of women. However, as the conflicts and ambivalence of their stands suggest,[5] defining different places in a hierarchy does imply other perspectives: Tops, as postmodernists know, require bottoms to exist. In specifically restricting the places of African Americans, non-Protestants, and women, the South, willy nilly, revealed an otherness within itself, new and separate places from which to observe and map its fictive contours.

Just as the South's "different" attachment to places constitutes an indispensable critique of American culture, the perspective of those Southern "others" provides a uniquely critical view of the values and significance of the South as a region. Indeed, being the Other of America, the alter ego where the struggle of American identity can by played out, the South already occupies the space that has typically been reserved for women, and for writing. The function of writing, Alice Jardine explains, is to fill (in) that space of otherness—to describe and "place" what is "outside of" "the conscious subject," to name the difference (1985, ll4-15).

Obviously, the conscious subject of Southern writing has typically been white, male, Protestant, and upperclass—in its perspective, if not in its actuality. (We should recall here, for example, that one of the major constructors of the Southern subject was Margaret Mitchell, who was white and upperclass, but also female and Catholic). But that subject could only become articulate when it recognized its difference, when, for example, the South had to defend its peculiar institutions, or later, in the nineteenth century, to explain its resistance to being "reconstructed" as indistinct from the progressive and materialistic North. It is when writers named their perspective as more Southern than American that the conscious subject of their writing gained access to itself as an alternative to the dominant culture.

Similarly, women and African Americans have access to a critical perspective on the cultures that define them as Other. The power of African American writing, for example, has lain precisely in its ability to confront the dominant white voice with an assertion of another self. The celebrated doubleness of African American writing is, in one way, a consequence of black writers identifying a place from within the culture and renaming it, reclaiming the subjecthood that the culture denies.[6] Women writers likewise can redefine their place in Southern culture, but as Elizabeth Fox-Genovese suggests, white women have more often tended not to resist their identity with white men, allowing their racial privilege to compensate for—and often blind them to—their exclusions as women (1990, 34). However, when Southern white women do choose to write out of a minority consciousness, they, too, effect a powerful refiguring of the Southern landscape.

In the remainder of this chapter I will examine how three Southern women writers have used the short story to confront and rename the most prominent—and perhaps the most limiting—story of the region: that of the old South. In this otherness—as a "limited" genre, typically defined in terms of its inferiority and difference from the novel—the short story parallels the otherness of women (as well as the South) in offering valuable spaces for criticism.

Short stories by Southern women writers might thus be said to occupy a particularly rich confluence of otherness, establishing a perspective on American culture that can enable us to see its defining myths with new clarity. In retelling the story of the old South, where their places are rigorously inscribed, other writers—be they black or women or homosexual or poor—have the opportunity, at least, to face head on the paradox of claiming an authority denied them by their social "place" but assumed in the act of writing (and perhaps also in being white or Protestant or heterosexual or middle class). Such a position offers a (sometimes ambivalent) perspective from which they can—perhaps must—rename their places, ultimately reshaping the narrative and cultural terrain of the South. In the confines of the short story, that act of reconstruction is intensified, exaggerated by the deliberate partiality of the form. Unable to contain the whole story and unsuited for the novel's totalizing claims of authority, the short story reveals in its limits the partiality of any story. Demanding silences and gaps, places where, in Valerie Shaw's phrase, "unwritten or even unwritable things" can stand (1983, 263-64), the genre offers its practitioners a congruous way of undermining the authority and universality on which hierarchies depend. Moreover, as a "lesser genre," the form also lends to its subversion the disguise of insignificance, its destabilizing challenge always already contained by its devaluation and difference.

The three writers I will discuss represent what I hope is a significant range of experience and era: one from Georgia, one from Mississippi, and one from Saint Louis who has signficant ties to Louisiana. Two are white, their fathers small businessmen, their mothers homemakers; one is black, the daughter of sharecroppers. One is Catholic. Two were only daughters; only one had many siblings. All three produced two or more major collections of short stories and wrote at least one novel. Of the three, Kate Chopin is the only nineteenth-century writer, a "local colorist" engaged by issues of women's identity and autonomy. Eudora Welty is identified with the mid-twentieth-century Southern Renaissance and its reactions to social change; Alice Walker, the only one of the three still writing, is associated both with the women's movement and the Civil Rights and Black Power struggles of the 1960s and 1970s. In all three, the topos of the old South appears rarely, even uniquely. For Welty or Walker, the lapse is not surprising. Welty, in fact, called "The Burning" (1955) "the worst story I ever wrote," pointing to its Faulknerian "curlicues" as evidence of its weakness (Gretlund 1984, 221). Alice Walker's interest in slavery in "Elitheia" (1981) is its link to Black Power issues of the 1970s. Even Kate Chopin, whose career was contemporaneous with the first literary reconstruction of the South, uses antebellum settings in only a handful of her nearly one hundred stories, of which "Ma'am Pelagie" (1892) is representative.

These stories about the old South suggest how writing as Other, even implicitly, can trouble the foundations of a familiar and authoritative mythology and then reconstruct it in ways that make it useful, even possible, as a place for survival. Each story depends upon a recollection of the past, which is, of course, both the characteristic act of Southern writing and an essential component of place making, of telling the history that has brought us here, the story that allows us to know where and who we are. In each case, the limiting form of the short story forces a refraction of that past, a foreshortening that both reveals the illusoriness of the past, its artifice and falseness, and offers a key to how it must be reconsidered or re-viewed if it is to become a serviceable place for the future.

In "The Burning," for example, Welty's modernistically dense and allusive tale of two white women, Myra and Theo, who face the burning of their home at the hands of raping Union soldiers, the past becomes focused in the image of the mirror, where the women first see the intruding men on their (ironically) white horse as it clambers into their virginal parlor. For them the mirror is a screen, "filled with dusted pictures," reflecting and refracting a reality they choose not to see. Reading "trash" novels, concealing a miscegenous child upstairs, failing to react to the official warning of the enemy's approach, the two women live in the darkness of their own romanticized visions of their power and status as "ladies." The core of that blindness is manifest when they offer their black servant, Delilah, for rape to the marauding soldiers: As a non-person, she is to be "preferred" by the beastly Yankees. Later, Delilah, having assisted in the sisters' despondent suicides, returns to the ruined house to find the mirror "flat and face up in the cinders," still "set between black men" who

now seem to "look back through a door" to a golden world. In a richly evocative passage, the brimming mirror compresses the chaos and dazzle of that lost
society, founded on African labor and now destroyed by the very violence its
white owners have perversely concealed from themselves.

In Walker's story "Elitheia," the past is contained by "Uncle Albert," a
dummy posed subserviently in the window of a "locally famous restaurant"
owned by "the grandson of former slaveowners [who] held a quaint proprietary
point of view where colored people were concerned." When Elitheia discovers
the dummy to be the stuffed corpse of a rebellious ex-slave, Albert Porter,
whose owners vainly tried to make him "forget the past and grin and act like a
nigger," she steals and cremates him and places his ashes in a small apothecary
jar that she always carries with her. The dummy, like the mirror, falsely images the reality: Albert Porter was no "nigger," but a radical, aggressive individual. But threats to white authority like this can be "colored" enough only
when they are relegated to an idealized past or to the kitchens, or, like Albert,
transformed into passive icons of servitude. The dummy embodies the false
consciousness of an internalized slavery, the "vicarious fame" that is "a com-
fort" to the old people who have acquiesced to their places, having been made
to doubt their own "memory and eyesight" about Albert by his servile misrepre-
sentation.

In Chopin's "Ma'am Pelagie," the past collapses into a dream of the future:
the efforts of two sisters, Pelagie and Pauline, to rebuild the mansion of their
childhood. Living in the literal shadows of its ruined shell, the sisters waste
themselves in imagining how to restore their father's house. At the story's climax, "that old life and that old splendor" are vividly conjured in a dream sequence, as Pelagie recalls for one last time the past she has decided to leave
behind. Chopin's fragmentary narrative forces us to reconstruct the history that
has given the house its power: Telescoped images evoke antebellum elegance
and intrigue, then wartime pain and destruction; names encode lost relationships; broken vignettes convey complex histories. However, Pelagie's dream,
like narrative itself, only pretends that the past can be replicated—"re-read"
again the same; the story, in fact, must go on. As Chopin understands, its
repetition is a distortion, like Welty's mirror, isolating and impoverishing the
lives of the sisters, foreclosing selfhood for either of them.

The South is imaged in these stories as sites of man-made illusions, the effects of which are violent and real: distorting both physical and social places,
isolating individuals from the hope of a community or the possibility of selfhood, and jeopardizing the present as well as the future. Myra and Theo commit suicide when the place for Southern white ladies no longer exists, and Pelagie quietly fades into age and death when she cannot replicate the past in the
future. But these same images also suggest how the past can be renamed, how
the places that have been emptied of meaning by a shallow and narrow perspective that confuses the particular with the whole can be reviewed, their
proper depths restored, and, finally, their potential for creating communities

with a common point of view revived.

The key to such reconstruction is typically a concrete act of remembering, a counter to the abstraction that is the enemy of place and of story. Places, like fictions, are undone by the failure to see what is there, to keep them specific, to maintain in stories and names the necessary connections with the physical. To lose that specificity (as contemporary America reveals) is to risk placelessness; when every mall and suburb is interchangeable, their inhabitants become disconnected, indistinct, "nowhere." As Welty has eloquently explained, "Place in fiction is the named, identified, concrete, exact and exacting and therefore credible, gathering spot of . . . feeling" (1978, 121-22). To get the details right is critical to places; to distort them is to risk losing the feeling and thought that fiction—or names—mean to illumine.

Accordingly, it is the detail of his fingernails and hair that discovers to Elitheia "the truth" about Albert. She responds not only by burning his corpse, but by carrying his real remains with her, a mystery that the story is told (in italics) to explain. But the ashes are a talisman to restore the other stories about Albert, those that name him as no uncle and not likely "to sit still for nobody to call him that either." Her apothecary jar contains a serious medicinal, a cure for the lies and Uncle Alberts Elitheia finds everywhere, "in her textbooks, in the newspapers and on t.v." Albert's ashes are—in Toni Morrison's elegant term—a token of re-memory, a way to reconstruct places of active resistance to the old enslaving stories of race and white hegemony. Elitheia and her army-trained friends can thus reaffirm stories of integrity and authority, never again "act[ing] like niggers" or dummies, forgetting themselves or their community. Through Albert, renamed and realized in his very specific identity, they know that "whenever you saw somebody acting like a nigger . . . you could be sure he seriously disremembered his past." And the ashes allow them never to disremember again.

Similarly, in Welty's story; the mirror's chaos at first "felled [Delilah] flat," but later she catches in it "the motherly image" of herself, a self-reflection that moves her to action and survival. She sifts from the rubble the bones of the miscegenous child, Phinny, and packs them away with Myra's rings, the Jubilee cup, and other repossessed remnants of the golden world. They become her treasure as she sets out "without dreams" toward "horses and fire, to men," emblems of another, more hopeful place. In contrast to the white women, who in their clinging to the inadequate roles of the past are now just "two stones," Delilah finds in the flattened mirror a new perspective on herself—as mother, a role slavery had stripped from her. By marking Delilah as the survivor, Welty—like Walker—implies that black women, undeceived by the status of "ladies" (or dummies) and released from the racist denials of selfhood, can refigure the legacies of the old South into new identities. Both stories, in fact, reflect what Peter Schmidt sees in Welty as the "reemergence of African American anger and pride in the Civil Rights movement," a moment he finds "prophesied" in Delilah's survival (1991, 256), but one that is consciously invoked in Walker's story.

Though Chopin's story fails to consider racial difference as a counter to the old places of the South, her story does provide a graphic image of how (white) women's places can be reconstructed. Pelagie's decision to relinquish the past is made in the dawning light of Venus, the sign of love. Her protective love for her sister Pauline, whose young life is being sapped away, allows Pelagie at last to exchange the hollow structures of life for living relationships. The new wooden house she constructs at once draws to it the sisters' wandering brother and his lively daughter: The "re-creation of Valmet" is in fact the recreation of a family, not merely a building. The past cannot replicate itself (resulting in imitations, dummies, and death), but must provide the "solid foundation" for new "shapely structures" that can support and nourish "a young and joyous existence." By reforming and internalizing the physical and social "places" of the old South for which Valmet had stood, Pelagie relocates herself and her sister, removing them from isolating ruins to a living community. Such reconstruction, admitting change and encouraging other perspectives (like that Pelagie views from her broad veranda, full of music and laughter; or Delilah's glimpse of the other side of the river; or Elitheia's wary vision of "hype"), reveals how the narrow bases on which the myth of the South was founded can indeed be reformed.

Writing in the South, as women (or as African American or as Catholic—like Flannery O'Connor) and in the short story, authors like these confront several explicit challenges of limit. "Only women" or "only regionalists," or "only short story writers," their perspective—their place—is already defined as partial, limited—less significant if not insignificant. As writers they must reauthorize the differences of their perspectives, protesting the right to write from their own places, resisting the fiction of universality and identity that authorship implies. In the stories themselves this resistance often appears as discontinuity and gaps: the past condensed by Welty's mirror or Pelagie's dreams; a "motherless" miscegenous child; the italicized, fairy-tale structures that decipher the hieroglyphic of an apothecary jar. Such ruptures and silences ultimately challenge the partiality of all narrative and cultural authorities, revealing how no perspective can be definitive, how illusory any place of authority is—whether fictional or cultural or social or political. In that partiality lies an authentic power, the power of limits to recall us to our place, to force us to see how much we cannot see, to remind us how incomplete any naming, any story must be. Such a power is one I would claim for these writers and for many others like them. Such power is, without question, large indeed.

NOTES

1. The principal river of what is now called the United States has had many names. Native Americans who lived along its lower stretches named in "Balbancha" or Balba-

hachas." See David I. Bushnell, *Drawings by A. De Batz in Louisiana, 1732-1735* (Washington D.C: Smithsonian Institution, 1927) 9.

2. Philip Fisher examines how James Fenimore Cooper and other "popular" writers continued this process of renaming the American landscape in *Hard Facts: Setting and Form in the American Novel* (New York: Oxford UP, 1985) 5-6.

3. See Michael Bradshaw's helpful discussion of the changing notion of region in *Regions and Regionalism in the United States* (Jackson: UP of Mississippi, 1988) espec. 3-8. See also David Lowenthal, "Past Time, Present Place: Landscape and Memory," *Geographical Review* 65 (1975): 1-36.

4. See George B. Tindall, "Mythology: A New Frontier in Southern History," in *The Idea of the South: Pursuit of a Central Theme*, ed. Frank E. Vandiver (Chicago: U of Chicago P, 1964) 15. See also the Introduction to *Encyclopedia of Southern Culture*, eds. Charles Reagon Wilson and William Ferris (Chapel Hill: U of North Carolina P, 1989) xv-xx.

5. The internal contradictions of the Agrarians' positions are examined by, among others, Richard Gray, *Writing in the South: Ideas of an American Region* (Cambridge: Cambridge UP, 1986) 143-44; and Daniel Joseph Singal, *The War Within: From Victorian to Modernist Thought in the South, 1919-1945* (Chapel Hill: U of North Carolina P, 1982) espec. 198-201.

6. See, for example, James Olney, "Autobiographical Traditions Black and White," in *Located Lives: Place and Idea in Southern Autobiography*, ed. J. Bill Berry (Athens: U of Georgia P, 1990) 66-77.

WORKS CITED

Bradshaw, Michael. *Regions and Regionalism in the United States*. Jackson: UP of Mississipppi, 1988.

Bushnell, David I. *Drawings by A. De Batz in Louisiana, 1732-1735*. Washington D.C: Smithsonian Institution, 1927: 9.

Chopin, Kate. "Ma'am Pelagie," *The Complete Works of Kate Chopin*. Ed. Per Seyersted. Baton Rouge: Louisiana State UP, 1970: 232-39.

Ferguson, Suzanne. "The Rise of the Short Story in the Hierarchy of Genres," *Short Story Theory at a Crossroads*. Eds. Susan Lohafer and Jo Ellyn Clarey. Baton Rouge: Louisiana State UP, 1989: 176-92.

Fisher, Philip. *Hard Facts: Setting and Form in the American Novel*. New York: Oxford UP, 1985.

Fox-Genovese, Elizabeth. "Between Individualism and Community: Autobiographies of Southern Women," *Located Lives: Place and Idea in Southern Autobiography*. Ed. J. Bill Berry. Athens: U of Georgia P, 1990. 20-38.

Gray, Richard. *Writing the South: Ideas of an American Region*. Cambridge: Cambridge UP, 1986.

Gretlund, Jan Nordby. "An Interview with Eudora Welty," *Conversations with Eudora Welty*. Ed. Peggy Whitman Prenshaw. Jackson: UP of Mississippi, 1984: 211-29.

Hobson, Fred. Prologue. *Tell About the South: The Southern Rage to Explain*. Baton Rouge: Louisiana State UP, 1983: 3-16.

Jardine, Alice A. *Gynesis: Configurations of Women and Modernity*. Ithaca, N.Y.: Cornell UP, 1985.

Leitch, Thomas M. "The Debunking Rhythm of the American Short Story," *Short Sto-*

ry Theory at a Crossroads. Eds. Susan Lohafer and Jo Ellyn Clarey. Baton Rouge: Louisiana State UP, 1989: 130-47.

Lewis, Pierce. "Defining a Sense of Place," *Sense of Place: Mississippi*, eds. Peggy W. Prenshaw and Jessie O. McKee. Jackson: UP of Mississippi, 1979: 24-26.

Lowenthal, David. "Past Time, Present Place: Landscape and Memory," *The Geographical Review* 65 (1975): 1-36.

O'Brien, Michael. *The Idea of the American South, 1920-1941*. Baltimore: Johns Hopkins UP, 1979.

Olney, James. "Autobiographical Traditions Black and White." *Located Lives: Place and Idea in Southern Augtobiography*. Ed. J. Bill Berry. Athens: U of Georgia P, 1990: 66-77.

O'Rourke, William. "Morphological Metaphors for the Short Story: Matters of Production, Reproduction, and Consumption," *Short Story Theory at a Crossroads*. Eds. Susan Lohafer and Jo Ellyn Clarey. Baton Rouge: Louisiana State UP, 1989: 193-205.

Rowe, Anne E. *The Enchanted Country: Northern Writers in the South, 1865-1910*. Baton Rouge: Louisiana State UP, 1978.

Schmidt, Peter. *The Heart of the Story: Eudora Welty's Short Fiction*. Jackson: UP of Mississippi, 1991.

Shaw, Valerie. *The Short Story: A Critical Introduction*. London: Longman, 1983.

Singal, Daniel Joseph. *The War Within: From Victorian to Modernist Thought in the South, 1919-1945*. Chapel Hill: U of North Carolina P, 1982.

Storace, Patricia. "Look Away, Dixie Land," *New York Review of Books* 38 (Dec. 19, 1991): 24-37.

Tindall, George B. "Mythology: A New Frontier in Southern History," *The Idea of the South: Pursuit of a Central Theme*. Ed. Frank E. Vandiver. Chicago: U of Chicago P, 1964. 1-15.

Tuan, Yi Fu. *Space and Place: The Perspective of Experience*. Minneapolis: U of Minnesota P, 1977.

Walker, Alice. "Elitheia," *You Can't Keep a Good Woman Down*. New York: Harcourt Brace Jovanovich, 1981: 27-30.

Welty, Eudora. "The Burning," *The Collected Stories of Eudora Welty*. New York: Harcourt Brace Jovanovich, 1980: 482-94.

—. "Place in Fiction," *The Eye of the Story*. New York: Random House, 1978: 116-33.

Wilson, Charles Reagon, and William Ferris, eds. "Introduction," *Encyclopedia of Southern Culture*. Chapel Hill: U of North Carolina P, 1989: xv-xx.

7

The Place of (and Place in) the Anglophone African Short Story

Roger Berger

I

The little criticism thus far directed toward the African short story—Anglophone or otherwise—has focused on theme or origin.[1] To provide a more symptomatic reading, I want to examine both the place of and place in the Anglophone African short story. This method reveals how the African short story resists the topographic and ethnographic tendency of many African and post-colonial novels.[2] African short stories in English, I want to argue, tend to assume place, marking it with signifiers of the "African" rather than with lengthy ethnographic or topographic passages; and this assumption heralds a confident, decolonized, truly postcolonial mode of fiction. Yet, even before I can discuss the place of (and place in) the African short story, some problems inherent in my title must be considered.

First, any essay that purports to discuss Anglophone texts must address the question of language. That is, can an authentically African narrative—short or long—be written in *English*—or even in what seems to be an Africanized English? On one side, of course, stands Chinua Achebe and in particular the first generation of colonial and postcolonial African writers and scholars. Achebe believes that "the English language [is] able to carry the weight of [his] African experience," although he admits that "it will have to be a new English, still in full communion with its ancestral home but altered to suit its new Afri-African surroundings" (1965, 30). On the other side may be found Obi Wali, Chinweizu, and, more recently, Ngugi wa Thiong'o who suggest that the use of English in African texts not only reenacts the epistemic violence of imperialism but also—in Whorf-Sapir terms—inadequately represents an African world (its landscape, its people, and its social life).[3] Such a position is particularly important to invoke in a volume on the short story in English. Does this volume acknowledge the very real literary achievements of the short story in English, or does it inadvertently celebrate centuries of English colonial conquest—with the English language both a remnant and a constant reminder of the continuing cultural imperialism of English?

I do not necessarily have an answer to this. In my own work I want both to acknowledge the difference inherent in literature from outside the Western tradition *and* to recognize the fundamental connections between African and world literatures. I want, that is, to affirm Cornel West's call for "a new cultural politics of difference" (1990, 19), while at the same time making use of what Edward Said terms "worldliness." Said writes that "By linking works to each other we bring them out of the neglect and secondariness to which for all kinds of political and ideological reasons they had previously been condemned" (1991, 28). The Anglophone African short story offers us precisely such a site for noting difference and universality.

Indeed, one of the major topics of critical debate over the African short story concerns seemingly opposed origins of the genre: Some critics point to the immense influence of the traditional African tale on the contemporary African short story, while others see it as emerging from the Western short story, the one invented by Poe, Hawthorne, Turgenev, and Gogol. My sense is that the African short story writer makes use of both—when it suits his or her needs. There are any number of "traditional" African short stories, as can be seen in Jomo Kenyatta's "Gentlemen of the Jungle" or the variously sutured myths that make up the work of Amos Tutuola. And there are innumerable "realistic" epiphany stories by Sembene, Aidoo, Achebe, Kibera, Ngugi, Gordimer, Mphahiele, Head, Ndebele, Okri and even what seem to be "postmodern," "metafixional" texts, especially by Taban lo Liyong.[4] African short story writers are brilliant improvisers and creators, making use of other fictional traditions and, of course, influenced by indigenous narrative traditions.

Another difficulty inscribed in my title concerns the seemingly natural move of lumping together all Anglophone African short stories—much less all African short stories—thereby reinforcing the essentialist notion of only one African narrative tradition, which may be discovered through a careful dissection of any number of African stories. Do Africa and African literature—like other "imagined communities" (see Anderson 1983) such as America, Asia, Europe and so forth and their "literatures"—constitute legitimate categories, or do they reinforce what Said terms the "epistemology of imperialism" (1991, 20) by discounting the very real differences that exist between and among the geographical and political sections in Africa?[5]

One final problem that is concomitant with the difficulty of a single African literature: Given the sheer number of excellent African short stories, one wonders how to select "representative" stories—much less *a* representative story. I have allowed the anthologies of African short fiction to make that selection, and for the most part I will refer only to stories in the Achebe and Innes anthology (1985). Yet it is clear that these two editors—like most anthologists of African short fiction—tend toward contemporary "realism" in their selections.

Indeed, the conspicuous absence of experimental short "fixion" writer Taban lo Liyong from the Achebe and Innes anthology reflects their "mimeticist" bias.[6]

II

The place *of* the Anglophone African short story is unfortunately clear. In his recent *Tradition and Modernity in the African Short Story: An Introduction to a Literature in Search of Critics*, F. Odun Balogun, himself an excellent short story writer, issues a reprimand and a challenge to scholars of African literature that will undoubtedly seem all too familiar to those interested in the short story in general. After outlining the general critical indifference shown toward the African short story, Balogun complains that this marginalization of the African short story endangers the genre: "No form of literature can flourish without the nourishment of informed critical analysis" (1991, 5). However debatable Balogun's notion of criticism's essential role in the production of quality fiction may seem, his point about the marginalized status of the African short story—in terms of both international scholarship and the novel—is well taken.

In terms of scholarship, the current place of the African short story is, it is sad to report, secondary, almost nonexistent. Aside from Balogun's one book, only a handful of articles may be found (compared to the increasingly large number of critical books and articles on the African and third-world novel). Although this state of affairs is a far cry from the time when an esteemed European critic of African fiction advised African writers to stick with the short story rather than the novel (he felt in the early 1960s that African writers had not yet attained the literary maturity to write what were nonindigenous longer works of fiction), it still bespeaks a curiously arrogant attitude toward some of the best writing to emerge from Africa.

In terms of place *in* the Anglophone African short story, what is particularly symptomatic is the near *absence* of place. Indeed, unlike the African novel (Anglophone and otherwise), which is known for its extensive "topographic" and "ethnographic" detail of place and people, the African short story in English tends to use very little—or sometimes virtually no—topographic or ethnographic description. Such an absence would seem surprising. As Stephen Gray suggests, "A sense of place is the only element a writer has at his [or her] command in a New Literature [in English] that has to be different. The elements of plot, character, action, use of dialogue, rhythm, and all the other techniques of making literature remain the same" (1986, 7). In his chapter on "Yeats and Decolonization," Said argues that "if there is anything that radically distinguishes the imagination of anti-imperialism it is the primacy of the geographical in it" (1990, 77). In terms of literature, Said suggests that the colonized writer, in order to repossess the appropriated land, tends toward the "cartographic" (1990, 79). Such a move—in the work of, say, Yeats, Neruda, Cesaire, and Darwish—imaginatively invents a place, one that replaces the lost and transfigured (or colonized) landscape. As such, place is *a*—perhaps even *the*—great theme of colonial and postcolonial literature (especially in European-language texts).[7] Yet in the Anglophone African short story, place is seemingly taken for granted.[8]

It must be emphasized that place is, of course, never entirely absent from these texts. Along with occasional topographical references, place *in* the Anglophone African short story is discursively marked in at least two ways. Place initially emerges in what Mary Louise Pratt terms "the literary speech situation" (1977, 100) that is, in the performative locutions of author, title, notes on contributors, and other speech-act elements that inform readers—even before they read a particular short story—that the short stories under consideration are African and are meant to be set within a recognizably African location. One of the covers of Achebe and Innes' *African Short Stories*, with its semiblurred photograph of either dawn or dusk over what appear to be African rural huts and part of what may be a large acacia tree, is meant to evoke an authentic (at least less urbanized) Africa, even though many of the stories concern characters who live in urban settings—or in places in which colonial and postcolonial intervention has fundamentally transformed the rural African landscape.

It is even more difficult to know what to make of the cover of Nadezda Obradovic's *Looking for a Rain God: An Anthology of Contemporary African Short Stories*. With a kind of ciphered African dancing or leaping in what appears to be cloud-covered foliage, the "Africanist" cover illustration and design by George Corsillo—probably not an African—again signifies Africa as a natural or possibly "primitive" environment.[9] Yet the story that provides Obradovic with his title, Bessie Head's "Looking for a Rain God," is located in rural, drought-ridden Botswana, a withered landscape. I do not want to suggest that Achebe and Innes or Obradovic are necessarily responsible for the cover designs and representations on their anthologies; rather, I want to describe the ways in which a sense of place—however problematically—is first invoked by the speech-act elements framing the texts. These covers, among other speech-act elements, contribute a sense of place to these stories, even though this sense of place is curiously based on a rather stereotypical and monolithic image of Africa—an image that many African short stories indirectly attempt to subvert.

Perhaps more significantly, Anglophone African short story writers also offer a sense of place with indexical signifiers of the "African" in the English text of the story.[10] Indeed, most of the stories in the Achebe and Innes collection focus immediately on a specific character whose characteristically "African" name clearly announces the story's setting. Consider the beginning of David Owoyele's "The Will of Allah," the title of which could suggest, at least for a Western reader, a Middle Eastern setting:

There had been a clear moon. Now the night was dark. Dogo glanced up at the night sky. He saw that scudding black clouds had obscured the moon. He cleared his throat. "Rain tonight," he observed to his companion. (Achebe and Innes 1985, 22)

Except for the protagonist's name, this story could be located almost anywhere. In fact, were one to replace "Dogo" with a name that signified another place, the location would be immediately shifted.

The same could be said for Chinua Achebe's "Civil Peace," a story about the difficulties of survival and the ironies of life in the aftermath of the Nigerian civil war. The first line reads, "Jonathan Iwegbu counted himself extraordinarily lucky" (Achebe and Innes 1985, 29). (The protagonist's name—Jonathan Iwegbu—perhaps clearly conveys the hybrid nature of the Anglophone African short story.) Very little topographical information is offered in the rest of the story, although indexical signifiers of place are given, such as "Nigerian shillings," "Biafran pounds," "Jonathan's zinc house of no regrets built with mud blocks," "mangoes," and "palm-wine."

But perhaps the most important signifier of place occurs when Achebe occasionally employs "pidgin" English—or even non-English words—in the story's dialogue. Such linguistic references function as "metonymic moments," as Bill Ashcroft, Helen Tiffin, and Gareth Griffiths suggest in their *The Empire Writes Back* (1989, 52), moments that indicate both the inadequacy of "standard" English to represent a non-English landscape and the untranslatability of certain aspects of culture and place in Africa. Indeed, unlike the novel, the Anglophone African short story seldom glosses these lingistic signifiers of place: Either the reader must make sense of them from the context, or the author assumes a shared linguistic and cultural knowledge. Ashcroft, Tiffin, and Griffiths claim a political significance in these moments: "Postcolonial writing abrogates the privileged centrality of 'English' by using language to signify difference while employing a sameness which allows it to be understood" (1989, 51). These disruptions of the English text may indeed be sites of textual resistance to a discursive imperialism. However, mainly they offer an economic means of suggesting place.[11]

The symptomatic absence of place in the Anglophone African short story may be attributed to at least two causes: genre and audience. In terms of genre, most of the Anglophone African short stories emphasize character, not setting. They are populated by what Frank O'Connor terms the "submerged population group" (1985, 18) that O'Connor believes characterizes the short story. A survey of Anglophone African short story collections—Aidoo's *No Sweetness Here*, Achebe's *Girls at War*, Ekwensi's *Lokotown*, Ngugi's *Secret Lives*, Ndebele's *Fools*, and Okri's *Stars of the New Curfew*—reveals any number of marginalized characters. In global terms, these characters are the marginalized of the marginalized—"the Other's other" (Miller 1985, 16).

This is not to suggest that political themes—as well as any number of other themes—are absent from the Anglophone African short story. Indeed, Balogun lists seven major themes: art, religion, tradition and culture, urban life, colonial and postcolonial reality, apartheid, and the ironies of life (1991, 9-25).[12] Rather, it is to insist that what makes these short stories compelling artworks is their relentless interest in what Northrup Frye terms the low mimetic hero or antihero. As O'Connor suggests, "The short story remains by its very nature remote from the community—romantic, individualistic, and intransigent" (1985, 21). Or, as the narrator of Can Themba's "Crespuscule," comments, "Those of us who have been detribalized and caught in that *characterless* world of belonging nowhere, have a bitter sense of loss" (1972, 8, italics added). Themba is, of course, referring to the cruel effect of apartheid, but he also points to a human condition often captured in the short story.

The lack of extensive descriptions of place also reflects the audience to whom the Anglophone African short story, unlike the novel, is addressed—not to outsiders but to an African reading and listening audience. These stories belong to what Stephen Gray defines as a third-phase of colonial and postcolonial narrative—a more assured, less anxious mode of writing. They

value an autochthonous readership first, for whom the advertisement of colourful landscape is simply ludicrous. Somehow the familiar is never strange. The sense of place . . . is . . . merely part of a shared, felt milieu, a familiar and meaningful backdrop, the cause of resonance. (1986, 9)

The Anglophone African short story—unlike the novel—is much more accessible to a general reader in Africa. It tends to appear in magazines, like *Okike* or *West Africa* (in Nigeria), *Joe Magazine* and *Zuka* (in Kenya), *Durm* and *Staffrider* (in South Africa), or *Darlite* (in Tanzania).[13] In short, the Anglophone African short story tends to be written and published *in* Africa, and thus there is a sense in which the short stories are more local than international, more closely connected to a place, and thus less likely to need to foreground location. The African short story is also the staple of high school and university literature courses in Africa. As Achebe comments in the introduction to his anthology:

My own experience from teaching African fiction for a few years at the University of Nigeria, Nsukka, had shown me that a majority of students came to the course with a poor background of reading and consequently tended to be intimidated by the sheer size of the novels they had to study. One way I found to alleviate their terror was to begin each course with the study of half-a-dozen or so African short stories. (1985, x)

These stories assume place and no longer feel it necessary to justify their existence.

The Anglophone African short story, then, provides a model for a new kind of postcolonial text. It suggests that we need not look hard to find what may well be the next phase of an already great literature. Indeed, perhaps one of the reasons why the African short story has been such a neglected genre is that foreign readers sympathetic to African literatures have difficulty locating in it *both* whatever sense of the exotic may have initially attracted them to third-world literature *and* an overt manifestation of the great anticolonial theme. That is, the general absence of place *in* the Anglophone African short story has much to do with the place *of* the genre. This "absence" of place makes the African short story quite possibly more difficult but, in the long run, more rewarding for the non-African reader because it demands that its readers pay attention to the people of the stories without romanticizing or sentimentalizing them. Readers are introduced to Africa mostly on its own terms. For this reason, the African short story may well displace—indeed, has always already displaced—the novel as *the* postcolonial genre.

NOTES

1. See de Grandsaigne and Spackey (1984); Balogun (1991); Feuser (1986). See Julien (1983) on the origin of the African short story.

2. For discussions of the ethnographic nature of postcolonial literature, see Ashcroft, Tiffin, and Griffiths (1989); Slemon and Tiffin (1989).

3. See also the special issue on the question of language, *Research in African Literature* 23. 1 (Spring 1992).

4. See lo Liyong's *Fixions and Other Stories* (1969).

5. See, for example, the debate between Jameson (1986) and Ahmad (1987).

6. See Gray (1991) for a discussion about the problems of anthology selection—particularly for anthologies of South African writing.

7. See, of course, Fanon: "For a colonized people the most essential value, because the most concrete, is first and foremost the land" (1961, 44).

8. There are, of course, exceptions to the generalization that African short stories in English eschew lengthy topographic or ethnographic description. See, for example, Bessie Head's lyrical "Snapshots of a Wedding" in which she begins the story with a lengthy description of place. It is possible that South African short story writers in general, undoubtedly as part of the ongoing antiapartheid campaign, tend to make more ethnographic and topographic references than short story writers from other African nations.

9. For a discussion of the use of the primitive in essentializing the other, see Torgovnick (1990).

10. Signifiers of place may also be usefully understood in terms of Barthes's notion (1968) of the "reality effect."

11. However, see Zabus who, in discussing the use of indigenous terms in Europhone African texts, argues that "indigenization [is] a double-edged weapon, a tortuous instrument of liberation. On the one hand, it appears as a valid strategy of decolonialization. . . . On the other hand, indigenization and its attendant methods help revitalize and recirculate a European language in need of syncretic transfusion" (1991, 44). For a discussion of the problems of multilinguistic texts, see also Dasenbrock (1987).

12. In European-language African short stories, Feuser notes twenty-eight themes (1986, 1110).

13. Ngugi, for instance, originally published his stories in little magazines in Kenya: *Penpoint, Kenya Weekly News, Transition, The New African, Zuka, Ghala*, and *Joe Magazine* (Nguugi 1975, Acknowledgments).

80   The Tales We Tell

WORKS CITED

Achebe, Chinua. "English and the African Writer." *Transition* 18 (1965): 27-30.
—. *Girls at War and Other Stories*. New York: Fawcett, 1972.
Achebe, Chinua, and C. L. Innes, eds. *African Short Stories*. London: Heinemann, 1985.
Ahmad, Aijaz. "Jameson's Rhetoric of Otherness and the 'National Allegory.'" *Social Text* 17 (Fall 1987): 3-25.
Aidoo, Ama Ata. *No Sweetness Here*. New York: Doubleday, 1971.
Anderson, Benedict. *Imagined Communities: Reflections on the Origin and Spread of Nationalism*. London: Verso, 1983.
Ashcroft, Bill, Helen Tiffin, and Gareth Griffiths. *The Empire Writes Back: Theory and Practice in Post-Colonial Literatures*. London: Routledge, 1989.
Balogun, F. Odun. *Tradition and Modernity in the African Short Story: An Introduction to a Literature in Search of Critics*. New York: Greenwood, 1991.
Barthes, Roland. "L'effet de reel." *Communications* 11 (1968): 84-89.
Chinweizu, Onwuchekwa Jemie, and Ihechukwu Madubuike. *Toward the Decolonization of African Literature*. Washington, D.C.: Howard UP, 1983.
Dasenbrock, Reed Way. "Intelligibility and Meaningfulness in Multicultural Literature in English." *PMLA* 102 (Jan. 1987): 10-19.
de Grandsaigne, Jean, ed. *African Short Stories in English*. New York: St. Martin's, 1985.
de Grandsaigne, Jean, and Gary Spackey. "The African Short Story Written in English: A Survey." *Ariel* (April 1984): 73-85.
Ekwensi, Cyprian. *Lokotown and Other Stories*. London: Heinemann, 1966.
Fanon, Frantz. *The Wretched of the Earth*. Trans. Constance Farrington. New York: Grove Weidenfeld, 1961.
Feuser, Willfred F. "French-English-Portuguese: The Trilingual Approach: 2. Aspects of the Short Story." *European-Language Writing in Sub-Saharan Africa*. Ed. Albert S. Gerard. Vol. 2. Budapest: Akademai Kiado, 1986. 1106-20.
Gray, Stephen. "The Politics of Anthologies." *Staffrider* 9.3 (1991): 43-50.
—. "A Sense of Place in the New Literatures in English, particularly South African." *A Sense of Place in the New Literatures in English*. Ed. Peggy Nightingale. St. Lucia: U of Queensland P, 1986: 5-12.
Jameson, Fredric. "Third-World Literature in the Era of Multinational Capitalism." *Social Text* 15 (Fall 1986): 65-88.
Julien, Eileen. "Of Traditonal Tales and Short Stories in African Literature." *Presence Africaine* 125 (1983): 146-65.
Komey, Ellis Ayitey, and Ezekiel Mphahlele, eds. *Modern African Stories*. London: Faber and Faber, 1964.
Larson, Charles, ed. *Opague Shadows and Other Stories from Contemporary Africa*. Washington, D.C.: Inscape, 1975.
lo Liyong, Taban. *Fixions and Other Stories*. London: Heinemann, 1969.
Miller, Christopher L. *Blank Darkness: Africanist Discourse in French*. Chicago: U of Chicago P, 1985.
Ndebele, Njabulo. *Fools and Other Stories*. New York: Reader's International, 1886.
Ngugi wa Thiong'o. *Decolonising the Mind*. London: James Currey, 1986.
—. *Secret Lives*. New York: Lawrence Hill, 1975.

Obradovic, Nadezda, ed. *Looking for a Rain God: An Anthology of Contemporary African Short Stories*. New York: Simon and Schuster, 1990.

O'Connor, Frank. *The Lonely Voice: A Study of the Short Story*. 1963. New York: Harper and Row, 1985.

Okri, Ben. *Stars of the New Curfew*. New York: Viking, 1989.

Pratt, Mary Louise. *Toward a Speech Act Theory of Literary Discourse*. Bloomington: Indiana UP, 1977.

Said, Edward W. "The Politics of Knowledge." *Raritan* 22.1 (Summer 1991): 17-31.

—. "Yeats and Decolonization." *Nationalism, Colonialism and Literature*. Ed. Seamus Deane. Minneapolis: U of Minnesota P, 1990: 69-102.

Slemon, Stephen, and Helen Tiffin, eds. *After Europe: Critical Theory and Post-Colonial Writing*. Sydney, Australia: Dangaroo Press, 1989.

Themba, Can. *The Will to Die*. London: Heinemann, 1972.

Torgovnick, Mariana. *Gone Primitive: Savage Intellects, Modern Lives*. Chicago: U of Chicago P, 1990.

Wali, Obi. "The Dead End of African Literature?" *Transition* 10 (Sept. 1963): 13-16.

West, Cornel. "The New Cultural Politics of Difference." *Out There: Marginalization and Contemporary Cultures*. Eds. Russell Ferguson, et al. Cambridge: MIT P, 1990: 19-38.

Zabus, Chantal. *The African Palimpsest: Indigenization of Language in the West African Europhone Novel*. Amsterdam: Rodolpi, 1991.

8

Generic Variations on a Colonial Topos

Ian Reid

I

Whenever we read or write, we are seeking significance by applying or creating interpretive frames.[1] More generally, perception itself depends on framing. In this broad sense, anything can serve as a frame if it is perceived as enclosing an area within which meanings take shape. Frames place things in relation to one another and mark off insides from outsides, albeit ambiguously. Without framing, signification itself would be impossible; so also would self/other distinctions, and so would any differentiation between types of text. This chapter will consider some shifting historical relationships between certain text types, or genres, and a colonial consciousness of place.

In most cultures, a primary perceptual frame for forming one's subjectivity is the familial house. That shared early experience of domestic self-placement has produced, in turn, a certain conventional set of ways of "framing" written narratives about children's emergent consciousness of their home environment. Of course, it is not the case that writers have always used a single and stable generic frame for this theme. Domestic framings of early childhood experience can, for instance, be reframed generically according to the kind of colonial situation about which they are written. This process is exemplified in the group of texts to be discussed here: British writer Walter Pater's "The Child in the House," the New Zealand stories of Katherine Mansfield, and Australian writer David Malouf's *12 Edmondstone Street*.

The starting point of my chapter is a nonfictional text: Malouf's autobiography *12 Edmondstone Street*.[2] What makes it relevant here is that, as its title indicates, Malouf attaches signal importance to the house, the familial home, as a shaper of memory and imagination:

First houses are the grounds of our first experience. Crawling about at floor level, room by room, we discover laws that will later apply to the world at large; and who is to say our notions of space and dimension are not determined for all time by what we encounter there, in the particular relationship of living-rooms to attic and cellar (or in my case under-the-house), of inner rooms to the verandahs that are open boundaries?

Each house has its own topography, its own lore: negotiable borders, spaces open or closed. (1985, 8)

It may seem from this excerpt that Malouf's *12 Edmondstone Street* shares the premises of *The Poetics of Space*, the phenomenological study in which Gaston Bachelard meditates on the theme that "all really inhabited space bears the essence of the notion of home" (1964, 5). Bachelard is invoking transcendent archetypes, linking house imagery with what he calls "Motionless Childhood, motionless the way all immemorial things are" (1964, 5-6). Malouf is much more particular; in *his* account, the formative role of one's childhood dwelling place has to do with the ways in which particular features frame one's emergent sense of the social world. Malouf describes a distinctively local Queensland architecture in which, "Verandahs are no-man's-land, border zones that keep contact with the house and its activities on one face but are open on the other to the street, the night and all the vast, unknown areas beyond" (1985, 20), and in which the nether regions also take a localized shape by placing indigenous culture outside the frame of civilization:

The whole space is closed in with vertical slats, painted nigger-brown on the outside and black within. . . . [If you dig the dirt beneath the house] you come upon debris, bits of broken china, bent forks, old tin pannikins, encrusted nails and pins, which suggest that human habitation here might go back centuries. History tells us, of course, that it does not (we discount the abos [aborigines]), but I don't believe it. History belongs to the world of light. The debris under the cinders, under the thin topsoil of under-the-house, bears the same relation to history as the dark of our stump forest to the lighted rooms above. They belong to different dimensions. (1985, 44)

Malouf's description of the area beneath the floorboards testifies eloquently to contemporary ethnocentric presumptions, just as features of the house interior disclose class and period values:

Our Front Room is a warning, richly put, against easy pleasures and the dangers of "the social life." The instruments of smoking and drinking are made visible, displayed and kept in a state of awful glitter, but only to demonstrate their attractiveness, and to show how firmly, in this house, they are resisted. (1985, 50)

Far from suggesting (as Bachelard does) that imagery of the childhood home remains "motionless" and "immemorial," Malouf's descriptions often incorporate a sense of historical variability, as in this passage:

Modern bathrooms are secular shrines. Under lights as brilliant as any theatre, the body is apotheosised. . . . Old-style bathrooms (of which ours was entirely typical) were the product of a simpler and poorer economy and served a body with simpler needs.

(1985, 57)

There is more to all this than just reminiscence about a physical habitation. Pervading the rooms is the superintendent influence of parental figures and their own cultural orientations. Thus Malouf's mother is placed in relation to her bedroom sanctum with its relics of the Edwardian English past:

Though it has no door, and the knee-high window to our verandah is always raised, we have learned early, my sister and I, that this room is not to be trespassed upon. Its thresholds are magic barriers. The drawers of our mother's dressing-table are full of temptations to small hands, and all its crystal is breakable. (1985, 24)

Here his mother has a box of family heirlooms; and here she keeps a spirit lamp burning in memory of her parents, giving this up only when the Malouf family leaves Edmondstone Street, whereupon she seems "freed at last from a whole troop of ghosts, including the ghost of England, that in our first house had kept her constrained" (25). In later passages we learn more about her background:

When she came to Australia she was thirteen, just the age perhaps when it is most diffi- cult to make a change. She clung to what she had left or lost and was more English than any of her brothers, who had all been grown men when they migrated and who prided themselves now on being local boys. English for my mother was right. She reproduced in our childhood what she remembered (minus a few housemaids) of her own life in Edwardian London. . . . Forbidden to use local slang or to speak or act "Australian," we grew up as in a foreign land, where everything local, everything outside the house that was closest and most ordinary, had about it the glow of the exotic. The effect on me was just the opposite of what my mother must have hoped. (1985, 33)

Malouf's paternal grandfather, on the other hand, had come to Brisbane in the nineteenth century from Lebanon—although his particular Old Country is not specified until the very end of the text. In the suburban shop run by his wife, he continued to play the role of "the exiled ruler of a minor kingdom still receiving courtiers in a far-off place" (6). His son, Malouf's father, "had, in his quiet way, adapted himself so completely to this new place that there was no link between them. But then, my father was born here, had grown up 'Aus- tralian' in the rough South Brisbane 'pushes' before the Great War" (7).

Is *12 Edmondstone Street* a colonial or a postcolonial text? The question is malformed. We need to separate the "I" character within the framed utterance from the framing I-narrator. The former still lives colonially within a British- dominated "age of certainties"; the latter is positioned outside it, postcoloni- ally. The colonial mentality can "discount the abos" and can sustain itself with

meals that defy latitude and the facts of climate and weather by reproducing the baked dinners, stews, hot-pots and boiled puddings of the Mother Country (our mother's country), which we continue to consume, after more than a century, as if a hundred de- grees of humidity constituted a strictly moral challenge, and we had our real existence in a cold place on the other side of the globe. (1985, 55)

The colonial mentality can also feed, during World War II, on clichés and complacencies that implicitly relegate questions of cultural difference to an unseen limbo beyond the frame:

Freedom. Destiny. The easy life we have grown up in, white for the most part, British almost entirely, in spirit Protestant, has never been under threat. If there are those among us whose freedom has been lost, who have been dispossessed, we do not see them. They are invisible—like the aborigines, who have not yet established themselves in our consciousness. Or they have not yet arrived, even if they are already living down the road or next door—like the migrants, whose sorrows we do not hear because we have not yet opened our ears to receive them. . . .
    We do not know it yet but the war is already won.
    The other thing we do not know is that all the values it was meant to embody, even in us, are already lost. (1985, 37)

    That proleptic incorporation of a later stage of awareness, the "present" of Malouf's act of writing, his standpoint in the here and now of composing the text, can appropriately be called postcolonial—and this partly a matter of generic choices. The basic textual strategy of *12 Edmondstone Street* is not subject to the compulsively iterative and centripetal journey structures that normally circumscribe representations of colonial dependence. Malouf's domestic autobiography stands apart from those narrative compulsions; indeed, its genre has less to do with storytelling in the strict sense than with describing. Although the book is not wholly static, its representation of place and displacement refuses to follow the typical contours of colonial narrative, which would move from outpost to center.
    It is in the historical interval and the imaginative space between those two perspectives, between the colonial and the postcolonial, that a classic structure in the modern short story takes shape. This is the structure of an incomplete journey away from home. The relevant dates of its appearance vary with the historical stages of different colonial societies: For instance, one finds this structural pattern in Nathaniel Hawthorne's early nineteenth-century American tales, registering the aftermath of the former colony's severance from England, but it occurs also in Franz Kafka's early twentieth-century tales, born from his experience of displacement as a German-speaking Jew living in Prague. Although in other respects the historical circumstances of their genesis obviously differed, quintessential short stories such as Hawthorne's "Young Goodman Brown" or "My Kinsman Major Molineaux" and Kafka's "A Country Doctor" typify a genre that has an affinity with the cultural condition of in-betweenness. Neither colonial nor yet quite postcolonial, Malouf's text alludes to that journey structure without actually embodying it. Although its genre is autobiography, *12 Edmondstone Street* seems to acknowledge ironically how compelling certain frames of narrative fiction can be.

II

Malouf's *12 Edmonstone Street* has a strong, though perhaps unwitting, affiliation with a once well-known nineteenth-century British text. This generic parent bears the signature of an aptly named Pater. Walter Pater's first piece of prose fiction, a third-person quasi-autobiographical portrait, was titled "The Child in the House." Most of this text is taken up with detailed description of a young boy's remembered images of the place where he grew up—description of "the process of our brain-building, as the house of thought in which we live gets itself together" (1928, 158). Although Pater's style is more elaborate, a passage such as the following could almost have come from the beginning of Malouf's book:

How insignificant, at the moment, seem the influences of the sensible things which are tossed and fall and lie about us, so, or so, in the environment of early childhood. How indelibly, as we afterwards discover, they affect us; . . . giving form and feature, and as it were assigned house-room in our memory, to early experiences of feeling and thought, which abide with us ever afterwards, thus, and not otherwise. . . . Our susceptibilities . . . belong to this or the other well-remembered place in the material habitation . . . [which] thus gradually becomes a sort of material shrine or sanctuary of sentiment. . . . (1928, 151-52)

"The Child in the House" opens with an image that has been read as allegorical: The young boy-protagonist, Florian, meets "by the wayside a poor aged man, and, as he seemed weary with the road, helped him on with the burden which he carried, a certain distance" (147). One Pater critic, G. C. Monsman, suggests that this opening episode evokes an Everyman allegory; he compares it with *Marius the Epicurean,* in which a spiritual relationship between house and occupant is described from the point of view of what Pater calls "the pilgrim soul" (42). Indeed "The Child in the House" goes on to refer to the child's "mental journey" (148). However, that journey is not so much a pilgrimage as a peregrination, a meander of "his wandering soul" (154) through ideas and sensations drawn from an urbane cultural past. True, the story ends with a picture of Florian on a country road, moving "far into the rural distance" (169), yet this is merely a fade-out; the text is not propelled by any journey structure. No one actually goes anywhere in Pater's fictions, and there is very little sense of momentum. His texts are firmly situated on home ground; the cultural securities of an educated elite in nineteenth-century England underpin what he writes. No doubt one might argue that the nostalgic humanism of Pater's Oxford education put him in a quasi-colonial relationship to an idea of classical and biblical antiquity. Monsman remarks, "Just as in his first portrait, 'The Child in the House,' Pater attempts to 'hark back to some choice space' in his own childhood, so in all [his] portraits we go back to an earlier age" (1967, 39). However, it would be imprecise to define this in colonial terms. Pater's imagination does not frame experience through a linear plot structure of the kind seen in stories such as those written by Hawthorne and Kafka. His writings register no impulse of urgent restlessness that would dictate a journey from home to "Home." This latter trajectory, shaping what one might regard as the typical narrative of colonial consciousness and thereby reframing the significance of the childhood house, is to be found in the writings of our third exemplary figure, whose work reveals something of the history of the short story proper.

III

Not long before her twentieth birthday, Katherine Mansfield left her native New Zealand for London, where she had already spent three years in her mid-teens. A few months after that return to London, she wrote in her journal:

I should like to write a life much in the style of Walter Pater's *Child in the House*. About a girl in Wellington, the singular charm and barrenness of that place—with climatic effects—wind, rain, spring, night—the sea, the cloud pageantry. And then to leave the place and go to Europe. To live there a dual existence—to go back and be utterly disillusioned, to find out the truth of all—to return to London—to live there an existence so full and strange that life itself seemed to greet her—and ill to the point of death return to W[ellington] and die there. A story . . . of the strange longing for the artificial. (Murry 1984, 37-38)

This "dual existence," as she calls it, produces a pattern recurrent in several Mansfield stories—characteristically late colonial—as a child's house memories are caught up in a to-and-fro movement that is quite different from the Paterian model. It is a movement of agitation, and in Mansfield's imagination it is often linked with different parental impulses.

Embarkation is an obsessive trope in Mansfield's fiction. In a story called "The Voyage," a child whose mother has just died sails away from Wellington; in "Six Years After," it is the child who has died and the parents who are traveling by ship. Their destination is uncertain, for a reason that is powerfully significant although the text does not make it explicit. "Six Years After" was written, and is apparently set, in 1921. As its title indicates, the bereavement that still overwhelmingly preoccupies the couple, although they cannot speak of it, is the death of their son six years earlier, during World War I. (Katherine Mansfield's own brother had been killed in action—fighting for the British Empire—in 1915.)[3] This brief story depicts the utterly disorienting experience of a colonial generation whose young men were slaughtered in response to imperial imperatives. The narrative figure for this bewilderment is the unimaginability of the ship's destination. The story ends with an incomplete sentence: "And the little steamer, growing determined, throbbed on, pressed on, as if at the end of the journey there waited. . . ." One is reminded of the final sentence of Malouf's book, evoking an "unnameable destination" for the protagonist as a result of his chance encounter during World War II with a group of Japanese prisoners of war.

The motif noted in "Six Years After" appears elsewhere in Mansfield's fiction. The child-in-the-house becomes minaturized as a doll's house in the well-known story of that title. The theme of restlessness and departure is sounded again in "The Wind Blows," which begins when a girl wakes up to the wind shaking the house. Later, with her brother, she goes for a walk on the esplanade; they watch a steamer put out to sea and imagine that they themselves are on board. The ship is "making for the open gate between the pointed rocks that leads to. . . ." Again, an incomplete final sentence implicitly marks the late colonial attitude.

Mansfield's New Zealand stories, beginning with "Prelude" and dealing so recurrently with scenes of the-child-in-the-house and with irresolute journeying, were written as a direct and conscious response to her soldier brother's death. However, her orientation remained in most respects a colonial one: "Oh, I want for one moment to make our undiscovered country leap into the eyes of the Old World" (Mansfield 1974, xiv).

IV

In the conclusion to their book *The Empire Writes Back*, Ashcroft, Tiffin, and Griffiths emphasize what they call the "subversive" aspect of "the postcolonial enterprise":

It has been the project of postcolonial writing to interrogate European discourse and discursive strategies from its position within and between two worlds: to investigate the means by which Europe imposed and maintained its codes in its colonial domination of so much of the rest of the world. (1989, 19)

I have suggested that one cannot identify *the* postcolonial so categorically. The tensions and transitions between different forms of coloniality have done much to shape the history of the modern short story. This can be seen in generic re-framings of the primal experiential frames—reframings, that is, of the textual types and imagery through which one's "first place" is represented. Those who write about spatial and familial figures that surround the child in the house will inevitably register differences of cultural and historical placement—and generic choices will tend to inscribe those differences. The short story, constructed in the distinctive journey-from-home form that I have briefly indicated, was particularly apt for framing one set of experiences.

NOTES

A longer version of this article, titled "Reframing 'The Child in the House': Short Stories and Neighboring Forms," appears in *Creative and Critical Approaches to the Short Story*, ed. Noel Harold Kaylor, Jr. (New York: Edwin Mellen Press, 1997) 325-38.

    1. See Gale MacLachlan and Ian Reid, *Framing and Interpretations* (Melbourne, Ausrailia: Melbourne UP, 1993).

2. Cf. also Paul Carter and David Malouf, "Spatial History," *Textual Practice* 3.2 (1989): 173-83; and David Malouf, "A First Place: The Mapping of a World," *Southerly* 45.1 (1985): 3-10.

3. Of Mansfield's other stories in which the trace of this family trauma can be seen, especially noteworthy is "The Fly"; cf. Ian Reid, "Framing Mansfield," *Short Story* 1.1 (1990): 83-95, in particular 87.

WORKS CITED

Ashcroft, Bill, Helen Tiffin, and Garth Griffiths. *The Empire Writes Back: Theory and Practice in Post-Colonial Literatures*. London: Routledge, 1989.

Bachelard, Gaston. *The Poetics of Space*. Trans. M. Jolas. New York: Orion Press, 1964.

Malouf, David. *12 Edmondstone Street*. London: Chatto and Windus, 1985.

Mansfield, Katherine. *Undiscovered Country: The New Zealand Stories of Katherine Mansfield*. Ed. Ian A. Gordon. London: Longman, 1974.

Monsman, G. C. *Pater's Portraits: Mythic Patterns in the Fiction of Walter Pater*. Baltimore: Johns Hopkins UP, 1967.

Murry, John Middleton, ed. *Journal of Katherine Mansfield, 1904-1922*. 2nd ed. London: Constable, 1984.

Pater, Walter. "A Child in the House." *Miscellaneous Studies: A Series of Essays*. London: Macmillan, 1928. 172-96.

Breaking Down the Boundaries: "Earth, Air, Water, Mind"

Leslie Marmon Silko

In *Storyteller* (1981), I pay tribute to all of the storytellers. Storytellers are anonymous. They live and they die. They serve the stories. Stories are what are alive and live forever. However, I also like putting, "she said," in my stories to remember that many of the storytellers I have heard were women.

I write in the mornings. By the end of the day I am ready to say, "Oh just push the big nuclear button and get rid of it all." But in the morning I still feel like there is hope. I cannot understand how people can jog or swim or do something really strenuous early in the morning. All of the words, all of the dreams, all of the valuable things that your dreams have created are in your tissue and sweat, and then the jogger jogs them out. In order to be a writer you cannot jar the body or move it around. The closer you can be to the dream state, to waking up, the better, and so nightgowns are good. Actually no clothes at all are it, but I try loose-fitting clothes. They are very important.

Dreams usually just give me a starting-off place. I have never had dreams that were so great that I could just sit down and turn them into stories—ever. But I have had dreams that had great elements, or disturbing elements, that then propelled me to write a story. For example, in 1981 there must have been helicopters going over my house in Tucson and I incorporated them into my dream. But in my dream the helicopters were flying in low. They were those Vietnam-vintage helicopters and the doors were rolled back and they were full of wounded U.S. infantrymen. And I could see in my dream that they were coming from Mexico. And I wondered, why am I dreaming about our fighting in Mexico? This was in 1981, and it was so powerful that in a sense much of what I ended up writing about in *Almanac of the Dead* was to try to figure how this dream came to me like that. The other dream I had that was important for *Almanac* was that two heads were floating in the Sochi Milko gardens in this wonderful grocery sack. There was this brightly colored braided plastic shopping bag. And then these two heads that belonged to the American ambassador to Mexico and his assistant were floating. That dream gave me things to write, to work around, or a place to take off from. I use dreams to guide me. That is how dreams work for me.

I love to work with narrative and with stories: things I hear, things I make up, things that occur to me. *Almanac of the Dead* (1991) is just full of stories. There were the little stories I heard: the story about the little ash-child by the fireplace, the story of a feud in my own family over a piece of backyard, the stories Simon Ortiz told me. I would say to Simon, "Have you written a story about the old man who died twice?" "Well, no," he would say. "I haven't gotten around to do it." Finally I said, "You know, I think—I just feel like—I'm probably going to write that story." Then there was the story about Pete's pig. This was something that actually happened in Simon's family, this daughter-in-law and sister-in-law fighting over the pig. Whoever fed the pig the most would get to have most of the meat.

I was fascinated with all of these little stories because they seemed to be sayng something about the whole notion of owning, or holding. I joined them all together under the title "Private Property," but what I was trying to do was to experiment with the way in which different sorts of things can be packed into a narrative poem and hold together. They hold together with certain repetitions of images. I was experimenting here with internal ways of joining. One example is the repetition of ashes—the ash-boy, and then later the adulteress whose excuse to go meet her lover is that she has to go dump the stove ashes. I was intrigued when those images reoccurred, or reappeared.

The other thing was that there were these horses that belonged to Bill Jeremiah, and the horses were always going through Laguna. They, too, of course were about private property. However, I also like the feeling which we all had at Laguna that almost everything that happened seemed to have those horses as a backdrop. They were somewhere. They were off in the sand hills in the distance, or they could be in the middle ground, or they were actually in the foreground. I had this urge to put all these stories together knowing full well all of the rules we have for the short story, and that is what happened.

I think there is something about narrative that is similar to the functions of mathematics, something called fractals that allow mathematicians to take just a few dimensions of the shoreline and project the actual shape of a coastline they have not seen. I believe some similar dynamic operates in language, in narrative, so that you are given a few things and you can tell what is going to happen. I got started on *Almanac of the Dead* because the Mayans said they could foretell the future and they had these almanacs made of narrative, and I got to wondering: How is it that this could be? I think some day people will figure it out.

When I started writing *Almanac of the Dead*, the issue my two old lady characters felt most strongly about was the irrelevancy of borders. The tribal people crossed over the Mexican border; the boundaries were irrelevant. That feeling is already in the air down in Tucson. Disregard of boundaries is very strong. And so I was amazed and gratified when the Berlin Wall went down. I was also amazed by the great migrations and displacements of people that have been going on, because I have that happen in the *Almanac*, but I did not really think that it would start to happen so soon.

The key image, the tip off was the images that were flashed around the world showing Filipino people standing up to Marcos's army. When those soldiers did not fire upon those people in Manilla, it seemed to me that the next thing that happened was Tienneman Square. I used to make fun of Marshall McLuhan when I was an undergraduate, but McLuhan was right about the effect of these global images. There are certain kinds of images that are so powerful that they enter the air.

Boundaries are falling in every direction. It is something that has been coming for a long time and human beings have a kind of collective awareness about what is happening. In *Almanac of the Dead*, I imply that there will be riots, so when the riots in Los Angeles came, as an author I was glad. A writer is always glad to figure something out. Riots are inevitable. That is how I could figure it out. The riots have been coming since 1640. You cannot have millions and millions of people dispossessed, enslaved, and exploited. To this day we still, all of us, live with the effects of what was done hundreds of years ago to the Native American people and the African American people. People are always saying that was a long time ago, that happened in the past, that was five hundred years ago. But that is using linear time. The colonialists loved to use a long time-string. Then they could say, "That happened a long way back. Why are you still mad?" But a lot of tribal cultures and peoples think of time as an ocean. We swim in it. African Americans were promised forty acres and a mule. The country never settled up. The riots in Los Angeles were, in a sense, absolutely necessary, absolutely unavoidable given the past.

I think the more boundaries that can be broken down, the better: political boundaries and intellectual boundaries. I think boundaries are disappearing, and they are disappearing because women are making them disappear. The impetus toward this is women's studies. I believe that it is we women who are making that step to try to see that all of this compartmentalization is marginal. I see compartmentalization coming to an end. These ridiculous groupings of African American, Native American, Latino. It is all American literature, after all. We are getting now to where we have men's and women's writing, and finally we will just have people writing. When I was invited to New York to read, it was still Native American night, but slowly, slowly, slowly, slowly, these sorts of ridiculous boundaries are being removed, and now that women are really aware of what that means, it is just going to go faster and faster.

One of the things I am most concerned about are the boundaries of genre. I have never paid much attention to these boundaries. I think the most important thing when you have something you feel you need to put down in language, is to get it down and get it going, and worry later whether it is a poem or a short story. *Ceremony* (1977) started out as a short story.

The law represents another form of boundary. I went halfway through law school, three out of six semesters, and it was a great eye-opener. There is no better way to understand a culture than to study what is expressed in the law. The law is a fascinating intellectual pursuit. The actual *practice* of law is the pits. In the first-year class you study the Anglo-American legal system. You find out that the feudal lords were the bosses; they were the judges. The feudal lords administered the law to their slaves basically, their vassals, and to the common people. If you study through the whole history of the Anglo-American legal system, you will see that the little person will always stay there and the mighty ruler will always stay there, and this system will not allow for the kind of justice that people—tribal people in the Americas and people in other places —are looking for. This is not a just system. Once you see that, then there is no point in going on. I might have advised my clients, "Throw a rock through the window; burn it down" because there would be no remedies for the little person. And so I decided that, in all good conscience, rather than have myself and my clients in jail, I would drop out and indict the law. In a way, *Almanac of the Dead* is a seven-hundred-and-some-odd-page indictment. It is my law-suit. It is my land claim lawsuit. I think that every so many hundred's of years dispossessed people have to reassert, or constantly assert, "we claim this," over and over again. We do not want to forget. In the last part of *Almanac of the Dead,* a character named Wilson Weaseltail says you'll find no justice in the law. So Wilson becomes a poet, and he composes poems that list lawsuits.

We are not more stupid than wild animals. Wild animals can tell when their own kind is dying, when their own kind is suffering. In point of fact, anyone who follows certain ways, no matter what color they are, no matter what their background is, if they become enamored with nuclear testing, if they are enamored with expanding petrochemical usage on earth, if they are enamored with having lawns and using up the precious water of the West—because the water's going to run out very soon—they will literally be changed by the land. This continent will literally change people. It already has and it continues to. What we will see is an eventual disappearance. This is what the whole Beyond Rio Conference held in Brazil was all about: one industrialized nation polluting the earth so much more than all the others. People are saying, "We can't keep living like this anymore." That is what is meant by "things European" or that style of living by tearing the earth apart, exploiting it, and polluting it. There is no question but that those ways and those days are numbered. And whether it will just end in destruction or whether there will be a change in the way we can manage, that is being determined right now. I do not see the end of Europeans, but the end of European behavior, values, and attitudes toward the land. There already is, and there will continue to be, a shift away from those old ways of behaving with the earth, the air, and the water. It has to be. However, I feel positive about what is happening. I think that the more boun-daries that fall, the better. I think that when Eastern European people come and see the West, and vice versa, that good can come. The great empires are broken.

Part III

Roles and Genres

9

Poe's Legacy: The Short Story Writer as Editor and Critic

Ann Charters

As a short story critic, editor, and teacher myself, I have found that the best commentators on short fiction are short story writers. When I teach writers as critics of (or as commentators on) the short story, it achieves at least four ends. I have found that authors who write about the writing of short fiction often give permission to students to think critically and even independently about what they have read. An example of this is Nathaniel Hawthorne's beautifully composed Preface to his second edition of *The Twice-Told Tales*. What Hawthorne writes that gives courage to my students is this: As he glances over long-forgotten pages and considers his way of life while composing them, he says he can very clearly discern why he was so ignored in his early years as a writer. He says he would have reason to be ashamed if he could not criticize his own work as fairly as another person's. He confesses that although it is scarcely his business, he can hardly resist the temptation to comment on his stories. Hawthorne even says that if writers were allowed to do so and would perform the task with perfect sincerity and unreserve, their opinions of their own productions would often be more valuable and instructive than the works themselves. That is the didactic Hawthorne speaking. Certainly, however, one of the strengths of the short story form is that it is short and thus can be collected, and such collections invite writers to comment on their own work in their introductions, as Hawthorne has.

Another reason I like commentaries by writers as critics of short fiction is that they give an immediate sense to students—much more quickly than I could in a course of fourteen weeks—of the direct transmission of a literary tradition. If a student reads Willa Cather describing how she was impressed by Sarah Orne Jewett's work and was empowered partly by Jewett's work to become a writer, there is a sense of writers listening to and reading and helping each other become writers.

A third reason why criticism or commentaries work is that the short story is an international form. It is fun to hear writers commenting on other writers, sometimes very critically. Genwilla Chavey's comment on Joseph Conrad's "Heart of Darkness" is not a rave for that story by any means. More neutrally, one can read D. H. Lawrence's review of Ernest Hemingway's *In Our Time* and discover what an English reader, a reader with his own agenda as a writer, found in reading Hemingway. Lawrence took Hemingway, of course, as fitting his own preconception of what Americans were like.

Finally, I like students to read writers on short fiction because often writers write beautifully about the creative act, or about what it means to be a writer. I know no better example than the essay by Raymond Carver called "Fires," which is a wonderfully illuminating explanation of the price a writer pays and the stamina it requires to make a life as a writer. Carver describes going into a laundromat in Iowa City and having to wait a long time for the dryer to become free. His wife had left him in charge of their two children and he did not know where they were and he could not leave the laundromat until he could dry his clothes. He realized in that moment, he said, that he could not have control over his life. He wanted to write more than anything else, but circumstances were dictating what he could do. It helped him, he said, to determine his course of writing short rather than long fiction. Such ordinary things determine choice of form.

10

"Stories with Real Names": Narrative Journalism and Narrative History

Gay Talese

As a boy growing up in the 1940s, I was drawn to writers of fiction, particularly those who had perfected the art of the short story. Among the writers I most admired were John O'Hara, Irwin Shaw, John Cheever, and F. Scott Fitzgerald (the latter's "Winter Dreams," a forlorn tale of romance involving a country club caddie and a lovely young female golfer who gives range to his vision, would thereafter take flight in my fantasies whenever I saw a slender woman swinging a club on the fairways); but the story that most influenced me as a writer was a Carson McCullers selection entitled "The Jockey."

I read this story in an anthology while I was in college during the early 1950s, and what caused me to read it a second time was the realization that, smooth and controlled as was its language and style, its strength was in the reality it evoked—and the fact that I could not tell if McCullers was writing fact or fiction. Her story was to me overwhelmingly *real*. She made it up, yes; but it read like a feature article in a newspaper, and it occurred to me that I might try to instill some of what she achieved in my own efforts as an aspiring young journalist and aspiring writer. I would not *create* situations, of course, as McCullers had so magnificently done, nor would I ever knowingly falsify any facts merely to heighten my readers' interest; but my approach to writing nonfiction would nevertheless be structured along lines of McCullers' fictional account of an embittered and overweight jockey.

Her story begins:

The jockey came to the doorway of the dining room, then after a moment stepped to one side and stood motionless, with his back to the wall. The room was crowded, as this was the third day of the season and all the hotels in the town were full. In the dining room bouquets of August roses scattered their petals on the white table linens and from the adjoining bar came a warm, drunken wash of voices. The jockey waited with his back to the wall and scrutinized the room with pinched, crepy eyes. He examined the room until at last his eyes reached a table in a corner diagonally across from him, at which three men were sitting. . . .

The three men at the corner table were a trainer, a bookie and a rich man. The trainer was Sylvester—a large, loosely built fellow with a flushed nose and slow blue eyes. The bookie was Simmons. The rich man was the owner of a horse named Seltzer, which the jockey had ridden that afternoon. . . .

"Had dinner?" Sylvester asked.

"Some people might call it that." The jockey's voice was high, bitter, clear. . . .

Sylvester turned to the rich man. "If he eats a lamb chop, you can see the shape of it in his stomach a hour afterward. He can't sweat things out of him any more. He's a hundred and twelve and a half. He's gained three pounds since we left Miami."

"A jockey shouldn't drink," said the rich man.

"The food don't satisfy him like it used to and he can't sweat it out. If he eats a lamb chop, you can watch it tooching out his stomach and it don't go down. . . ."

What I chose to do from the very beginning of my days as a young journalist was to avoid writing about people who were newsworthy. I did not ever want to be on the front page of a newspaper, and for the most part, I succeeded. If you write about people who are newsworthy, you are writing about people who will die tomorrow, and I was interested in work that would live long after tomorrow. I think I had, even as a young man, a vain sense of myself that might be akin to the sense of the fiction writer who is, after all, writing for eternity. I wrote about ordinary people, people who were not known, people who were obscure. I identified very much with obscurity because I thought of myself as a rather obscure person on earth.

My own work as a journalist was to try to emulate the short story, but to do so in a place where the short story was all but unacceptable: the newspaper. I wanted to write stories with real names. I managed to a degree to get away with this, which is to say to get some of the pieces that I wanted to write into the newspaper. If I was a .200 hitter, that was probably all I could be in those days. If ten stories were thrown out, once in a while there would be one or two that would be allowed in *The New York Times*. But I quit *The Times* after a while because I found a place that suited me better, *Esquire* magazine, which published some of the great short stories of the 1960s and 1970s. I managed to get into *Esquire* nonfiction short stories about people not so well known—and sometimes people who were well known—but all employing many of the tactics and weapons of the fiction writer: scenes, dialogue, details suggesting psychological mood, even interior monologue.

I try to follow my subjects unobtrusively while observing them in revealing situations, noting their reactions and the reactions of others to them. One of my ambitions is to remain with my subjects long enough to see their lives change in some way. This becomes my story. I attempt to absorb the whole scene, the dialogue and mood, the tension, drama, and conflict, and then I try to write it all from the point of view of the persons I am writing about, even revealing whenever possible what these individuals are *thinking* during those moments I am describing.

It is possible to do interior monologue in nonfiction if you know a person very, very well. However, very few nonfiction writers take the time to know a person so well that they know what and how that person thinks. I had the advantage of knowing certain people well enough to know both what and how they thought. One of them was a professional prizefighter, the heavyweight champion back in the 1960s, Floyd Patterson. I knew Floyd Patterson, for I had written thirty or forty articles about him. I spent great amounts of time with him in private—before fights, after fights, during those long periods when there were no fights—and I knew how he thought. In 1964 I wrote a piece on Floyd Patterson called "The Loser" which is as close as you can come to getting inside the head of a person who is a real person. The interior monologues I presented in "The Loser" were real and verifiable thoughts.

Quoting people verbatim, however, has rarely blended well with my narrative style of writing or with my wish to observe and describe people actively engaged in ordinary but revealing situations rather than to confine them to a room and present them in the passive posture of a monologist. Since my earliest days in journalism, I have been far less interested in the exact words that came out of people's mouths as in the essence of their meaning. More important than what people say is what they think, even though the latter may initially be difficult for them to articulate and may require much pondering and reworking within their minds. This is what I gently try to prod and stimulate as I query, interrelate, and identify with my subjects as I personally accompany them whenever possible, be it on their errands, their appointments, their aimless peregrinations before dinner or after work. Wherever it is, I try physically to be there in my role as a curious confidant, a trustworthy fellow traveler searching into their interior, seeking to discover, clarify, and finally to describe in words (my words) what they personify and how they think.

There are times, however, when I do take notes. Occasionally there is a remark that one hears—a turn of phrase, a special word, a personal revelation conveyed in an inimitable style—that should be put on paper at once lest part of it be forgotten. That is when I may take out a notepad and say, "That's wonderful! Let me get that down just as you said it"; and the person, usually flattered, not only repeats it but expands upon it. On such occasions there can emerge a heightened spirit of cooperation, almost of collaboration, as the person interviewed recognizes that he or she has contributed something that the writer appreciates to the point of wanting to preserve it in print.

At other times I make notes unobserved by my subject—such as during those interruptions in our talks when the person has temporarily left the room, thus allowing me moments in which to jot down what I believe to be the relevant parts of our conversation. I also occasionally make notes immediately after spending time with my subject, when things are still very fresh in my mind. Then, later in the evening, before I go to bed, I sit at my keyboard and describe in detail (sometimes filling four or five pages, single-spaced) my recollections of what I saw and heard that day—a chronicle to which I constantly add pages with each passing day of the entire period of research.

I have never felt that there is a great barrier between fiction and nonfiction. I believe writing can be elevated to the level of art—whether you are being as true as you can be to the facts of a real person's story, or if you are working with materials totally "created"—if there are materials that are ever totally created. The fiction writer takes private imaginings and makes them public. The fiction writer invents characters, who, if artfully elaborated, become part of the art of the ages: a Madame Bovary or a Captain Ahab. The nonfiction writer usually deals with public life, deals with people who are fairly well known, and brings added information to make them better known—or more reviled, as the case may be. I think, however, that it is possible for a nonfiction writer also to delve into the private life of both famous and ordinary people. If nonfiction writers "re-present" their worlds truthfully and artfully, their stories can (and have) become a permanent part of our human chronicle. And so I think it is all in *how* it is done, not whether it is done under the label fiction or nonfiction.

11

Story in the Narrative Essay

Mary Swander

In the intense heat of the 1987 drought, my co-author Jane Staw and I climbed into the cab of a pickup truck, with cooler, computer, sleeping bags, and two dogs, and set off across seven Midwestern states to interview gardeners for our book *Parsnips in the Snow* (1990). A year later, we had talked to fifty gardeners and profiled twelve in our collection, including a mail carrier in Omaha, an African American philanthropist in Topeka, a stockbroker in Chicago, and a Trappist monk in Dubuque. Between our first stop for gas on Interstate 35 and our publication party, we journeyed through a writing process that struggled not only with the form of the interview as essay, but with the essay as narrative akin to the short story.

Once home, we had pools of melted ice cubes in the cooler and boxes of interviews on cassette tape, but we were a long way from having a book. Diligently, painstakingly, we put the pedal to the tape recorder metal and made transcripts of the information we had gathered. Then the real work began. We read and reread, searched and pulled out the best quotes from the interviews themselves. Because people often speak in non sequiturs, jumping from subject to subject, from place to place, we attempted to stitch the best quotes together, ordering them in a logical fashion, eliminating irrelevancies and redundancies.

After months of work, we found we were getting closer to the idea of the interview, the heart of a story about each one of these gardeners, the hearts of the gardeners themselves. We had created Studs Terkel-like oral histories that developed a dramatic tension of their own, a rise and fall of action, a peak moment of insight or epiphany. There before us was the raw material for a good essay, but we wanted something more.

We had strolled through acres of prairie at the New Melleray Abbey in Iowa, where yellow and purple coneflowers were scattered among the little and big bluestem grasses. We had tasted the sweetness of fresh sugar snap peas eaten right from the vines in Minnesota. We had heard the roar of a bulldozer rip up one hundred gardens brim-full of ripe strawberries in Old Town Chicago. In our writing, we wanted to include these sensual images—the visual, auditory, tactile, and olfactory experiences of our trip.

Of course, we wanted to reflect upon our subjects' lives and their reasons for gardening, how they accrued and sustained their passion for plants and grow-ing things. The essay best allows one to meditate, ruminate, speculate, but we wanted to do more. We wanted to dramatize, build up that tension we felt coming through to us from the transcripts. We wanted to develop more charac-terization, flashback and flesh out our gardeners' lives, let something happen to them, find more plot—or, plot within a plot. So in order to achieve richer, livelier, more fully realized prose, we borrowed narrative from the short story and brought summary and scene to our nonfiction.

After we had interviewed the spunky and self-sufficient Edith Cone, we were anxious not only to recreate her setting, but also to collapse the facts of her back-ground into a paragraph of summary that might help point toward the roots of her passion:

Edith left Ferncrest [her childhood farm] when she was twenty years old. She is now eighty-one, widowed, and living on her own farm ten miles north of Independence, Iowa. Her white salt-box house sits close to Highway 150 with its hum of combines, pickups, tractors and automobiles. But her garden is set back from the road, a half-acre she still maintains herself, lush with zinnias, marigolds, black-eyed Susans, comfrey, basil, oregano and chives, as well as the more predictable cauliflower, broccoli, peas, beans, beets and corn.

The roots of this garden stretch all the way back to Ferncrest—past Edith's three chil-dren, her marriage and the egg farm she and her husband, Floyd, managed for forty years, past her 1928 master's degree in organic chemistry at Iowa State University, to her childhood, when as soon as she could walk, she picked strawberries alongside her father and sat beside him on the buckboard on the road to the Barlett railroad station with shipments of eggs destined for Council Bluffs. (1990, 5)

At the same time, we wanted to describe Edith physically and the way she figures in her setting:

The first time we saw Edith she was crouched in her broccoli patch, a giant sunflower head drooping above her. She looked like part of the landscape, her head bent to one knee, her gray hair pulled into a tight bun, the dowager's hump on her back in the shadow of the sunflower leaves. Beyond the garden, a cluster of outbuildings, two full henhouses, an old slatted corncrib bursting with cobs, and two forty-cow barns an-nounced the business of everyday farm life. Further off, a pasture sloped toward the horizon, emerald here, chartreuse there, kelly green in the distance where Edith's Guernsey, Belle, a brown-and-white blur, grazed. (1990, 5, 7)

Yet, if we only concentrated on summary, we would miss the close-up shot of Edith in action. We would miss her voice, the energy she put into her work, the tension, poignancy, and release of humor that her own words rendered. In the following scene, she spots a single lambsquarter in her football-field-sized garden:

"A weed! A weed! I spotted a weed!" she shouted, and continued along the row on her hands and knees, stabbing and gouging, stabbing and gouging, puffs of dirt flying up around her face, then drifting back down into the garden as she worked. "You know a little weed gets to be a big weed mighty quick, and I spend quite a lot of my time pulling them out and using them as mulch on the rest of my garden. Since my stomach surgery in 1981, my muscles aren't good. And if I stand for very long, I just get worn out. But I can work on my knees for half a day." (1990, 10)

Ultimately, a good writer of nonfiction, just like a good writer of fiction, aims to blend summary and scene. Here, a description of Edith's chicken operation flips right into her monologue dramatizing her role in the birds' demise:

Edith's slaughtering apparatus, a two-by-two nailed across two four-foot stakes, defined the outer limit of the farmyard. On one side sprawled the barns and chicken coops, surrounded by stretches of bare earth punctuated with tufts of crab grass. The air was filled with high-pitched fussing of the hens. . . .

"See, I hang the chickens on here by their legs. Then I kill them. I like to take a knife and go right into the brain. That gets them immobile. Next I take off the heads so the blood drains out. Then I have a pail of hot water and get them ready to pluck." (1990, 11)

We close Edith's chapter with yet a faster leap back and forth from scene to summary. In the final few paragraphs, we further develop her characterization and capture her strength and determination. Here, Edith wants to send us home with a bag full of zucchini:

In the barn, Edith seesawed up a ladder to a stack of brown paper bags piled on a high shelf. Then, hanging onto a rung with the other hand, she looked down. "You see, I so seldom go to the grocery store that I never have any sacks. People have to bring these to me."

Friends might bring Edith paper bags, but they bring her little else. Instead, she is the one who shares her bounty with the world. Meat, milk, fruits, vegetables, healing herbs —on a rural route in the middle of Buchanan County, Iowa, just at the bend where the road jogs north toward Oelwein, Edith has created her own Garden of Eden. And there she remains.

"No, I won't give it up. Imagine strawberries by the nineteenth of May. And in Iowa. I refuse to leave. Gardening is going to keep me going. If you sit down and do nothing, what are you going to end up with?" (1990, 17-18)

12

Hemingway's "Indian Camp":
Story into Film

H. R. Stoneback

I

"Is dying hard, Daddy?"
"No, I think it's pretty easy, Nick.   It all depends."
Ernest Hemingway, "Indian Camp"

This chapter examines Ernest Hemingway's "Indian Camp" and Brian Edgar's 1990 film adaptation of the story. Edgar's film had its world premiere at the "Hemingway and the Movies" Symposium held at the State University of New York—New Paltz in 1990; since then it has been featured at the International Hemingway Conference at the Kennedy Library in Boston and at various international film festivals. My treatment of the story and the film will be rooted in certain facts, stances, and experiences: (1) I served the filmmaking process in the capacity of script and location consultant; (2) I brought to that function a certain logocentric skepticism and "textual purism" grounded in my primary academic identity of Hemingway scholar-critic; (3) I learned a good deal in the process of the making of the film about the risks, the extraordinary difficulties and delicacies of making a film from a classic short story; (4) I hold no brief here as film critic, and even if I were sufficiently endowed with filmic vocabulary and categories of perception and analysis, I would resist their full deployment in such a discussion, for my primary concern, professionally and personally, is fiction, not film.

For two years I have watched and studied, over and over, the Brian Edgar film of "Indian Camp," trying to see truly what is there, trying to form an exact constatation, trying also to block out the simultaneous unrolling in my mind of Hemingway's text, which I know by heart, which I have taught and discussed hundreds of times. I have lately begun to feel that I know less and less about the making of fiction into film, that the process is far more enigmatic, far more mysterious, than I could have guessed before my initiation as a consultant in the "Indian Camp" film project. To all of this add the memory, the resonance as I write these words, of long wet cold all-night location shooting of the film, in October-frosted mountains, from dark to chilled dawn, and I believe I have given the honest critic's account of bias, intention, and personal engagement with the subject at hand.

We might begin with certain facts and analyses concerned with the fiction and then attempt to locate the film within these contexts. One of Hemingway's earliest stories, "Indian Camp" is the very first short story for which he was paid—less than ten dollars (1924). There is general agreement that it is one of his finest stories. Paul Smith, in his recent comprehensive study of Hemingway's short fiction, sums up the matter as follows:

["Indian Camp"] has never been seriously challenged as the profound and original work of fiction it is. It has appealed to all the critical schools and survived them all with something left unanswered, perhaps, unanswerable. It has invited and evaded psychoanalytical and archetypal analyses. Sociological interpretations seem dated confessions of the 1960s. . . . And, finally, the story, as we all know, cast a long shadow, which Hemingway witnessed four years later and at the end of his life. (1989, 41)

Smith's reference to the story's concern with suicide and the subsequent suicides in the Hemingway family remind us that biographical soundings have often been taken from "Indian Camp." Biography aside, the story has attracted a broad range of readings, most of which agree that (1) it is a tale of initiation with a father-son focus, (2) the heart of the story is Nick's epiphany—or lack of epiphany—derived from the shocking experience of a birth/death juxtaposition, and (3) although the violent sequence of birth and death is much richer when "Indian Camp" is viewed in the full context of *In Our Time* (1925), still, the story stands rather well on its own. That may be as far as general agreement goes, for certain details of this brief tale have elicited radically divergent views.

For example, there is the question of why Uncle George, when the white men arrive at the lakeshore, gives out cigars to the Indian men. Those cigars have generated a great deal of heated discussion (more smoke than fire), with one side arguing that Uncle George is obviously the father of the Indian baby (see, e.g., Bernard 1965, 291; Brenner 1988, 239; Tanselle 1962, no. 52). This reading is then used as a foundation for arguments about the white man's "rape" of the Indian world, the white man's "intrusion" in and "destruction" of that "primitive" Native American life and culture. There is not space here to go into the problems of such readings. It must suffice to say that a tremendous burden of social guilt is imposed upon the white men in this misreading of the actual story. As Paul Smith suggests, such politicized or "sociological interpretations" now carry a strong whiff of the 1960s (e.g., Brenner 291; DeFalco 1963, 28-30; Tanselle no. 53). More recent discussions of the story have stayed closer to the text, have dismissed or ignored the question of Uncle George's putative fatherhood; some view those cigars as a ritual gift of tobacco, a perfectly normal event in traditional societies, American or Native American (e.g., Monteiro 1973, 146-52; Penner 1975, 195-99). This certainly seems to be the more accurate view, although the properly trained Hemingway reader with a disciplined awareness of the writer's attention to allusive detail will continue to wonder whether Hemingway produced those cigars to tease the paternity question and thus suggest another motive for the Indian man's suicide. In any case, the cigar question has so vexed generations of readers that Philip Young, one of the fathers of Hemingway criticism, finally confessed that he, not Uncle George, was the father of the Indian boy (Young 1966, ii-iii). Nice try, but no cigar.

How does Edgar's film adaptation deal with the cigar question? Straightforwardly—a cigar is a cigar is a ritual gift of tobacco. The film does not treat Uncle George from the paternity angle. Since I was an understudy for the film role of Uncle George I can assert categorically that the director does not have in mind a phallocentric reading of George's cigars. In an interview published after the release of the film, Edgar said that it is a "fascinating idea" that might make an "interesting version" of the story; however, as Edgar also suggests, this "could become too easy a resolution."

Another vexing question is why does the Indian man commit suicide? Some critics have viewed this question as central to the story's main concern. Does he slit his throat because he has a painful wound, a badly cut and infected foot? Because he cannot bear his wife's suffering, her screams of labor? Because he cannot bear, as some observers would have us believe, the presence of the white men in his world? Or the white doctor cutting his wife? For a very few critics, the Indian father is the central character in the story. He is variously seen as the symbol of the "death of a civilization" (Bernard 1965, 291), as a kind of last noble warrior, resisting the white man's "intrusion" in this "primitive" world, rejecting the conventional white man's role of the "proud father," or as a man whose "cut foot suggests an unconscious desire for castration deriving from his guilt for his wife's suffering" (Smith 1989, 39; Tanselle 1962, no. 53). For one biographical critic, the Indian man is the symbolic equivalent of Hemingway himself, and the story is the autobiographical record of Hemingway's agony over the birth of his first son; of course, for such a critic, the Indian's suicide is a prophecy of things to come in Hemingway's life (Lynn 1987, 229). Still other readings see the Indian father's role as peripheral; he is there simply to underline the sudden, violent, and inexplicable juxtaposition of life and death, which is Hemingway's primary theme throughout *In Our Time*.

How does the film treat the question of the Indian man and his suicide? This may be the crux that, depending on how the viewer responds and how well that viewer knows the story, makes or breaks the film version. At any rate, it is in this matter that Edgar's film departs most radically from Hemingway's story. In the story we are told that the Indian man is suffering his own pain; he has a very badly cut foot. We do not know this from the film; there is, at most, a fleeting and extremely minimalist suggestion of the wound. (When I asked viewers of the film who did not know the story about the Indian man's wound, they all said, "What wound?") In the text, the Indian man plays almost no role. He is actively present for a very brief passage before he rolls over "against the wall" and out of the angle of vision of the narrator and reader until his quiet suicide is later discovered. In the film, however, he holds center stage in sustained and foregrounded sequences, first in the intensity with which he regards his wife's screaming, and then in the eye contact he makes with Nick. In his screenplay, Edgar renders this as follows:

Slowly, he turns his head. His eyes meet Nick. Closer angle on Nick, looking up at the man. HOLD. The man looks straight at him: an expression steeped in a pain and knowledge Nick can't understand. An unspoken connection. The man smiles. Nick, next to his father, smiles back. (1990, 13)

None of this is in Hemingway's text, of course, not the faintest hint of this sense of "connection" between Nick and the Indian man. Put another way, the story devotes four brief sentences (out of a total of 146 sentences) to the Indian man before his suicide is discovered; the film gives at least five separate camera shots of the man, including point-of-view close-ups and hold shots; in addition, he is omnipresent in wide-angle shots. Of the film's elapsed action time, the Indian man is the center of more than 10 percent of it, which roughly quadruples the focus on the man that is present in the text.

This intensification of the Indian man's presence may be seen by viewers of the film who know the story as serious skewing of Hemingway's story line. The film's emphasis could be interpreted as visual underlining of Nick's ultimate concern with how hard dying is; more likely, the foregrounding of the Indian man allows a filmic metamorphosis of the tale into the "metaphor of intrusion" which, for Edgar, is the "meat of the drama" (Edgar in Stoneback 1990, 6). When I asked Edgar if he had decided, before making the film, why the man committed suicide, he said that he "came to believe that this man had lost face when his child could not be born, and amidst his wife's screams, the arrival and touch of the white man became too painful." Given this response, which echoes the responses of some of my student viewers of the film, it seems a useful corrective to stress what Joseph Flora sees as the "affection," mutually felt, in the "commerce between the Indians and the Adamses" (1982, 33-34). In any case, crucial questions of taste, of concrete historical knowledge or the lack of it, of ethnic abstractions and politics are most likely involved here; it is manifest, however, that Edgar's version of Hemingway is very much a post-1960s "Indian Camp," a Native American tale for the 1990s.

Another rubric which has generated sharply divergent critical views is this: What kind of man, what kind of father, is Dr. Adams? Such views tend to date from the 1960s, although I gather the story is still being taught in this fashion. Paul Smith sums up the false "charges" that have been brought against the doctor—"arriving improperly prepared, ignoring his patient's pain, belatedly consi-dering the husband's suffering"—and concludes that these strained readings "have been answered as they deserved to be" (1989, 39). Still, the attacks on Dr. Adams continue; he has been charged with racism; he has been, as Flora notes, found "culpable in the emergency at the Indian camp for practicing such professional procedures as the careful washing of his hands and asking George to lift the blanket so that his hands would remain clean while he operates." Such "vilification," Flora concludes, "is excessive" (1982, 33). To say the least.

Perhaps it is necessary to identify such excess as a kind of political inversion, a kind of Shining Path critical terrorism that seeks to turn inside out, to destroy the actual text and author under discussion. In any case, most recent critics have acquitted Dr. Adams of the charges brought by earlier commentators. George Monteiro, for example, stresses the necessity, for a physician, of that "affective neutrality" that enables "one's medical training and objectively learned technique to control one's behavior" (1973, 147). Those screams are not important to any doctor worth the name. Moreover, I would insist that Dr. Adams, far from being some insensitive racist villain, is Hemingway's earliest instance of an exemplary character performing with "grace under pressure"— performing well even though improperly equipped, doing the best he can, based on discipline and knowledge—in difficult and violent circumstances. And it is important to stress, too, as some recent observers have, that Dr. Adams is a loving father to his son.

Given some of the apparent tendencies of the film, it is a relief to see Dr. Adams characterized in the screenplay as a man "with a kind but weathered face." In fact, Dr. Adams is one of the film's strongest points: He is not convicted of the silly charges brought against him by some Hemingway critics. Both Brian Edgar, the director, and George Dickerson, the actor who portrays Dr. Adams, understand precisely his character and his role in the story, and the film brings Dr. Adams vividly and tellingly to life.

One more crux in the literary criticism of the story has been the question of Nick's epiphany. What does he learn? Or fail to learn? Obviously, this central concern is far too complex to treat in detail here. There has been a good deal of subtle discussion of the matter, most of it hinging on those famous last words of the story: "he felt quite sure that he would never die." Critical battles have been fought over Hemingway's final sentence. One side sees there an indication that this is an ironic tale of Nick's failed initiation, his lack of epiphany, or his romantic and illusory epiphany. For this side, Nick's assertion of immortality is a mere "romantic reaction to the experience" (DeFalco 1963, 32) revealing that he has not comprehended "the tragedy he has witnessed" (Waldhorn 1972, 54). The opposing side sees the ending as "neither illusory nor ironic" but very apt, especially because Nick here apprehends his father's love which reinforces his sense of being, and of immortality (Penner 1975, 202). This is right on target, I think, and such a reading is reinforced by Paul Smith's report on the "Indian Camp" manuscript, on Hemingway's addition, in his final revisions, of that entire last sentence: "In the early morning on the lake sitting in the stern of the boat with his father rowing, he felt quite sure that he would never die" (Smith 38). Smith stresses that the introductory phrases here are "necessary conditions for the rest of the sentence"; that is, at that mo-

ment and in that place with his father, Nick feels "sure" he will never die.
Clearly, this delicate ephiphany is the most difficult matter to translate from
fiction into film. Edgar brings a sufficiently complex and subtle reading of the
matter to the film's final scene. Nick's awareness, his implicit comprehension
of what he has just witnessed, is handled with skill by Sean MacLean, the actor
who portrays Nick, and with delicacy by Edgar, whose primary decision here is
to treat the conclusion with even greater understatement than the story does. I
will come back to this point in my conclusion.

II

> "The nurse should be here from St. Ignace by noon and she'll bring
> everything we need."

There are, of course, certain things that a text can do and film cannot
even attempt. The more the reader-viewer knows of Hemingway's techniques
of omission and understatement, of his "iceberg" theory of writing, of his
strategies of allusion, especially historical and geographical and religious allusion, the more difficult it will seem for the filmmaker even to aspire to translate
the fullness of text to screen. Take one small example from "Indian Camp."
After the operation is over, Dr. Adams says he will return the next morning and
adds: "The nurse should be here from St. Ignace by noon and she'll bring everything we need" (1938, 94).   Consider the implications of this sentence:
First, it is the story's only direct clue to setting, suggesting that the location of
the action is the Upper Peninsula of Michigan, somewhere within a morning's
travel from St. Ignace, which is on the northern side of the Straits of Mackinac.
It is possible that the setting could be on the south side of the Straits—quite
possibly in the Cross Village area—and the nurse from the Indian mission and
hospital at St. Ignace is the nearest available nurse. Historically, St. Ignace is
the old French port town and center of missionary activity among the Indians of
northern Michigan.

Hemingway, of course, is aware of this, as he is well aware of the other resonances of the name: St. Ignace for Ignatius of Loyola. St. Ignatius is an important figure in Hemingway's pantheon of saints, and significant allusions to him
are made elsewhere; for example, in *Death in the Afternoon* (1932) Hemingway
notes that at the Siege of Pamplona Ignatius received the leg-wound, the war
"wound that made him think." That is to say, the wound that led to his con-
version. Elsewhere I have documented in great detail the ways in which Hemingway deploys allusions to symbolic places and persons intertwined with resonances and nuances that require the reader's active sense of history, especially
Catholic history—all serving to create the symbolic landscapes that give his
fictions one of their most powerful if least understood modes of signifying (see,
for example, Stoneback 1986). So we have St. Ignace, in northern Michigan,
and the attendant reverberations of Catholic history, of French missionary activity among the Indians, echoing in some subterranean zone of the story.

However, quite typically, Hemingway's Catholic subtext, his anagogical level, also requires local geographical knowledge to be fully understood. To wit, in northern Michigan, St. Ignace is pronounced St. Ignis.

Now we may return to the part of the iceberg that shows above the surface. After his successful operation, and before he discovers the Indian man dead in his bunk, Dr. Adams says that the nurse will come from "St. Ignis," bringing "everything we need." In context, this is an *ignis fatuus*, a misleading hope, a deceptive light hovering over the watery night-ground of the story. If Dr. Adams has his fatuous moments anywhere in the tale, they occur precisely here, right after his St. Ignace remark, when he feels "exalted and talkative" in his "postoperative exhilaration" (1938, 94). In the ultimate context of the story, the *ignis fatuus* is the delusion that anyone, anywhere, will ever "bring everything we need." The Indian man, with his quasi-Ignatian "wound that made him think" too much, will not get what he needs from the nurse from St. Ignace. In the most immediate ironic sense, of course, the reader knows that the nurse from St. Ignace needs to bring along one of the Indian mission priests to say the last rites for the Indian man whose warm corpse is about to be discovered just after Dr. Adams makes his remark.

Such multilayered passages, a Hemingway trademark, can never be rendered in film, even if the actors and directors are aware of the resonances. In this case, since George Dickerson (as Dr. Adams) mispronounces the place as St. Ignace, the question, with its rich implications, was not even considered. But Nick, and Dr. Adams, and Uncle George, and all the Indians in the story, and Hemingway would have said St. Ignis. Thus Hemingway plays subtly on the cluster of associations released by the *ignis fatuus*, from all those glowing lights—cigars, lanterns, stove-fire, sunrise—to the fatuous hope that all needs will be fulfilled in the light of the next noon, or any noon.

Another potential problem for the viewer of the film who knows—shall we say—too much Hemingway is the impossibility of bringing into play in the film of this story the powerful and shocking juxtapositions, the manifold contexts of "Indian Camp" placed in its proper setting, in the fullness of *In Our Time*. For the viewer who knows the "Indian Camp" manuscripts and the deleted material which was published separately as a story called "Three Shots," there may be the same problem of knowing too much. This so-called story, "Three Shots," presents a brief scene which, chronologically, immediately precedes the action of "Indian Camp." Most important, it yields another angle on Nick's epiphanic feelings of immortality. It focuses on Nick's fear of death as he experiences it in church, singing the hymn he calls "Some day the silver cord will break." Hemingway's work evinces a lifelong concern with Christian categories of the soul and its disposition, here and hereafter, and he weaves a design in "Three Shots" and "Indian Camp" that traces Nick's movement from fear of the loss of the soul (the "silver chord" breaking) to a sense of being "saved by grace" ("Saved by Grace" is the actual title of the hymn). In "Indian Camp," the grace may inhere in Nick's witness to his father's saving grace, his "grace under pressure" in cutting that umbilical cord and bringing new life into the world; and a subsuming grace may be present in a larger religious sense, as it so often is—though so seldom recognized—in Hemingway's later fiction.

If these then are matters that the film cannot render, it should be added that there are also things that film can do and text cannot. The most obvious example is, I suppose, the visual power and effects, which in this film are remarkable. And then, somewhat less obvious, there is sound. Consider the many sounds of this short film; here are a few of them as indicated in the brief screenplay:

Crickets and cicadas are HEARD . . .
Crickets BUZZ loudly.
A strange, ETHEREAL SOUND has begun—a presence which suggests something unknown.
The SOUND of the paddle is heard through the water, the rowboat is HEARD ahead.
A DOG is HEARD barking, but not seen.
MOANING SOUNDS can be heard . . .
She SCREAMS.
Birds can now be HEARD with the crickets.
A STRANGE SOUND can also be heard. . . . The SOUND continues, now joined by a low AMBIENT TONE, which rises in intensity . . .
The ambient tone PEAKS, continues.

These are just a few of the sounds included in the aural subtext of this short film. Perhaps the most striking and memorable sound of all is not even indicated in the screenplay; this occurs when Dr. Adams drops the knife in the basin of water, and the camera point-of-view is on the blood drifting from the blade. The knife makes a loud metallic clang as it hits the basin, and this tone is picked up and intensified by the sound-track sequence of bell-like sounds as Nick's "unspoken connection" with the Indian man is visually defined. Clearly and effectively, the sound delivers the deep textuality of what the film shows: "never send to know for whom the bell tolls; it tolls for thee."

III

> "I'll probably get stoned for saying this, but I feel the last exchange between Nick and his father is the weakest part of the story." Brian Edgar

What kind of reviews and critical responses has the film elicited? It may be a bit early for formal reviews to have appeared in print; at least, I am not aware of any. However, since I have introduced the film on various public occasions and have moderated discussion sessions afterward, with audiences ranging from the Hemingway scholars and critics gathered for the Fourth International Hemingway Conference at the John F. Kennedy Library to upstate New York citizens, farmers and fishermen gathered at rural and small-town local libraries, I have compiled an extensive dossier of "oral reviews." Hemingway purists have responded diversely: Some are skeptical of the very premise that film can possibly do justice to Hemingway's alchemy but, with that reservation, they have praised this film.   General audiences, with no particular Hemingway knowlege or background have praised the film more generously.   Such responses and "reviews" could fill many pages here, but I shall merely list the most often repeated responses. Under the rubric of the film's strengths, much admiration has been expressed for (1) the acting and the directing in general, and especially the portrayal of Nick and his father; (2) the invention of the scene with Nick in the dark forest outside the cabin, a useful, necessary, and powerful scene that covers a time lapse in Hemingway's text; (3) the broken beads sequence, another Edgar invention; (4) the film's visual power, the light and the cinematography; (5) the film's sound and its silence, the way it captures a haunting sense of Hemingway's silence (that quality of Hemingway's prose which may be attributed to his "iceberg" principles of writing).

As far as regrets or disappointments with the film, the prevalent responses are these: (1) the politicization or "Indianization" or "Native-Americanizing" of Hemingway's actual story, insisting on a "metaphor of intrusion" and thereby diminishing the power of the father-son initiation story that Hemingway is telling; (2) excessive cutting of dialogue, in particular the final passage between father and son; (3) a certain blurring of Nick's epiphany; 4) the loss of the story's famous final image, with Nick's hand trailing in the water as he feels sure "that he would never die."

Refutation of the first critical charge is not easy: The film does invent, some would say, and insistently project the metaphor of the white man's intrusion. It could be argued that this emphasis accurately reflects neither Hemingway nor history. The Ojibways of Hemingway's Michigan were assimilated into the rural life of the region; they did not wear feathers and beads and buckskin as they do in the film; they did not have names like "Running Elk" and "Silent Bear" and "Echohawk" (as Edgar names them in his screenplay); Hemingway's Indians do not use the cliché canoes of the film, but rowboats; Uncle George does not carry a rifle into the Indian camp as he does in the film—he is on a fishing trip; and the edge of threat, the tense atmosphere (as indicated in the film, for example, by one Indian's sharply and ominously presented knife), is definitely not a part of Hemingway's story. "Indian Camp" is about a boy and his father, a doctor on a fishing trip, a doctor who knows and loves and gets along well with the Ojibways, who comes to them immediately when he is summoned, a generous and decent man and doctor answering a call for help, doing his best in difficult circumstances, presiding skillfully over the birth of new life in the Indian camp.

Rebuttal of the second critical objection of viewers is also rather difficult, for it involves the radical surgery performed on one of the most cherished dialogues in Hemingway's fiction—perhaps in American literature. Here is how it reads in the story:

"Do ladies always have such a hard time having babies?" Nick asked.
"No, that was very, very exceptional."
"Why did he kill himself, Daddy?"
"I don't know, Nick. He couldn't stand things, I guess."
"Do many men kill themselves, Daddy?"
"Not very many, Nick."
"Do many women?"
"Hardly ever."
"Don't they ever?"
"Oh, yes. They do sometimes."
"Daddy?"
"Yes."
"Where did Uncle George go?"
"He'll turn up all right."
"Is dying hard, Daddy?"
"No, I think it's pretty easy, Nick. It all depends." (Hemingway 1938, 95)

And in the film all this is reduced to:

"Why did he kill himself, Daddy?"
"I don't know Nick."
"Is dying hard?"

Thus Hemingway's sixteen lines of dialogue, carrying masterfully most of the story's gravity and resonance, are reduced to three lines. It would be difficult to explain to a non-Hemingway audience how much esteem—indeed reverence—centers on these lines exactly as Hemingway wrote them. Even the disappearance of the "Daddy" after the final "Is dying hard?" has been construed as pointless meddling with the essential poetic form of the passage. This problem, which seems to be the major one that Hemingway aficionados have with the film, is sharply underlined when we consider that the story's 401 words of spoken dialogue are cut to 259 words in the screenplay, and further reduced to a mere 169 spoken words in the film. Somebody should tell the director, one Hemingway purist remarked, that "you don't mess with Hemingway's dialogue just as you don't mess with or modernize Shakespeare's."

In fact, I told the director just that in prefilming discussions; I also raised the question in the postfilming interview. He responded, in part: "I'll probably get stoned for saying this, but I feel the last exchange between Nick and his father is the weakest part of the story." Well aware that Hemingway's dialogue was his "biggest single challenge," Edgar held the view that "the real significance lies in what is not said," and he sees the final scene essentially as the "father's inability to answer" (Stoneback 1990). This view of the matter may well both overstate and overvalue, in a very postmodern 1990ish fashion, the father's uncertainty. Surely it disregards that aspect of the story that Joseph Flora characterizes as Hemingway's "catechetic" technique: "The questions are profound, beyond the comprehension of the questioner ultimately, and so are the answers. Yet the answers, if uncomprehended, carry authority and assurance" (1982, 23). Indeed, the "authority and assurance" of the father-son catechism is a core matter that is greatly diminished in the film.

In addition, as I gathered in prefilming conversations with the director, Edgar's advisor, the legendary Milos Forman, helped to confirm the feeling that Hemingway's dialogue was a bit windy, a bit too talky for film. In any case, for Edgar, the weakest part of the story is the sequence that Hemingway readers and critics tend to see as the strongest part, the one indispensable, unalterable scene. Maybe we can account for this disparity by suggesting the existence of an unbridgeable chasm between the literary sensibility and the film sensibility.

Another critical disappointment often registered concerning the film, the so-called blurring of Nick's epiphany, seems inextricably bound up with the loss of the concluding dialogue. Nevertheless, I do not agree completely with those who feel that Nick's epiphany is blurred. Certainly, the amplitude of such an epiphany is greater in the medium of the written word, and especially so with the full context of Nick's fear for his soul and the larger questions of immortality which are present in the complete contexts of "Three Shots" and "Indian Camp" and *In Our Time*—a large and rich and complicated terrain that Edgar could not possibly cover in a short film based solely on "Indian Camp." Given what I take to be the more limited possibilities of film in this respect, Edgar does bring across rather sharply as much as he can of Nick's epiphanic realization. And this is particularly true, I gather, for viewers who do not know the fiction.

And that final regret for some viewers, the loss of the image of Nick's hand trailing in the lake at sunrise, together with the content of the story's wonderful final sentence, is explained by Edgar as follows:

This image [Nick's hand trailing in the water] I desperately wanted, but unfortunately time and money kept me from having it. I had intended to shoot this last scene at dawn, as it appears in the story. But we had only two nights to shoot at the lake, and to have done this scene would have required consecutive dawns after shooting from 8 p.m. – 4 a.m. Nick and his father would have been zombies. We had to compromise with a pre-dawn scene, shot the last morning. (In fact, Nick's hand was trailing in the water, but you can't see it.) (Stoneback 1990)

Thus we see that some of the intricacies and difficulties of making this film and some of the objections of Hemingway purists are rooted in literary and aesthetic problems, some in political and historical visions and realities, and some in dollars.

In conclusion, still speaking as a novice in the country of film, I must say this: in the process of serving as a consultant in the making of this film, I learned a good deal about the physical and fiscal realities of filmmaking, about the necessary risks, the creative courage, and the extraordinary delicacies involved in making a film from a classic work of fiction. Brian Edgar tells me that he was first drawn to "Indian Camp" by its "visual poignancy," by its "profoundly compelling" visual power. Watching his film, I understand, but still cannot articulate, this quality better than I did before. It is, I think, visually stunning. I will not pretend to understand what I can only call the mystery of the transformation of a great story into a fine film. In spite of all the reservations of the Hemingway purists—some of which are my reservations, too—this film works, and it works beautifully. One viewer, a hierophantic guardian of the Hemingway mysteries, summed it up: "Edgar changes much, omits some, and misses some of Hemingway's story. Still, it is by far the best Hemingway film yet." I think of the bone-chilling all-night shooting on location, of the physical difficulties dictated by terrain and weather, of the burden of knowledge that, in a project already entangled in cost overruns, it would cost thousands of dollars more merely to film a few seconds of a boy's hand trailing in the lake, and I say, oh yes, Edgar's "Indian Camp" is a great success. I think of Hollywood's horrendous mishmash of high-budget Hemingway movies, of Anthony Quinn's recent disastrous *Old Man and the Sea* on television and of Joan Didion's morally confused and aesthetically bungled screenplay for HBO's flat and laughable version of "Hills Like White Elephants," and I conclude that Edgar's film is indeed the best Hemingway movie yet. It has the courage of its brevity and its silences. It has, more than any other Hemingway film, the lean alchemy and economy of Hemingway's style and vision. And somewhere in the back of my mind I hear this dialogue:

"Is film-making hard, Daddy?"
"It all depends, Nick."

WORKS CITED

Bernard, Kenneth. "Hemingway's Indian Camp." *Studies in Short Fiction* 2 (Spring 1965): 291.

Brenner, Gerry. *Concealment in Hemingway's Works*. Columbus: Ohio State UP, 1988.

DeFalco, Joseph. *The Hero in Hemingway's Short Stories*. Pittsburgh: Pittsburgh UP, 1963.

Edgar, Brian, "'Indian Camp': Screenplay." *English Graduate Review II* (Apr. 1990): 8-18.

Flora, Joseph M. *Hemingway's Nick Adams*. Baton Rouge: Louisiana State UP, 1982.

Hemingway, Ernest. "Indian Camp." *The Short Stories of Ernest Hemingway*. New York: Scribner's, 1938. 91-95.

Lynn, Kenneth S. *Hemingway*. New York: Simon and Schuster, 1987.

Monteiro, George. "The Limits of Professionalism: A Sociological Approach to Faulkner, Fitzgerald and Hemingway." *Criticism* 15 (Spring 1973): 145-55.

Penner, Dick. "The First Nick Adams Story." *Fitzgerald/Hemingway Annual* (1975): 195-202.

Smith, Paul. *A Reader's Guide to the Short Stories of Ernest Hemingway*. Boston: G. K. Hall, 1989.

Stoneback, H. R. "From the rue Saint-Jacques to the Pass of Roland to the 'Unfinished

Church on the Edge of the Cliff.'" *The Hemingway Review* 6.1 (Fall 1986): 2-29.

—. "Interview with Brian Edgar." *English Graduate Review II* (Apr. 1990): 5-7.

Tanselle, G. Thomas. "Hemingway's 'Indian Camp'." *Explicator* 20 (Feb. 1962): Item 53.

Waldhorn, Arthur. *A Reader's Guide to Ernest Hemingway*. New York: Farrar, Straus and Giroux, 1972.

Young, Philip. "Letter to the Editor." *Studies in Short Fiction* 3 (1966): ii-iii.

13

An Unfilmable Conclusion:
Joyce Carol Oates at the Movies

Brenda O. Daly

In 1966, three years before the shocking stories of Charles Manson and his "family" emerged, *Life* magazine carried the story of a murderer named Charles Schmid.[1] With the help of teenage "followers," Schmid murdered three young women and buried them in the desert outside Tucson. "The Pied Piper of Tucson" was later exposed by a sidekick, tried and sent to prison. Locking Schmid up did not, of course, make America a less violent or safer place to live. It was to explore this "senseless" violence in terms of its cultural implications that Joyce Carol Oates wrote her well-known short story "Where Are You Going, Where Have You Been?," first published in the fall of 1966. In the story Charles Schmid, renamed Arnold Friend, retains his too-large cowboy boots and pan-cake makeup, as well as his "Golden Car" and his habit of using "high falutin' language." But Oates transforms him into a friend/fiend—a harbinger of Death—whose significance has since been widely discussed in introductory literature classes in colleges and universities.

Twenty years after its first appearance, this widely anthologized story was made into a movie called *Smooth Talk*, released in 1986. Directed by Joyce Chopra, it stars Laura Dern as Connie, William Treat as Arnold Friend, and Mary Kay Place as Connie's mother. This intense interest in senseless violence—evident in the translations from fact into fiction and film—raises a number of questions: Why, for example, has yet another woman artist resurrected a tale of violence against women? Whose story is being told, and what are its larger cultural implications? Any response to these questions requires analysis of the relationship among many different texts: popular music, magazines, and books (some of which Schmid drew upon to create his persona), as well as medieval art, nineteenth-century American literature, and critical essays on Yeats.

One problem that Oates and Chopra emphasize—the psychosocial implications of space—is not a new preoccupation of women artists. For example,
Sandra Gilbert and Susan Gubar argue in *The Madwoman in the Attic: The
Woman Writer and the Nineteenth Century Literary Imagination* that "anxieties
about space seem to dominate the literature of the nineteenth century by women
and their twentieth-century descendants" (1979, 83). For women writers, this
anxiety about space is not simply metaphysical, but social, according to Gilbert
and Gubar. The fact that most agoraphobics are women supports this argument, as does the fact that male readers tend to resist the gothic genre whose
claustrophobic spaces have long been recognizable to women readers.[2] The
gothic spaces of works such as *Jane Eyre* and *The Yellow Wallpaper* further
illustrate Gilbert and Gubar's point, and in "Where Are You Going, Where
Have You Been?" it is easy to recognize Oates as a twentieth-century descen-
dant. Oates is, in fact, frequently described as a "gothic" writer, although this
term, sometimes used pejoratively, is too limited. Spatial inequalities are apparent even in Oates's title, "Where Are You Going, Where Have You Been?"
Such questions are often put to teenagers by parents, many of whom grant
greater freedom of movement to boys. Probably one reason that parents continue to constrain their daughters is that it is still possible for a girl—out late at
night and in public places—to be put on trial and found guilty of her own rape/
murder.[3] At one level, then, both Oates and Chopra are examining a woman's
lack of freedom and her vulnerability to male violence in our culture. Indeed,
spatial limitations are of "crucial concern" in Oates's story, as Christina Marsden Gilles has noted, and the "invasion of personal, interior space" occurs at
many levels (1981, 65). I see similar concern with spatial limitations and in-
vasions of personal space in Chopra's film.
  Both women use space to signify Connie's lack of sexual and social equality,
but what is lost in the translation from fiction to film can be understood only by
moving beyond the realistic plane of interpretation to allegory. In a review of
Chopra's film, Oates explains that her allegorical intentions were perhaps "too
explicit" in an earlier title, "Death and the Maiden."[4] Despite the loss of this
title, borrowed from a fifteenth-century German engraving by Albrecht Dürer,
critics have noted Friend's Satanic appearance and Connie's role as Everyman.[5] As I will illustrate, Oates's allusions to Emily Dickinson's poem
"Because I Could Not Stop for Death" also suggest that the story may be read as
allegory. Finally, it is perhaps in the lyrics of Bob Dylan's "It's All Over Now,
Baby Blue"—and Oates has dedicated the story to Dylan—that the historical
and political implications of "Where Are You Going, Where Have You Been?"
can best be understood. At this level of meaning the question of the title, addressed to readers, asks us to consider how an act of violence—apparently
without motive—can teach us something about our culture. Oates's tale of rape
may also be compared to Yeats's "Leda and the Swan," an allegory of power
and knowledge that preoccupied Oates in the 1960s in both her fiction—*A
Garden of Earthly Delights* (1966)—and in critical essays on Yeats. Although

these allegorical allusions are, understandably, lost in the film, Oates nevertheless credits Chopra with "an accomplished and sophisticated film." Noting Chopra's change of her story's ending, Oates described her own ambiguous conclusion as "unfilmable." The loss is significant, however, since at this moment in Oates's story Connie sees beyond Arnold Friend's limited, though powerful, vision.

Yet *Smooth Talk* certainly deserves praise, particularly its fidelity to Oates's spatial analogies. Nevertheless, one film critic has complained that Oates's "predictably nasty" story has, in Chopra's medium, become a formulaic cautionary tale for girls. B. Ruby Rich argues that, through its spatial vocabulary, the film warns girls to stay home and "keep a lid on their sexuality."[6] Chopra uses "the whole bag of cinematic tricks," complains Rich, to enforce a sexual/spatial system of inequalities:

Every time Connie is on screen, she's shot close-up, tightly, claustrophobically, with no space around her, pinned into that tiny unmoveable frame. Every time Arnold is on screen, he's in a middle-shot framed against an ample landscape, lots of space around him, master of the territory. The music surges on the sound track. It isn't long before high spirited Connie is a quivering puddle on the hallway floor. (1986, 69)

Rich exaggerates only slightly. In fact, at moments we do see Connie in a wider frame—at the beach or the shopping center, for example—but it is also true that each time Connie moves into public spaces, traditionally male territory, danger lurks in the form of a shadowy male who, as the movie progresses, becomes increasingly more threatening. And each time Connie crosses over into new and larger spaces—such as the moment when she crosses the highway to the drive-in—she becomes increasingly more vulnerable. Also, at each crossing she becomes more isolated as, one by one, her girlfriends drop out of the adventure, usually under orders from a parent.

The "high spirited" Connie is indeed trapped by the rapist in an isolated house where she has been left alone by her parents and sister. Yet, just as Oates and Chopra did not invent the spatial inequalities they depict, they also do not simply repeat a horror formula which, at a woman's expense, will titillate an audience. Rich claims that when Friend arrives at Connie's door-step, the film "turns into a familiar product, the stock in trade of the horror genre: woman alone, trapped in empty house, terrorized, raped or killed or left insane" (1986, 69). The innovative dialogue that Oates locates at this threshold—much of which Chopra employs in the film—is certainly not formulaic, nor is the conclusion of either the film or the story, as I shall demonstrate. Furthermore, when Rich says that the appeal of the formula, merely repeated by Oates and Chopra, is "the spectacle of lust delivered into the audience, and then punishment of its embodiment, again for audience pleasure" (1986, 69), she forgets that in the film Connie survives and in fiction, though not likely to survive, Connie "awakens" spiritually and, thus, sees beyond F(r)iend. What she sees, "the vast sunlit reaches of the land behind him and on all sides of him," is alive

(Oates 1974, 31). In a profound sense, then, Oates's Connie is as "high spirited" as Chopra's assertive survivor. Oates makes this comment about the
film's ending: "Laura Dern's Connie is no longer 'my' Connie at the film's
conclusion; she is very much alive, assertive, strong-willed—a girl, perhaps, of
the mid-1980s and not of the mid-1960s" (1986, 22).

The evolution of Connie's consciousness—as she faces death—is the focus of
Oates's story. Schmid was the central figure in *Life*, but in successive drafts of
the tale, Oates shifted Friend to the margins as Connie's consciousness became
central. Chopra's title, *Smooth Talk*, gives star billing to Friend, but Connie
has the last, assertive word. Neither artist blames the victim; instead, they tell
her story, breaking the silence imposed upon rape victims. Connie's story is
one of joy in her awakening sexuality, a "goodness" that challenges the con-
vention of virginal goodness. It is Connie's mother, whose morality is conventional, who forces Connie to disguise her sexuality. Thus Connie has "two
sides" that "looked one way when she was at home and another way when she
was away from home. Everything had two sides to it" (Oates 1974, 13). Yet in
her Preface, Oates explains that neither side is "evil" according to her moral
vision:

A new morality is emerging in America which may appear to be opposed to the old but
which is in fact a higher form of the old—the democratization of the spirit, the experiencing of life as meaningful in itself, without divisions into "good" and "bad,"
"beautiful" or "ugly," "moral" or "immoral." (1974, 9)

Younger readers seem to understand this evolution in consciousness, says
Oates, and Chopra shares this vision. Chopra has invented some wonderfully
amusing scenes that illustrate her pleasure in Connie's "trying on" her new
sexuality: Connie practicing boy/girl dialogue before her bathroom mirror;
Connie changing her clothes in the shopping center bathroom; or Connie trying
on a revealing outfit to wear to the drive-in.

The film audience is certainly not meant to share the attitude of Connie's
mother, who describes the "good" June and the "bad" Connie on the phone,
who rejects Connie when she tries to join the family card game, and who expects Connie to fulfill her own emotional emptiness. The mother's sexual jeal-
ousy is obvious. One scene especially shows the limits of her older morality:
When Connie's mother asks about "the Pettinger girl," Connie confronts her
mother with her own premarital sexualty. In return for this remark, Connie is
slapped. Despite her motherly love for Connie, she cannot express a more
genuine concern—that Connie's early sexual maturity may trap her into a
loveless marriage—because she thinks judgmentally, in terms of the old morality. A failure of imagination is evident in other family relationships as well.
The father—invented by Chopra—cannot seem to "imagine" what his wife
does all day. Their lives are gendered; their imaginations limited to the material world. They cannot move into one another's minds—past boundaries of
gender and generation—and this failure of imagination has harsh consequences

for Connie. For example, when Connie lies to her father, telling him her mother knows of her crossing the highway to the drive-in, he does not check her story, probably because he talks rarely with his wife. Such divisions in the family—including those between the two sisters—lead to Connie's isolation in the house on the day of Friend's visit.

Arnold Friend will challenge the very limits of Connie's consciousness. At the doorway, the threshold of Connie's body/consciousness, Oates intensifies the crisis. As Christina Marsden Gilles suggests:

The seduction motif functions successfully in "Where are you going?" because the delineation of interior space figured in the female analogizes invasion at several levels; the domestic space, the state of childhood consciousness associated with the home, and, of course, the individual consciousness. (1981, 65)

The house = body equation operates on yet another level in both fiction and film: house = culture. It is not, finally, Connie's house, but her father's. As Friend warns, "your daddy's house—is nothing but a cardboard box I can knock down any time" (Oates 1974, 29). Connie's quick submission to Friend reveals her attitude toward masculine authority. Connie begins to suspect that Friend is not what he pretends to be: an ordinary teenager dressed in blue jeans and cowboy boots. At least some of Friend's strangeness is lost when Chopra omits his makeup and wobbly boots. Given Chopra's realistic mode, these details would have seemed too bizarre—despite their origin in fact—but the camera accentuates Friend's potential for violence, as well as his role as a double. In the shadows outside the house, Friend's face looms at the window; then his body darkens in the doorway. Friend speaks softly, as if romantically, with Connie, but he yells in harsh, angry tones at his "other" side, Ellie Oscar, whose name suggests the fiend's "feminine" aspects. Then Ellie acts out his role as sidekick, or double, by ransacking Connie's bedroom while, off-screen, Friend violates Connie's body.

Chopra retains the rapist's "civility," his manner of invading Connie's romantic daydreams before claiming her body. When Connie protests that she does not know him, he demonstrates his rhetorical skills and possibly psychic power by knowing her music, her friends, her family, and even her private thoughts. He appears as unhurried as Dickinson's "civil" gentleman caller, who "knew no haste," but this very mixture of civility and threat creates the ambiguity—and terror—for his victim. When Friend says, "Connie, this is your day set aside for a ride with me, and you know it," she first thinks this man might fulfill her "the way it was in the movies and promised in songs" (1974, 16). Yet the sudden strangeness of the man—his face appears much older and his romantic promises become threats—leads Connie to feel estranged from the material world—her house, her body—and increasingly aware of an invisible realm of which Friend is the emissary. The recognition is violent: Forced to imagine her own rape/murder, Connie becomes detached from her own breathing, her own cries:

She felt her breath jerking back and forth in her lungs as if it were something Arnold Friend was stabbing her with again and again with no tenderness. A noisy sorrowful wailing rose all about her and she was locked inside it the way she was locked inside this house. (29)

Connie calls out to her mother, but finally hangs up the phone, obeying Friend so that he will keep his promise not to "come inside" the house. At the same time Friend also promises to "come inside . . . where it's all secret" (24).

Yet in both fiction and film perhaps Friend's most persuasive moment occurs when he implicates Connie in imagining her absent family. Like an artist, he sketches in just enough detail so that Connie, along with readers, begins to fill in missing details. Gazing into the distance, like a storyteller does, Friend creates this scene:

"Right now they're—uh—drinking. Sitting around," he said vaguely, squinting as if he were staring all the way to town and over Aunt Tillie's backyard. Then the vision seemed to get clear and he nodded energetically, "Yeah, sitting around. There's your sister in a blue dress, huh? and high heels, the poor sad bitch—nothing like you sweetheart! And your mother's helping some fat woman with the corn, they're cleaning the corn—husking the corn—"
"What fat woman?" Connie cried. (24)

And he has got her. She is trapped by his language, mastered by his vision. However, in their different texts, both Chopra and Oates "steal the language" from Friend, redefining the encounter, revising Connie's "end." Oates's ambiguous conclusion does not reflect one of the greatest social changes in the past decade: the feminist movement. Had Connie lived in the 1980s she might have been a "resisting reader"—a girl less vulnerable to lines from movies and lyrics from popular songs, a girl who insists upon defining reality in her own language. Let me now turn to the different visions of Connie's end, first in the film, then in the fiction.

Chopra's "Golden Car" does not turn into what Oates calls "Death's Chariot (a funky souped-up convertible)." However, when Connie returns from her ride, after being raped by Friend, the car has certainly lost its glitter, its glamour. Chopra does criticize the consumerism that disguises a greater American dream by emphasizing, as Oates does, the cars, houses, and hamburgers that define her characters' desires. Little wonder, then, that Connie's awakening sexuality is shaped by the values expressed by popular music, advertising, and movies. Chopra also suggests with her camera what Oates implies in Arnold's sinister behavior—his "sniffing" at Connie as if "she were a treat he was going to gobble up" (1974, 19)—that Connie herself may be perceived as a consumer object. Connie clearly rejects Friend's vision when, at the end of the film, she warns him not to return. Furthermore, when Connie dances with her sister June—in space Ellie Oscar has ransacked—she gains back some territory. Significantly, the music is the same that Connie and her mother had danced to earlier, though in separate rooms. In the end, then, Connie and her family are "musically" reunited, though Connie understands that she cannot tell her "innocent" family her story—that she has been raped. What Connie realizes is that, given her family's view of morality, she will be regarded as a "bad girl," as somehow to blame for the violence she has suffered.

It is precisely this morality that Oates believes we must move beyond. The ambiguous conclusion of "Where Are You Going, Where Have You Been?" prompts readers to analyze the question posed by the title and to move beyond the more obvious answers—those that remain within the realm of the visible world—just as the rhetoric of Arnold Friend forces Connie to move beyond the borders of her father's house. Connie knows, for example, that when Friend calls her "my sweet little blue-eyed girl" it "had nothing to do with her brown eyes." Oates carries this psychological complexity even further, linking the rapist's "little blue-eyed girl" to the "vast sunlit reaches of the land" (31). Readers who know Dylan's "It's All Over Now, Baby Blue" may interpret this vague phrase as reference to Connie's death: Connie will soon be buried in the ground. The film, of course, cannot develop this allusion, except through its sound track, but once again, death is not consistent with Chopra's revised ending. Yet, in framing the movie—which begins at the beach, moves for its climax (his/not hers) to the mountains, then returns to Connie's home—Chopra does suggest a power greater than the so-called civilized world. What had seemed a mere backdrop for human activity does "come alive" for Connie, even in the film.

Oates's story suggests that this consciousness of the "vast sunlit land" is repressed—like evil—by our civilized minds. But the unconscious threat of the earth, to which we must one day return, shapes our desire for a sense of belonging. Both the victim and the victimizer share this desire to be part of something larger: a family, a community, a country. Their shared music hints at this, as does their shared vision of the picnicing family. Chopra emphasizes this similarity through parallel scenes, both of which show Connie and Friend as "outsiders." Just as Arnold had stood alone in the darkness outside the drive-in, Connie stands alone in the darkness outside her home while her family plays cards. Significantly, Connie's isolation from her family increases as her sexuality becomes stronger, as if her father's house cannot contain, cannot allow, this erotic disturbance, and therefore relegates a woman's sexuality to the "outside," defining it as "evil." Yet both Oates and Chopra move behond this binary morality—and beyond the formulaic horror show—in their endings. When Connie asserts herself in the film, she moves beyond her rapist, but her victory—unlike his conquest of her—does not violate him. No simple reversal of roles occurs. Oates achieves a victory for Connie by implying that she chooses to sacrifice herself to protect her family from Friend. Despite her impending death, strongly foreshadowed in Oates's dialogue, one way to interpret the story is that Connie acts heroically.

Oates articulates Connie's "higher consciousness" through allusions to Dylan's music and Dickinson's poetry. Dickinson's carriage becomes the vehicle by which one imagines what Connie "sees" behind and on all sides of the f(r)iend. In "Because I could not stop for Death," Death seems to be in the driver's seat, like Friend. But Dickinson's carriage also has a passenger named "Immortality." This immortality becomes visible when the poem raises the question of what moves, what sees:

> We passed the School, where Children strove
> At recess—in the Ring—
> We passed the Fields of Gazing Grain—
> We passed the Setting Sun—

And, in the next line, "Or rather—He passed Us." Now the speaker's point of view, and consciousness, seem to have altered: If Grain is "Gazing," it must be alive. If what "passed" is not the carriage, but the "Setting Sun," then it, too, is alive. From this larger perspective, humankind appears circumscribed, like "recess—in the Ring," like the striving of "Children." Dylan makes a similar point in "It's All Over Now, Baby Blue." His lyrics describe a world alive, a world in motion. The carpet moves beneath Baby Blue's feet, and in lines eerily suggestive of Arnold Friend at Connie's door, Dylan even questions the certainty of one's own identity when he sugests that the vagabond at the door may be wearing clothes one wore before. Nothing stays, nothing is solid, not Connie's house, not even her heart: "That feels solid too but we know better," Friend tells her (30).

Like Death—Dickinson's unhurried gentleman caller—Friend easily destroys mere things: houses, cars, bodies. What Dickinson implies, however, is that Death does not have the power to destroy the invisible realm. In this realm, a grave becomes a new house:

> We paused before a House that seemed
> A swelling in the Ground
> The roof was scarcely visible—
> The Cornice—in the Ground—

To compare a grave to a house is to suggest that one "lives" in a grave. Like Oates, then, Dickinson implies that the earth itself is "alive," a form of life that, though it may absorb individual identities and human consciousness, nevertheless lives. And the "voice" of Dickinson's poem does achieve a kind of Immortality, just as the voice of Connie and her assailant become Immortal through the creative consciousness of Oates and Chopra. Of course, audiences must animate these artistic creations and, thus, this consciousness is never simply individual. Connie mistakenly assumes that her lover will affirm her individual fantasies, her vision of herself. Friend disabuses her of that faulty notion. However, by destroying her romantic fantasies, Friend awakens in her a consciousness of powers greater than the self—family, community, and "the vast sunlit land." As Oates says in her Preface:

There are cultures in which divinity is spread out equally, energizing everyone and everything; there are other cultures—unfortunately, ours is one of them—in which the concept of "divinity" was snatched up by a political/economic order, and the democratic essence of divinity denied. (1974, 8)

As Oates interprets the violence of a Charles Schmid, then, his acts, para-doxically, affirm a higher consciousness: the democratic essence of divinity. For this greater reality, a spiritual reality, the material world is a text to be read as the medievalists interpreted their world. At the same time, Oates's insis-tence upon the democracy of the spirit challenges medieval hierarchies, and thus, her story, "Death and the Maiden," is radically revisionary. By emphasiz-ing the relationship between past and present artists, however, Oates illustrates that her "new morality" is not "opposed to the old but . . . a higher form of the old" (1974, 9). Within the context of this new morality, Connie's death is not an "end," but the sign of a cultural change. As Connie moves across the threshold of her old house to her new house in the "sunlit land," she thus be-comes a harbinger of a new consciousness.

What is this new consciousness? In her essays on Yeats, both written in the late 1960s, Oates describes it as "the tragic fact of metamorphosis . . . at the heart of Yeats's poetry," a belief also at the heart of Oates's fiction during this period ("Tragic Rites" 169). Oates—again in her essay on Yeats—views the human personality as fluid. She says of Yeats's poetry:

Half consciously he seems to have chosen this primitive "logical thought" over the more commonplace and sanitary belief in the permanent isolation of human beings from one another and from the world of nature, whether animals, plants, or inanimate matter. The primitive imagination accepts totally the fact of miraculous change: what would be miraculous to them is our conception of a conclusion, an ending of spirit and energy. ("Tragic Rites" 169)

Oates's thought, I believe, is similarly "primitive," presenting Connie at the point of metamorphosis from one state of being to another, from one conscious-ness to another. By analogy, this moment of rape or violent metamorphosis, like the rape in Yeats's "Leda and the Swan," signals the violence of our cul-tural metamorphosis.

The difference between Oates's Connie and Chopra's Connie is but one in-stance of our cultural metamorphosis during the past twenty to twenty-five years. For such change, the conception of a conclusion—"an ending of spirit and energy"—would indeed seem "miraculous." In this sense, Oates's nonending is certainly "unfilmable," for it portrays an energy—an erotic, spiritual energy signaled by violence—that cannot finally be contained by a work of art. The conventions of realism especially—the insistence upon endings, and on "character" bounded by material realities including anatomical features—do not allow this higher consciousness to be invoked in Chopra's film. Oates has suggested its mystery by the use of a question in her title, "Where Are You Going, Where Have You Been?" and in the ambiguous conclusion of her story. She has also said, in a *Newsweek* interview in 1972: "I write about things that are violent and extreme, but always against a background of something deep and imperishable. I feel I can wade in blood. I can endure the 10,000 evil visions because there is this absolutely imperishable reality behind it" (Clemons 1972, 72). Perhaps this imperishable reality is present, not in a permanent "Connie," but in her metamorphosis through fiction, film, and, of course, American life.

NOTES

A longer version of this essay appeared in the *Journal of Popular Culture* 23.3 (Winter 1989): 101-14.

1. "The Pied Piper of Tuscon," *Life* 4 Mar. 1966: 18-24, 80-90. In the mid-1970s Charles Schmid was stabbed to death by inmates at the Arizona State Penitentiary. No one was convicted of his murder, according to a corrections officer at the prison.

2. "Gothic Possibilities" by Norman N. Holland and Leona F. Sherman in *Gender and Reading*, eds. Elizabeth A. Flynn and Patrocinio P. Schweickart (Baltimore: John Hopkins UP, 1986) 215-33. In their essay, Holland and Sherman compare their gendered responses to the gothic. For example, Holland says, "For me, both identifying with a female and imagining being penetrated call into question my male identity" (220). Sherman notes that "the gothic novel provides a polarizing of inside and outside with which an adult woman, particularly in a sexist society, might symbolize a common psychosocial experience; an invaded life within her mind, her body, her home, bounded by a social structure that marks off economic and political life as 'outside'" (226).

3. "The Donahue Show," 25 May 1988. Donahue's guest, Ellen Levin, mother of Jennifer Levin who was raped and killed by Robert Chambers in a New York City park, described how her daughter was put on trial by the media and by the lawyers. Without proof, according to Levin, newspapers asserted that Jennifer's diary contained descriptions of "kinky sex." During the 1980s violent crimes against women, including rape, increased.

4. "When Characters on the Page Are Made Flesh on the Screen," *The New York Times*, Sunday 23 Mar. 1986: 1, 22. All Oates's comments about "Smooth Talk" are from this essay.

5. Marie Mitchel Olesen Urbanski, "Existential Allegory: Joyce Carol Oates's 'Where Are You Going, Where Have You Been?'" *Studies in Short Fiction*, 15.3 (Spring 1978): 220-23. I disagree with Urbanski's view that Oates is telling the old story of "the seduction of Eve" in a contemporary setting. Oates is revising this story significantly. I also disagree that Connie's is a story of "Everyman's transition from the illusion of free will to the realizaton of externally determined fate." Connie does choose to walk through the door, however circumscribed this choice may seem. Other essays that examine the religious connotations of this story include Mark B. Robson's "Joyce Carol Oates's 'Where Are You Going, Where Have You Been?': Arnold Friend as Devil, Dylan, and Levite," in *Publications of the Mississippi Philological Association*, 1985:

98-105; Mike Tierce and John Michael Crafton's "Connie's Tambourine Man: A New Reading of Arnold Friend," *Studies in Short Fiction*, 22.2 (Spring 1985): 219-24, which interprets Friend as a Christ figure.

6. "Good Girls, Bad Girls," *The Village Voice*, 15 Apr. 1986. This review is, in part, a reply to an earlier review by Andrew Sarris called "Teenage Gothic," 4 Mar. 1986 . The controversy continued in a later edition (25 Apr. 1986) when Sarris replied to Rich.

WORKS CITED

Clemons, Walter. "Joyce Carol Oates: Love and Violence." *Newsweek* 11, Dec. 1972: 72-77.

Dickinson, Emily. "Because I Could Not Stop for Death." *The Poems of Emily Dickinson*. Vol. 2. Ed. Thomas H. Johnson. Cambridge, Mass.: The Belknap Press of Harvard UP, 1955. 546.

The Donahue Show. 25 May 1988.

Dylan, Bob. "It's All Over Now, Baby Blue." *Bob Dylan's Greatest Hits*. II, #7 on Compact Disc, Columbia Records, 1967.

Gilbert, Sandra, and Susan Gubar. *The Madwoman in the Attic: The Woman Writer and the Nineteenth Century Literary Imagination*. New Haven: Yale UP, 1979.

Gilles, Christina Marsden. "'Where Are You Going, Where Have You Been?': Seduction, Space and a Fictional Mode." *Studies in Short Fiction* 18 (1981). 65-70.

Holland, Norman N., and Leona F. Sherman. "Gothic Possibilities." *Gender and Reading*. Eds. Elizabeth A. Flynn and Patrocinio P. Schweickart. Baltimore: Johns Hopkins P., 1986. 215-33.

Oates, Joyce Carol. "Tragic Rites in Yeats's A Full Moon in March." *The Edge of Impossibility: Tragic Forms in Literature*. New York: The Vanguard P., 1972. 163-87.

—. "When Characters on the Page are Made Flesh on the Screen." *The New York Times*. Sunday 23 Mar. 1986: 1, 22.

—. "Where Are You Going, Where Have You Been?" *Where Are You Going, Where Have You Been? Stories of Young America*. Greenwich, Conn.: Fawcett, 1974: 11- 31.

—. "Yeats: Violence, Tragedy, Mutability." *The Edge of Impossibility: Tragic Forms in Literature*. New York: The Vanguard P., 1972. 139-61.

"The Pied Piper of Tucson." *Life* 4 Mar. 1966: 18-24, 80-90.

Rich, B. Ruby. "Good Girls, Bad Girls." *The Village Voice* 15 Apr. 1986: 69.

Urbanski, Marie Mitchell Olesen. "Existential Allegory: Joyce Carol Oates's 'Where Are You Going, Where Have You Been?'." *Studies in Short Fiction* 15.3 (Spring 1978): 200-203.

Storying in Hyperspace: "Linkages"

Robert Coover

Although I would like to present a kind of personal "short story of the short story" from oral tales to hyperfictions, I am not altogether sure I know, even as an alleged writer of short stories, what a short story is. I'm not alone in this, of course. It's as common a complaint as writer's block, and has perplexed half the papers I've read on the subject.

I *think* a short story is a fixed form of some kind, circumscribed and out-dated—or "exhausted," as my friend Jack Barth would say—and is related somehow to the Victorian novel and American writing workshops. Or at least that was how I was thinking when I started writing my own first breakaway fictions, bedazzled in those days by the likes of Kafka, Beckett, and Borges, who were not, so far as I could tell, writing "short stories."

So when my publishers finally agreed to bring out *Pricksongs & Descants* (1969), I followed Borges and insisted on describing its contents as "fictions." I thought of them, in short, as belonging to a broader deeper mainstream, and as something newly made, something fashioned. I didn't even call them "short fictions," just "fictions," meaning, I think, that these were as long as they could be, were complete: fictions. Ditto, *A Night at the Movies* (1987), though else-where, especially in catalogues and bibliographics, both of these books are often subtitled, though not by me, "short fictions."

But what is "short"? It is publishers who decide that usually, but what do they know about writing? What they know about—or pretend to know about—but don't trust them at any length in that department either—is book produc-tion, and it is largely the packaging that distinguishes novels from novellas and short novels from short stories, though where any one of these forms begins and the other ends, no one can say.

Likewise "short shorts" or "minifictions" or "quick fictions," "minute fictions," "flashers," and the like. A couple of anthologizers wrote to me from
Arizona one day, asking if I had any one- or two-page fictions for a collection
they were going to call Blasters. Just like Arizonans to call a book of fictions
"blasters." I wrote back in reply. The first time I ever visited that state was
when I went to the Tuscon Poetry Center for one week, and the night I arrived
three guys who had picked up some powerful rifles from a yard sale had got up
a game of trying to shoot through a steel door to set off some dynamite stored
away there for road works. They succeeded, much to the entertainment of the
neighborhood for several blocks around, though, afterwards, two of them were
dead and the third was forever after a quadriplegic. Still, helluva lot of fun, a
real blast and all that. The anthologizers came back with a new idea, which I
think the poet and fabulator Robert Kelly thought up: *Sudden Fiction* (1986). I
liked that better, so I wrote them one, or what I thought of as one, and called it,
in fact, "A Sudden Story." It is about a hero and a dragon, a narrative situation
that goes back several millenia, at least as far as the Epic of Gilgamesh and his
battle with the monster of the forest Humbaba, and probably much further . . .

Once upon a time, suddenly, while it still could, the story began. For the hero, setting
forth, there was of course nothing sudden about it, neither about the setting forth, which
he'd spent his entire lifetime anticipating, nor about any conceivable endings, which
seemed, like the horizon, to be always somewhere else. For the dragon, however, who
was stupid, everything was sudden. He was suddenly hungry and then he was suddenly
eating something. Always, it was like the first time. Then, all of a sudden, he'd remember having eaten something like that before: a certain familiar sourness . . . . And,
just as suddenly, he'd forget. The hero, coming suddenly upon the dragon (he'd been
trekking for years through enchanted forests, endless deserts, cities carbonized by
dragonbreath, for him suddenly was not exactly the word), found himself envying, as he
drew his sword (a possible ending had just loomed up before him, as though the horizon
had, with the desperate illusion of suddenness, tipped), the dragon's tenseless freedom.
Freedom? the dragon might have asked, had he not been so stupid, chewing over meanwhile the sudden familiar sourness (a memory. . . ?) on his breath. From what?
(Forgotten.) (vii)

Not everything in that anthology, interesting as it was, was what I would have
called a "sudden fiction," there being a number of prose poems, fables,
sketches, meditations, fragments from longer narratives, and what we call
"slice of life" stories—which are, of course, not "slice of life" but "slice of
novel" stories. The editors did, however, set a word limit of 1,500 words, so
certainly the pieces they published were short-short in that respect at least, but
somehow physical length did not seem an adequate or even relevant way of
categorizing them. The trouble is, see, I still think of *Gerald's Party* as a
"sudden fiction," long as it is on the printed page. I thought of it suddenly and
suddenly I wrote it, nonstop and without narrative breaks, and it suddenly took
me eight years to do that.

The point of course is, as many have said before me, that the structuring metaphor of a piece of fiction, the "mythos" as Aristotle might have it, determines the length and shape of the narrative, unless the author lacks the courage and intransigence and means to carry it through, and then it is merely a failed narrative, long or short. It has something to do with the narrative's centripetal force, as opposed to the power of its buried paradoxes to shatter that force and send the narrative hurtling outward into a more troubled trajectory. Finally, I've decided that a work is long when it can be excerpted. Otherwise, it's short.

The argument that the short story, even when narrowly defined, is somehow peculiarly American is one I have more trouble with. Oh yes, there are a lot of reasonable cultural and historical arguments: the popular magazine culture, our hasty toilet and subway and poolside reading, our bargain-hunting mentality— more for the price of one—the impact of film and television, limited literacy and even more limited attention spans, Poe's how-to-do-it influence, the O'Henry success story, our pluralistic ideology, and our impatience with attention-hogs, our rude holler to "say your piece and sit down!" But, still, short tale-telling is just too universal. I don't see how we can arrogate this ancient form unto ourselves without looking like parochial dreamfield bush-leaguers, unregenerate yahoos. The only thing truly American about the short story is the American effort to possess it, to colonialize it and add a new state to the union.

All of this is meant to lead, by way of composite characters, character types (like the picaro), framing devices (such as nested narratives), medieval interlacings, and suchlike, to thoughts about the future of short narratives in computerized hyperspace. Linking, one of the peculiar features of hyperfictions, is perhaps its most radically new, yet most profoundly traditional, element, hyperfictions being the new nonlinear, nonsequential, multidirectional, interactive, polyvocal narratives being produced on the computer nowadays in what is called hypertext. Unlike printed text, hypertext provides multiple paths between blocks of text and graphics—not to mention bits of film, music, and animation as well. The artist creates in this space by preparing text or other blocks just as she would compose on paper; then, by linking these blocks by way of various structuring and navigational devices provided by the software system of choice, she creates pathways, alternate readings and trajectories, maps for the reader and other aids, finally turning this webwork of possibilities over to the reader to create his own reading experience, and perhaps writing experience as well, why not, as he clicks creatively from window to window. I say, "he," "she"—but in this medium it can as easily be "they."

So if I were preparing this little essay in a hypertext format, I would now be offering you a variety of linked routes out of here, depending on what most interests you and keeps you awake. That hint I just dropped, for example, about the tendency in hyperspace toward collaborative projects. Or the relation between what I have just called the structuring and navigational devices of hyper-

text applications and what I earlier called the structural metaphors of fiction.
Or perhaps to a hypertext document, where you could see all this for yourself.
However, here on the page and in oral performance, which are the ways, until
now, all stories have been told, I can provide only one link, the next one in linear sequence. It's my call. You've no choices. So I am going to take a return
link and talk about a few of the many ways we have taken short fictions and
linked them up in the past, moving from disparate short narratives toward
longer, more complex ones.

In Genesis it was done by gathering up a mass of traditional tales, widely
available, and attaching them, linking them, to a name, to a character. Thus
Abraham, the Bible's first genuine character: sometimes weak, sometimes he-
roic, smart and dumb, proud and resilient, in fact pretty inconsistent to tell the
truth, such a grabbag of stories borrowed to create him. But thus, too, all the
Civilizing Heroes of the world, even our own frontiersmen. And thus Odysseus, thus King Arthur, thus Br'er Rabbit and the Saturday morning TV car-
toons: webworks of borrowed fragments.   Another linking device, brilliantly
used in our time by John Barth, is to build a storytelling frame, as in Boccaccio's *Decameron*, Basile's *Pentameron*, Chaucer's *Canterbury Tales*, or the
Arabian Nights, which might be thought of as a kind of group novel, snowball-
ing through time, and the more ingenious the framing mechanism is, the more
fun it is and the wider the range of enclosable stories, although the best frames
perhaps always reshape somehow the stories they tell and retell, as of course
John Barth's do.

Medieval romance does that. It also has a fascination for ingenious design,
having the need to embrace a great variety of popular and well-known but
wildly inconsistent narratives, but the design here is largely at the service of the
pursuit of meaning, more so as the years go by, as the form falls increasingly
into the hands of learned moralists or else of those vulgar sensationalists
thrown out of Don Quijote's library.

But Chretien de Troyes, the inventor of the form, had a freer, less program-
matic approach to his manipulation of the Breton tales, and so his own long
loose narratives are much more playful and full of unexpected, sometimes dis-
sonant, but often very creative juxtapositions, including a number of wildly
improbable linkages that through creative displacement helped to generate a
whole new literary form. This was the era, you'll remember, when everyone
was clicking on Ovid, the poet's poet. The troubadors loved him, the goliards
and minnesanger, Dante and Boccaccio and Chaucer—and Cervantes, Spenser,
and Shakespeare, for that matter—and Chretien had himself translated some of
Ovid. Now, as a writer, he made use of Ovid's brilliant way of weaving tales
together in a constant polytonal flow that was nevertheless carefully structured.
It was called "interlacing" and became a principle, a beautiful principle, of romance writing, achieving even greater power in the deep structures of the sym-
bolist, modernist, and surrealist movements.

Cervantes used all of these devices, and more besides—the ancient idea of books buried in books, for example, and the sequential parodies of conventional forms, the use of paired characters to produce or make use of standard comic routines, and so on—to invent the novel. *Don Quijote* Part I is still essentially a loosely linked collection of short fictions based on sequential parodies of contemporary literary forms, but Cervantes gets the whole package integrated and put together in Part II, and the novel, the classic form of the Gutenberg era of the printed book, is born. It's interesting that he accomplishes this, or so I believe, by working on an impressive variety of innovative short fictions before finding the large structures that will satisfy him for the longer haul, implicitly ironic structures with multiple levels that set a standard that holds to this day. Cervantes, of course, dreamed up this new, this novel thing, all by himself, with a little help from the great literary traditions of his day—and from the innovative breakaway authors of the *Celestina* and *Lazarillo de Tormes*, who gave him character type as a linking device—but he wasn't the first to accomplish this. The Epic of Gilgamesh (*click*), written three or four millenia earlier, exhibits many of the same integrative features, including the organization of disparate tales under the theme of one man's quest for transcendent meaning, the use of framing mechanisms, the questioning and testing of the conventional wisdom as a way of provoking narrative movement, even the creative invention of a sometimes comic and often complaining sidekick, Enkidu, the wild man from the steppes, with whom Gilgamesh, like Don Quijote with Sancho Panza the peasant, entered the enchanted forest to do battle with the legendary giant. And thus, you see, if you can remember how we started, I've made another sudden link. It would be much easier to follow all this on a screen.

So what have we got?

A world of stories, most short, like the windows on a computer screen, linked together by various principles, sometimes loose and encyclopedic—like the Stith Thompson Folk Motif Index, for example, a grand if totally unreadable maxi-fiction, at least in its present printbound state, but one I recommend to any of you out there suffering from writer's block (click)—and sometimes tightly bound by theme or character or symbol or ontology, and so on, and always, until now, presented in linear fashion, whether orally or in print, no matter how clever the devices of a Sterne, a Joyce, a Cortazar, or a Calvino who once said that: "The book in which I think I managed to say most remains *Invisible Cities*, because I was able to concentrate all my reflections, experiments, and conjectures on a single symbol; and also because I built up a many-faceted structure in which each brief text is close to the others in a series that does not imply logical sequence or a hierarchy, but a network in which one can follow multiple routes and draw multiple, ramified conclusions."

This, of course, was hypertext that he was talking about, though he was never able to write there. Even so, he called his *If on a winter's night a traveler* (1981) a "hypernovel" . . .

And though hypertext cannot be converted to print, what I have tried to do here is to give you an intimation of what it might be like to read fiction in hyperspace, fiction short or long, but I think ever lengthening even as the windows grow smaller, my effort here having been from the beginning (and here, at the end, by way of Calvino) to show that we could have reached here by multiple routes "aimed at tracing the lightning flashes of the mental circuits that capture and link points distant from each other in space and time."

WORKS CITED

Calvino, Italo. *If on a winter's night a traveler.* Trans. William Weaver. New York: Harcourt Brace, 1981.

Coover, Robert. *A Night at the Movies, or, You Must Remember This.* New York: Linden Press, 1987.

—. *Pricksongs & Descants: Fictions.* New York: Dutton, 1969.

Shapard, Robert, and James Thomas, eds. *Sudden Fictions.* Frontistory by Robert Coover. Salt Lake City: G. M. Smith, 1986.

Part IV

Cognition and the Short Story

14

HyperStory:
Teaching Short Fiction
with Computers

Charles May

The use of computers in the college English classroom has largely focused on word processing for the teaching of writing because such programs make tangible and more manageable an essential writing process that was previously elusive—the creation of a virtual page that is more solid than what goes on in the mind yet more flexible than what goes on a piece of paper. Other computer programs have not been so successful. Faculty have largely rejected drill-and-practice grammar programs because they do not embody an essential paradigm of learning how to write; indeed, research has shown that the conventions of English usage are better mastered within the context of the reading/writing process than in the isolated memorization of rules. Other programs, such as grammar and style checkers are less than helpful because they are not sensitive to context and therefore can flag only the most rule-bound violations of grammar and usage. No application has been created that embodies or objectifies an essential but previously elusive element of that other significant skill English faculty have traditionally taught—the reading of literature.

What it means to "teach literature" has become problematical in the last few years as graduate student and faculty interest in literary theory and cultural studies has pushed undergraduate instruction in literature classes farther and farther out to the fringes of the English curriculum. In the special January 1997 issue of *PMLA* on The Teaching of Literature, a panel discussion begins, predictably, with the graduate student question: "Is there such a thing as literature?" Although the discussion raised the usual theoretical, cultural, and gender-based considerations on this issue, there was little disagreement with one participant's conviction that literature, whatever it is, must be experienced, and that teachers should find ways to engage students in that experience. Another discussant, again without any disagreement, argued that teaching literature, regardless of the level, involves teaching reading skills, and that particular skills are needed for particular kinds of texts.

Although this very idea seems old fashioned nowadays, reeking too much of the formalism of analysis and the Platonism of genres, most teachers, if pressed, will admit that their central concern is that students learn how to read literature in some meaningful way. And a central concept of both literary and reading research, in spite of the current trend toward the flaccid plot summaries and polemical Marxist arguments of much cultural criticism, is that the fictional text is not simply an encoded message, no matter how politically privileged, lying on the page waiting to be deciphered, but rather a formal pattern or "intertext" that we read by applying cultural and cognitive codes or schemas which enable us to infer or create a text. As William H. Gass has said in his 1996 collection of essays *Finding a Form*, the artist's fundamental loyalty is to form: "Every other diddly desire can find expression; every crackpot idea or local obsession, every bias and graciousness and mark of malice, may have an hour; but it must never be allowed to carry the day" (35).

For literature teachers the central paradox that plagues the teaching of narrative fiction is that it is a linear form that must ultimately be read in a nonlinear way. When literature teachers ask students to read stories, they dutifully do so in a straightforward fashion: they scan the letters, words, sentences, and paragraphs, translating them into mental images—watching things happen, hearing people talk—trying desperately to satisfy the demands of the assignment, which means getting to the end of the damned thing. And the "end" for them often is no more than the conclusion of a series of events that occur "one damned thing after another." Thus, when we ask them what happened in a story and they begin summarizing the events one after another, we say, "No, that's not what I meant at all."

Both the cognitive scientists and the literary theorists agree that reading is possible because of codes—arrays of rules and protocols of inference-making that have become conventionalized into the institution we call literature. Only those students who become aware of these rules and protocols and are able to transform a linear series into a meaningful configuration can be said to have mastered the reading process. In order to learn to read, readers must not only possess adequate and appropriate schemas of cultural knowledge, events, actions, and processes, but they also must have internalized schemas of typical discourse structures, that is, clusters of conventions by which the story communicates its configurational meaning.

However, even if we agree that regardless of what other pedagogical or political agendas we may have in the classroom we are primarily interested in teaching students how to read, the problem still remains how best to guide students to that point when they can go beyond the first reading that simply finds out "what happens next" to subsequent readings that transform context into code.

The most common classroom method is of course to model this procedure, showing students how to read a story by publicly "reading" a story, spicing up demonstration by interspersing Socratic queries. The problem with the method is that students are not fooled; the personality of the teacher in front of the class is too strong, and the students are frustrated that they will never be able to read a story in the complex way the teacher does.

In 1989, I developed a modest software application, which I named *Hyper-Story*, to help my students learn how to read short fiction "on their own," without the overpowering "guidance" of the teacher at the front of the class. The application won first prize in the Liberal Arts category of Zenith Corporation's Masters of Innovation competition. A few years later, when D. C. Heath published my short story anthology *Fiction's Many Worlds* (1993), it packaged a modified version of the software with the book. Created with the hypertext authoring programs of HyperCard for the Macintosh and Toolbook for Windows, *HyperStory* is technically quite simple. However, the more than five hundred students who used it in my classes between 1990 and 1995 indicate that it is successful in teaching them how to read literature in meaningful ways.

HyperStory uses several unique features of the computer to compel students to "slow" down their reading and construct spatial nets out of the temporal flow of the story. The way the program does this is to force students to pause at possible nodal points that thematically connect to other points of the story where they are asked to consider questions about structure, the conventions, the motivation, and the theme of the story. Periodically, after students have paused and responded to these points on the computer, they are asked to pull these suggestions together and formulate some ideas about their relationship.

Although it is easier to demonstrate this than it is to describe it, perhaps it will be better understood by using an example of a story often "taught" in introduction to literature classes, Edgar Allan Poe's "The Cask of Amontillado." The story begins with the following sentences: "The thousand injuries of Fortunato I had borne as I best could, but when he ventured upon insult, I vowed revenge. You who so well know the nature of my soul, will not suppose, however, that I gave utterance to a threat" (Poe 1978, 1252). A small light bulb icon in the margin of the story, when clicked with the mouse, pops up a window that asks the following question: "Why are we not told what the injuries to the narrator are?" The window also asks: "Who is the 'you' who knows so well the nature of his soul?"

A bit later on when Montresor meets Fortunato, another light bulb popup, when clicked, asks: "Why does the story take place at carnival time? Consider the theme of 'supreme madness' and the way Fortunato is dressed." When Montresor begins his efforts to lead Fortunato down into the catacombs, still another light bulb popup asks the reader to notice the method by which Montresor makes sure that his servants will not be home. And when Montresor has chained Fortunato to the recess in the wall, a light bulb popup asks the reader to note Montresor's "echoing" Fortunato's shouts and to consider the theme of "mocking" and how it relates to other themes in the story. At the end of the story, a light bulb popup asks the reader to note the fact that the events described took place fifty years before and to consider why Montresor might be telling about it after all these years.

At each one of these popups, readers are encouraged to click on a button labeled Notes at the bottom of the screen which links them to a notepad where they can respond to the light bulb questions by brainstorming their responses in an open, free-writing way. At certain points in the story, after having responded to several light bulb prompts, readers find another icon on the screen of a hand writing on a piece of paper. By clicking on one of these icons, they are taken to a screen where a writing prompt asks them to pull together some of the brainstorming ideas and write one or two organized paragraphs based on their brainstorming. For example, at one point readers are asked to do the following: "Write a paragraph in which you discuss the relationships between the following themes in the story: Montresor's coat of arms, the motto of Montresor's family, the criteria for a successful revenge, the basic relationship between Fortunato and Montresor." At another point, a writing prompt asks the reader to write a paragraph about Montresor's jokes about the Masons and to try to tie together the Mason themes with the other basic themes and techniques of the story; specifically, the reader is asked to relate Fortunato's inability to understand the meaning of the trowel with the fact that the Masons are a secret brotherhood.

By responding to the light bulb popups in the Notes section of the program through free-form brainstorming and then by synthesizing these brainstorming ideas through linking various themes, motifs, and techniques in the story in the Writing Prompts sections, readers gradually begin to develop some understanding of the basic pattern in the story.

Part of the success of *HyperStory* results from having students read text on a computer screen rather than on the pages of a book. Reading text on a computer screen is less "efficient" than reading text in a book; that is, one cannot read as fast. As a result, reading text on a computer, by its very medium, slows readers down, not allowing them to skim hurriedly to the end of the story. Moreover, *HyperStory* exploits student familiarity with video screens for providing information, as well as the irresistibility of interactive "hot spots" or buttons on a screen such as are common in video games. One student said: "I was always curious about what lay behind the light bulb or writing prompt symbols."

Students who read text on a computer screen put themselves in a more serious analytical state of mind than when they read from a book. One student reported, "I would have preferred reading these stories curled up in my bed with tea and a book," but grudgingly admitted that "*HyperStory* made me think more carefully." It makes reading fiction a different kind of experience than just processing linear events, an experience in which readers get caught up in the analysis of ideas. Moreover, students are apt to feel more "captive" to text on the computer screen, more bound to it and less apt to drift off to other matters, than they are when reading a book. One student wrote, "Being on the computer made me focus more on the story. Once I started, I felt compelled to finish it." Students are also apt to feel a closer sense of interaction with the computer than with a book. As one student said, "Because I was involved with the computer I felt a closer relationship to the story. When asked to consider an idea I was by the nature of the interactive relationship with my computer more involved."

Part of the success of the program is a result of providing students with queries at specific points in the story. Because many students do not know where to pause and reflect in a story, they are motivated to move quickly to the end. One student said, "Rather than read the story like a newspaper article, *HyperStory* forced me to slow down." Another suggested that "if you skim the stories there is no way you can answer the questions." Another noted: "With *HyperStory* you feel you are more a part of the story because you are working within it. Without *HyperStory* I don't believe I would have felt as involved in my work as I have." Another pointed out: "The pop-ups and prompts occur at the exact place in the story that your mind is most involved with a particular idea or concept. I doubt I would have done half as much thinking about these stories without it."

Finally, *HyperStory* provides a nonjudgmental method whereby students can freely brainstorm their experience, allows them to brainstorm in an effortless way, and gives them the sense that they are making discoveries on their own without the interference of the teacher. Although the questions embedded in *HyperStory* may be very similar to those a teacher might pose Socratically in a discussion class, embedded as they are in the text, the student has no fear of making the wrong response and receiving a negative reaction from the teacher or the rest of the class. Another reason for this increase in students' willingness to brainstorm lies in the relative ease of doing the reading and responding in one seamless activity. One student noted that *HyperStory* was effective "because it is easier to write more on a computer than on a sheet of paper. It was fun to do the *HyperStories* for they were unlike anything I have ever done before. I wouldn't have gotten involved in any stories without the *HyperStory* homework." Another noted: "It was easier to work on the computer because you didn't have a lot of materials to sort through. Everything was right there on the screen."

Students are apt to read stories hurriedly and casually if they think that they can come to class and get "answers" from the teacher. As one student put it, "Without *HyperStory*, I would have relied on the teacher to spoon-feed us what the stories were about. By using *HyperStory* I was forced to come up with my own ideas." Another said, "Without *HyperStory* I would have left all the explaining up to the teacher, but I liked figuring out the stories and knowing I could do it."

HyperStory creates the illusion that it is the story, not the teacher, that is asking the questions. I know this may sound absurd, for if pushed, students would admit that they knew someone had to program the queries and popups into the story, but somehow when they begin working they forget that. This is a common phenomenon; computer users often refer to the computer itself as if it had some innate intelligence, and indeed some CAI programs encourage this illusion. The effect of this illusion in *HyperStory* is that the students do not think that a teacher is leading them along to a preconceived conclusion, but that the story itself is trying to help them understand. As one student noted: "Without *HyperStory* I would not have developed my own analytical skills; I would have learned only how you saw the story. This way, without your guidance I came to my own conclusions."

Student use of *HyperStory* indicates that students can learn how to read short fiction meaningfully if the teacher provides them with a means of engaging in the process of converting linear events into configurational meaning by making their own discoveries about the story's meaning and way of meaning. Although simple in design, *HyperStory* indicates that practical pedagogical value may be derived from a blending of old-fashioned literary theory and newfangled technology.

WORKS CITED

Gass, William H. "Finding a Form." *Finding a Form: Essays.* New York: Knopf, 1996. 31-52.

May, Charles. *Fiction's Many Worlds.* Lexington, Mass.: D. C. Heath, 1993.

Poe, Edgar Allan. "The Cask of Amontillado." *Collected Works of Edgar Allan Poe.* Ed. Thomas Olive Mabbott. Cambridge, Mass.: The Belknap Press of Harvard UP, 1978. 1252-66.

15

Interdisciplinary Thoughts on Cognitive Science and Short Fiction Studies

Susan Lohafer

When we read a short story, what cognitive strategies come into play? Do we "process" short stories differently from other literary texts? Do we know what "storyness" is—how we recognize it, how it mediates the meaning of a given text, how it functions in a cultural context?

In the past, questions like these have been asked separately and differently by psychologists on the one hand (often working with simple folk tales or texts written by the investigator) and by literary scholars on the other (usually working with canonical, "high culture" texts). There has been little interaction between the scientists and the humanists, partly for practical reasons, but partly because each group felt the other would not understand or value its materials, methods, language, or goals.

Nevertheless, anyone looking at the larger paradigms of academic study knows that "text" is a word that turns up everywhere. "Narrative," as a fundamental human activity, is studied by almost everyone interested in the behavior of the brain. There is, for example, Theodore Sarbin's influential volume called *Narrative Psychology: The Storied Nature of Human Conduct*, with an introductory essay called "The Narrative as a Root Metaphor for Psychology" (1986).

Coming from the other direction, there is Norman Holland, the name most literary people associate with a "cognitive approach." Like I. A. Richards and Stanley Fish, Holland introduced a degree of empiricism into his work by experimenting with real readers. Unlike the psychologists who study text processing, he was interested in the cognitive "style" or "personality" of his subjects, and how this "identity" controlled their responses as readers (Holland 1975). More recently, literary scholars who have worked with frame theory (Reid 1989) and discourse analysis (Lohafer 1989, 1993, 1996) have begun modifying the empirical methods of science in other ways, developing new "experiments" in reader-response.

What is called for, I think, is not only a willing suspension of disciplinary boundaries, but a motivated curiosity to discover what nonliterary scholars are doing with short narrative forms. For this brief discussion, let me point to only two of the more common questions in cognitive research of the 1990s: (1) how do children learn what a story is and how to tell one, and (2) how do competent readers construct mental models which help them process and remember narrative texts?

Before children reach school-age, they tend to produce "sequential lists of events," whether asked simply to tell what happened in a brief film they have just witnessed ("on-line narrations"), to transform those events into a news story, or to use them to create a "more embellished" story (Hicks 1990). Although pre-schoolers can recognize these varied genre prompts, they cannot respond to them in fully-differentiated ways because they cannot choose or vary their narrative stance.

Some researchers, assuming that autobiographical memories are the earliest materials of story, say that "event memory" begins early, but narrativity comes later, after exposure to adult talk about past and future scenarios. Margaret S. Benson argues for a developmental progression in the ability to use plotted narrative. Three-year-olds can recount events, but without a central theme. Four-year-olds may supply a theme, but without purpose or goals. A goal-plan does appear in stories by five-year-olds. Older readers, beginning at about nine, are able to construct hierarchical goal-plans—and thus full-fledged stories, by one commonly accepted definition (Benson 1993; Trabasso and Nickels 1992).

The literary scholar will probably not be interested in these rudimentary steps toward narrativity, but even (or perhaps especially) in the face of the most complex and opaque literary text, it is worth remembering where and how the sense of storyness originates. In my own work, I have tried to bring together primary cognitive models of what a story *is* with sophisticated examples of what a story can *mean*.

But perhaps the most interesting research into the way we process stories has to do with the mental models we use in order to comprehend what we read. The story-grammarians and those working with artificial intelligence helped us understand how story-schemas and event-scripts organize, make sense of, and store incoming information. In the 1980s, the focus shifted to causal and/or goal-outcome relationships, but, to my way of thinking, the most suggestive work for the literary scholar is the recent development of "situation models." Processing a text is not a matter of decoding one sentence after another, stringing together a sequence of "locally cohesive" units; rather, it is a multi-layered, multifaceted process of constructing and revising mental representations of "situations" suggested by spatial, temporal, causal, and emotional information provided by the text (Zwaan, Magliano, and Graesser 1995).

This general shift away from text-based, local phenomena toward more global mental representations shows up in many quarters. One example is Erwin Segal, Judith Duchan, and Paula Scott's 1991 study of interclausal connectives (such as "and," "then," and "but"). After reviewing the more limited way story-grammarians, cohesion theorists, and causal-chain advocates view these words, Segal and his associates argue that connectives work on both local and global levels. These words reflect and determine "where" the reader sees him- or herself within the story-world (a vantage-point called the "deictic center"). Connectives like "and" usually supply continuity, while "then" or "but" signal discontinuity in the reader's vantage point (which may be identified with a narrator, a character, or no one in particular). The conclusion serves quite well as a summary of a general trend in text-processing theories: "The notion of deictic continuity recasts the issue of local versus global away from text-based notions towards an evolving mental-model one."[1]

Among those "text-based notions" are a pair of terms beloved by New Critics and their formalist and structuralist heirs: "linear" versus "spatial." Cognitive scientists can offer a more flexible, reader-response-oriented, "situational" framework for talking about the reciprocity between the sequentiality of print literature and the networking, interactive, model-building activities of the reader. The burden of many of these studies is that readers bring all sorts of prior knowledge to the act of reading a given text: story schemata learned at a very early age (Benson 1993); scripts for repeated, commonplace activities in their culture (Mandler 1984); "goal-plans" (Trabasso and Nickels 1992); "just world" expectations (Dorfman and Brewer 1994); and the kind of personal association and inference-making that causes different readers to describe the appearance of a character differently, often in terms not found in the text (Cothern, Konopak, and Willis 1990).

Scientists are more and more often using "natural" stories (those occurring in the real world, including literary texts) rather than artificial narratives created in the lab; they are looking at models for emotional and aesthetic, as well as cognitive, experiences in reading; and they are giving more and more weight to the prior knowledge readers bring to the text—in other words, to culturally-coded assumptions.

The work I have been mentioning is empirical; it is often loaded with statistics, graphs, even "mathematical-looking" symbols. Nevertheless, I believe it can spark inquiries, engender fresh perspectives, and yield insight even to those who are, as I am, utterly committed to the short story as a work of art. It can help define the primariness of narrative while avoiding the essentialism and elitism of some formalist theories. It can throw light on the cultural conditioning of literary comprehension while avoiding the ideology of some cultural criticism.

In the border country between narrative theory and cognitive science, scholars can find new heuristics and mutual inspiration.

NOTE

1. Erwin M. Segal, Judith F. Duchan, and Paula J. Scott, "The Role of Interclausal Connectives in Narrative Structuring: Evidence from Adults' Interpretations of Simple Stories," *Discourse Processes* 14 (1991): 51.

WORKS CITED

Benson, Margaret S. "The Structure of Four- and Five-year-olds' Narratives in Pretend Play and Storytelling." *First Language* 13 (1993): 203-23.

Cothern, Nancy B., Bonnie C. Konopak, and Elizabeth L. Willis. "Using Readers' Imagery of Literary Characters to Study Text Meaning Construction." *Reading Research and Instruction* 30 (1990): 15-29.

Dorfman, Marcy H., and William F. Brewer. "Understanding the Points of Fables." *Discourse Processes* 17 (1994): 105-29.

Hicks, Deborah. "Narrative Skills and Genre Knowledge: Ways of Telling in the Primary School Grades." *Applied Psycholinguistics* 11 (1990): 83-104.

Holland, Norman. *5 Readers Reading*. New Haven: Yale UP, 1975.

Lohafer, Susan. "A Cognitive Approach to Storyness." *Short Story* 1 (Spring 1990): 60-71.

—. "Preclosure and Story-Processing." *Short Story Theory at a Crossroads*. Eds. Susan Lohafer and Jo Ellyn Clarey. Baton Rouge: Louisiana State UP, 1989: 249-75.

—. "Preclosure in an 'Open' Story: Julio Cortázar's 'Orientation of Cats'." *Creative and Critical Approaches to the Short Story*. Ed. Noel Harold Kaylor, Jr. Lewiston, N.Y.: The Edwin Mellen Press, 1997. 215-34.

—. "Stops on the Way to 'Shiloh': A Special Case for Literary Empiricism." *Style* 27 (Fall 1993): 395-406.

Mandler, Jean M. *Stories, Scripts, and Scenes: Aspects of Schema Theory*. Hillsdale, N.J.: Lawrence Erlbaum, 1984.

Reid, Ian. "Destabilizing Frames for Stories." *Short Story Theory at a Crossroads*. Eds. Susan Lohafer and Jo Ellyn Clarey. Baton Rouge: Louisiana State UP, 1989. 299-310.

Sarbin, Theodore R., ed. *Narrative Psychology: The Storied Nature of Human Conduct*. New York: Praeger, 1986.

Segal, Erwin M., Judith F. Duchan, and Paula J. Scott. "The Role of Interclausal Connectives in Narrative Structuring: Evidence from Adults' Interpretations of Simple Stories." *Discourse Processes* 14 (1991): 27-54.

Trabasso, Tom, and Margret Nickels. "The Development of Goal Plans of Action in the Narration of a Picture Story." *Discourse Processes* 15 (1992): 249-75.

Zwaan, Rolf A., Joseph P. Magliano, and Arthur C. Graesser. "Dimensions of Situation Model Construction in Narrative Comprehension." *Journal of Experimental Psychology: Learning, Memory, and Cognition* 21 (1995): 386-97.

16

A Map of Psychological Approaches to Story Memory

Steven R. Yussen

From early childhood to late adulthood, a common way people exchange information is through stories. Stories are used for entertainment, for inspiration, for dramatizing ethical and moral lessons, for sharing newsworthy happenings, and for explaining concepts in concrete and personal terms, to name just a few obvious purposes. It is no surprise, then, that there has been an explosion of interest and research by cognitive psychologists on how people remember and understand stories (Bower and Morrow 1990; Mandler 1987; Stein and Trabasso 1982; Yussen, Mathews, Huang, and Evans 1988; Stein, Trabasso, and Liwag 1994; Yussen and Ozcan, in press). In this chapter, I will consider, in turn (1) the nature of stories; (2) the major theoretical models used to describe stories and story comprehension; and finally (3) the influence of story coherence on processing stories. We recognize that stories are consumed both by listening and by reading. For convenience, I will refer to the story "consumer" primarily as a reader throughout the remainder of this essay, confident that most (but not all) of what I have to say about reading and remembering stories can be generalized to listeners as well as to readers.

Stories come in many forms. Some recount true events; others are fiction. Some are short and simple, as in the experimental narratives used by many cognitive psychologists; other stories are long and complex as in literary short stories or novels, with thousands of words, many events, and many levels of intended meaning and purpose. Some stories are designed to be told; they are part of an oral tradition. Other stories are meant to be read. Finally, some stories have a simple linear structure which is easily discerned. One or more characters engage in a series of actions that follow logically from one to the next, the characters' motivations are openly revealed in the text, and there is a logical conclusion to the problem(s) set for the characters. Other stories have a structure less readily discerned by the reader. The logic of characters' actions may be unclear and their motivations obscure, the connections among events made confusing because key information is missing, the order of events inverted, or many subplots are present to keep straight.

Given this diversity in narrative form, can we distill the essence of "story" or "narrative" for the purpose of scientific study? Cognitive psychologists believe we can, and they have proceeded accordingly. Their approach has been to identify a small set of defining elements to a story, to study these elements with simple narratives, and to examine a range of implications about how people of various ages remember, understand, and otherwise think with these narratives.

Stories occur in a physical world that can be imagined by the reader. If the story in question is true, if it takes place more or less in our present time, and if it involves locations known to the reader, then representing this physical world is relatively straightforward for the reader. To the extent the story departs from these hypothetical features, and of course most stories do, its audience must work harder to create a representation of the story world and the characters acting in it. Our contemporary human experiences will dominate this representation, even as the story forces the reader to depart from these contemporary experiences and imagine the fictional world purposefully created in the story.

The story may be thought of as an abstraction constructed from the interplay of the written text of the author and the considerable knowledge (of language, of people, of the world, of stories and storytelling, and so on) brought to the text by the reader. It follows that there is no such thing as a single story, a fixed text for a narrative; each reader constructs his or her own story. However idiosyncratic this representation may be for each reader, nonetheless we should be able to divine some general features of the story that each reader does or does not remember, understand, or otherwise process. The search for commonality, of course, is one task for science; it does not preclude the equally challenging task of discovering the unique story representations held by different people for the same text.

A considerable body of work has accumulated over the past two decades on how adults remember stories that they read or hear (e.g., Black and Bower 1980; Kintsch 1977; Stein and Trabasso 1982; Thorndyke 1977; Trabasso and Van den Broek 1985; Yussen, Mathews, Huang, and Evans 1988). One group of investigators (e.g., Bower, Black, and Turner 1979; Nelson 1978; Schank and Abelson 1977) has amassed evidence to show that if a story conforms to a familiar script, subjects will recall it better than if the story is unscripted or contains improbable events. A "script" is the cognitive representation of a frequently occurring event in the culture, such as eating at a restaurant or visiting the doctor. Scripts contain events that unfold in a predictable, highly prescribed manner. For example, when we eat at a restaurant we customarily enter, sit, eat, and leave, in that order. If any of these elements are left out or arranged in an unusual order when the story is presented, our memory for the story may be distorted as we actively attempt to fit it in to a more predictable form.

Another group of investigators (e.g., Mandler 1987; Stein and Trabasso 1982) has attempted to understand the internal structure of stories, using "grammars" and hierarchical tree structures. In this approach, a story is divided into contexts, events, and subevents (e.g., Mandler 1987; Stein and Glenn 1979), and the propositions that capture these elements are described with respect to the hierarchical "level" they occupy in a text hierarchy of propositions. The level of a proposition in a hierarchy and the number of other propositions to which it is directly linked in the hierarchy will predict the likelihood of a reader's remembering the proposition. Consider the president story used by Yussen and his colleagues (1991). It tells of someone who becomes interested in learning more about a famous political figure. She next attempts to find a book about him, fails in the attempt to find such a book in a library, and finally succeeds in locating and purchasing a book in a local bookstore. There are at least five recognizable levels: the setting (first level) dominates the initial motive to learn (second level), which in turn directs the first episode where the character goes to the library and fails to get a book (third level). The failure leads to a second goal attempt of searching in a bookstore (fourth level), which in turn leads to a successful outcome (fifth level). If a good hierarchical arrangement is not present in the story or if the arrangement is "camouflaged" (by, for example, scrambling the presented propositions), the story as a whole will prove more difficult to recall.

Yet a third view of story form is based on a "causal network model" (e.g., Trabasso, Secco, and Van den Broek 1984; Van den Broek 1988, 1989). In this view, particular propositions in a narrative are connected logically to other propositions in the narrative. Connections may vary both qualitatively and quantitatively. A character's motivation or overall goal may be linked to several subgoals which unfold until the final goal is accomplished. This produces a hierarchical quality to the story. An example is a story about Danny, based on one written by Van den Broek and Trabasso. Danny wants to have a bike he sees in a store (overall goal). He first attempts to obtain money to buy it from his parents (subgoal 1) but is unsuccessful, so he finds a job (subgoal 2) to earn money (subgoal 3) to buy it eventually. With a little rewriting, the same propositions can be reordered to create a sequential version of the story where the separate goals are not connected to an overriding super goal or primary purpose. In the sequential version, Danny wants to find a job (goal 1). Next he wants a bicycle (goal 2). He works (goal 3). He asks his parents for money (goal 3) but is unsuccessful. After learning the cost of a bicycle, Danny accumulates money from work (goal 4) and buys the bicycle (goal 5). The hierarchical version of the story is qualitatively different from the sequential version because it links the goals of the separate episodes while the sequential version does not create an overall linkage among the goals. The hierarchical version also differs quantitatively from the sequential version, because there are more links among the goal statements and to the various action propositions in the story than are present in the sequential version. The goals and action propositions will, therefore, be remembered better in the hierarchical version than in the sequential version of the story.

A fourth and final view was offered by Bower and Morrow (1990). They suggest that to understand a story fully, the reader's principal task is to create a mental model for the story. The model includes a spatial representation of the people, places, and events described in the story. A kind of "scene" representation occurs in working memory, they claim. As the story unfolds, the reader's working memory continually updates this scene, with the earlier scenes pushed into longer term storage or forgotten. The scene representation is used to access necessary information and to draw appropriate inferences. For example, if a story mentions that two people stand facing each other on the porch of a large mansion, the reader can use this information to interpret a conversation between the characters and to understand that conversations held elsewhere in the house may not be heard. This spatial focus also means that the reader will be quicker to access information about these two characters or something about their immediate space, since this "scene" is at the moment "on-stage"; that is, in working memory.

What makes a narrative readily understandable and memorable? What increases the likelihood that a reader will remember most of the information contained in a story? No doubt, there are at least three important factors. One is the knowledge that the reader brings to bear on the story. If the story itself trades on events commonly known in the culture, for example, "scripted events" (e.g., Bower, Black, and Turner 1979), or if the story deals with specific people, places, and events that are well known to the reader (e.g., Anderson and Pearson 1984), the story is likely to be remembered and understood better than a story without these features.

A second quality is that the story generates engagement and interest in the reader, perhaps because one of the characters is valued and liked by the reader (Brewer and Lichtenstein 1982), because particular details are regarded as novel and unusual, or because the topic of the story is one that has great appeal to the reader (e.g., Asher 1980).

A third quality is the structural adequacy of a story. For convenience, we refer to this quality as "story form." We regard a story written with a high degree of structural adequacy as having "good form"; in contrast, a story written with a low degree of structural adequacy is regarded as having "poor form." In principle, we should also be able to identify stories whose form is of some intermediate structural adequacy.

What do we mean, though, by structural adequacy or "good form"? If we restrict our attention to the four different models of text comprehension discussed earlier, there are four apparently different answers. First, consider a script-based perspective. Given a story based on one or more scripted events, the story is well structured if elements of the script occur in their expected order and if there are no incongruous elements. By contrast, a story would be considered poorly structured if it contained scripted elements whose order is seriously violated and if it contained a number of incongruous elements.

Next, consider a story grammar description. Story grammars also contain particular categories of information ordered in particular ways (e.g., Setting + Event 1 + [Event 2] + . . . + [Event N]; Event = Initiating Event + Internal Response [Motive] + Attempt + Consequence + Reaction). Good form results from most or all of the categories of expected information occurring in their predicted order. However, if much of the expected information is missing or if the order of the expected information is seriously violated, great confusion can be the result.

Third, consider an answer based on the causal network theory. In this view, individual propositions in a story will be well understood and remembered if they have many causal links to other propositions in the story. Good story form results from many propositions in the story linked causally to many other propositions in the story. By contrast, poor story form results if more propositions in the story have infrequent or few causal links to other propositions in it.

Finally, consider an answer based on the Mental Model theory. In this view, a good story is one readily represented and with a succession of "represented scenes" easily linked to one another. Factors that interfere with the buildup of good mental representations and linkages among "represented scenes" contribute to poor story form.

WORKS CITED

Anderson, R. C., and P. D. Pearson. "A Schema-theoretic View of Basic Processes in Reading Comprehension." *Handbook of Reading Research*. Eds. R. C. Pearson et al. White Plains, N.Y.: Longman, 1984. 255-91.

Asher, S. R. "Topic Interest and Children's Reading Comprehension." *Theoretical Issues in Reading Comprehension*. Eds. R. J. Spiro, B. C. Bruce, and W. F. Brewer. Hillsdale, N.J.: Lawrence Erlbaum, 1980. 525-34.

Black, J. B., and G. H. Bower. "Story Understanding as Problem Solving." *Poetics* 9 (1980): 223-50.

Bower, G. H., J. B. Black, and T. J. Turner. "Scripts in Memory for Text." *Cognitive Psychology* 11 (1979): 177-220.

Bower, G. H., and D. G. Morrow. "Mental Models in Narrative Comprehension." *Science* 247 (1990): 44-48.

Brewer, W. F., and E. H. Lichtenstein. "Stories are to Entertain: A Structural-Affect Theory of Stories." *Journal of Pragmatics* 6 (1982): 473-86.

Kintsch, W. "On Comprehending Stories." *Cognitive Processes in Comprehension*. Eds. Marshall Adam Just and Patricia A. Carpenter. Hillsdale, N.J.: Lawrence Erlbaum, 1977.

Mandler, Jean M. "On the Psychological Reality of Story Structure." *Discourse Processes* 10 (1987): 1-29.

Nelson, K. E. "How Children Represent Knowledge of their World in and out of Language." *Children's Thinking: What Develops?* Hillsdale, N.J.: Lawrence Erlbaum, 1978.

Rumelhart, D. E. "Notes on a Schema for Stories." *Representation and Understanding: Studies in Cognitive Science*. Eds. Daniel G. Bobrow and Allan Collins. New York: Academic P, 1975. 211-36.

Schank, R. C. E., and R. Abelson. *Scripts, Plans, and Goals*. Hillsdale, N.J.: Lawrence Erlbaum, 1977.

Stein, N. L., and C. G. Glenn. "An Analysis of Story Comprehension in Elementary School Children." *New Directions in Discourse Processing*. Ed. R. O. Freedle. Vol. 2. Norwood, N.J.: Ablex, 1979. 53-120.

Stein, N. L., and T. Trabasso. "What's in a Story?: An Approach to Comprehension and Instruction." *Advances in Instructional Psychology*. Ed. R. Glaser. Vol. 2. Hillsdale, N.J.: Lawrence Erlbaum, 1982. 213-68.

Stein, N. L., T. Trabasso, and M. D. Liwag. "The Rashomon Phenomenon: Personal Frames and Future-Oriented Appraisals in Memory for Emotional Events." *The Development of Future-oriented Processes*. Eds. M. Harth, et al. Chicago: U of Chicago P, 1994.

Thorndyke, P. W. "Cognitive Structures in Comprehension and Memory of Narrative Discourse." *Cognitive Psychology* 9 (1977): 77-110.

Trabasso, T., T. Secco, and P. Van den Broek. "Causal Cohesion and Story Coherence." *Learning and Comprehension of Text*. Eds. H. Mandl, N. L. Stein, and T. Trabasso. Hillsdale, N.J.: Lawrence Erlbaum, 1984.

Trabasso, T., and P. Van den Broek. "Causal Thinking and the Representation of Narrative Events." *Journal of Memory and Language* 24 (1985): 612-30.

Van den Broek, P. "Causal Reasoning and Inference Making in Judging the Importance of Story Statements." *Child Development* 60 (1989): 286-97.

—. "The Effects of Causal Relations and Hierarchical Position on the Importance of Story Statements." *Journal of Memory and Language* 27 (1988): 1-22.

Yussen, S. R., S. Mathews, T. Huang, and R. Evans. "The Robustness and Temporal Course of the Story Schema's Influence on Recall." *Journal of Experimental Psychology: Learning, Memory and Cognition* 14 (1988): 171-79.

Yussen, S. R., and N. Ozcan. "The Development of Knowledge about Narratives." *Issues in Education: Contributions from Educational Psychology*. Greenwich, Conn.: JAI P, in press.

Yussen, S. R., A. D. Stright, R. L. Glysch, C. E. Bonk, I. Lu, and I. Al-Sabaty. "Learning and Forgetting of Narratives Following Good and Poor Text Organization." *Contemporary Educational Psychology* 16 (1991): 346-74.

17

Short Story Structure
and Affect:
Evidence from Cognitive Psychology

William F. Brewer

This chapter is the preliminary report of the results of an experiment examining the psychological properties of a sample of short stories. Most work on stories in the area of cognitive psychology and cognitive science has focused on problems of text comprehension and text memory (for a discussion, see Brewer 1982; Brewer and Lichtenstein 1982). However, it seems to me that an adequate psychological theory of stories must incorporate such constructs as plot, suspense, and resolution. During the last decade a group of us at the University of Illinois has been developing a structural-affect approach to the study of stories which attempts to capture a much broader range of characteristics of texts (Brewer 1980; Brewer and Lichtenstein 1982).[1] This research has been strongly influenced by work in the humanities, particularly by literary criticism, narratology, and by rhetorical and structural approaches to text. Within the structural-affect framework we have carried out research on artificially constructed texts (Brewer 1996a, 1996b; Brewer and Lichtenstein 1981); on Hungarian and American short stories (Brewer and Ohtsuka 1988a, 1988b); on children's responses to texts (Jose and Brewer 1984, 1990); on fables (Dorfman and Brewer 1994); and on cross-cultural studies of texts (Brewer 1985). It should be noted that the structural-affect theory attempts to capture the structural and affective properties of texts designed for entertainment and has only limited application to the literary and aesthetic properties of texts.

The structural-affect theory relates particular structural features of narratives to particular affective responses in the reader and then relates these structural-affect relationships to story liking. The structural-affect theory is based on the assumption that there is a distinction between the events that underlie a narrative and the linguistic presentation of these events. We refer to the organization of the events in the underlying event world as *event structure*, and we refer to the temporal arrangement of these events in the text as *discourse structure*.

We have hypothesized that three of the most important discourse structures used in entertainment stories are: surprise structures, suspense structures, and curiosity structures. We hypothesize that each of these structures is based on a different arrangement of the discourse with respect to the underlying event structure and that each is designed to produce a unique affect in the reader. Figure 17.1 gives an overview of the predicted affect curves:

Figure 17.1
Text Characteristics and Predicted Patterns of Affective Response for Suspense, Surprise, and Curiosity

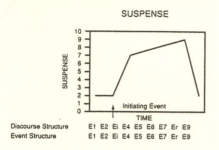

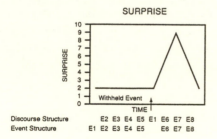

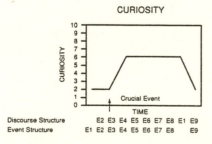

We propose that *surprise* is produced by including critical expository or event information early in the event structure, but omitting it from the discourse structure. This information is critical in that it is necessary for the correct interpretation of the event sequence. In a surprise discourse structure the author withholds the critical information from the early sections of the text and does not let the reader know that something has been withheld. Then the author, later in the text, reveals the unexpected critical information, producing surprise in the reader and leading the reader to give a new interpretation to the events in the text.

For example, consider the following event structure: (1) Morris Zapp puts a letter bomb in the mail; (2) a letter is delivered to Jacques Derrida; (3) Derrida opens the letter; and (4) the letter explodes seriously injuring Derrida. A possible surprise discourse structure from this event structure would be: (3) Derrida opened a letter; and (4) the letter exploded injuring Derrida. In this text the author has deliberately omitted telling the reader that there was a bomb in the letter. When the letter is opened and explodes, the reader should be surprised and must rethink the assumption that the object was simply an ordinary letter.

We propose that *suspense* is produced by including an initiating event or situation in the event structure. We define an *initiating event* as an event that has the potential to lead to a signficant outcome (either good or bad) for one of the main characters in the narrative. We also hypothesize that the event structure must contain the outcome of the initiating event. In general, a suspense text is organized with the initiating event early in the text and with considerable intervening material before the outcome is presented. The initiating event causes the reader to become concerned about the potential consequences for the character; the intervening material prolongs the suspense; and the eventual occurrence of the outcome resolves the suspense.

A possible suspense *discourse structure* for the bomb *event structure* would be: (1) Morris Zapp puts a letter bomb in the mail; (2) the letter bomb is delivered to Jacques Derrida; (3) Derrida opens the letter; and (4) the letter explodes injuring Derrida. The action of placing the bomb in the letter is the initiating event since it has the potential to lead to a very significant outcome for one of the characters in the text. In this suspense discourse structure, the author has given the reader the information about the initiating event early in the text, causing the reader to be in suspense about the potential outcome of this action. The suspense is resolved when the reader is told that Derrida was injured.

We propose that *curiosity* is produced by including a crucial event early in the event structure. In a curiosity text, the author withholds the significant event from the reader, but, unlike the surprise discourse structure, the author provides enough information about the earlier events to let the reader know that the information has been omitted. This arrangement of the discourse structure causes the reader to become curious about the withheld information, and the curiosity is resolved by providing enough information in the latter section of the text to allow the reader to reconstruct the missing event.

A possible curiosity *discourse structure* for the bomb *event structure* would simply be: (4) Derrida is injured when a letter he was opening exploded. Given a text describing this event, the reader should be curious about the cause of the explosion. The remainder of the text might consist of having a detective try to uncover who sent the letter bomb. Toward the end of the text, the author could resolve the curiosity by having the detective reveal the information that Morris Zapp had placed the bomb in the letter to Derrida.

In the structural-affect theory, it is assumed that different arrangements of discourse organization lead to different forms of story liking. In particular, we have hypothesized that readers will enjoy narratives with discourse organizations that produce surprise and resolution, suspense and resolution, and curiosity and resolution.

The goal of our present experiment has been to study the psychological responses of undergraduates reading a broad range of short story types. The data allow a test of structural-affect theory with a new sample of texts offering very diverse structures. In addition, the data should give some insights into the responses of undergraduate readers to different types of short stories.

The basic design of this study was to have undergraduates read a short story and then to have them rate the short story on a number of relevant variables. Three types of short stories were used: popular, classic, and postmodern. *Popular* short stories were defined as those that substantial numbers of people would pay to read. Thus, the sample of popular short stories was obtained by going to a news stand in Champaign-Urbana and buying a sample of magazines that contained short fiction. One story was sampled from each of five magazines by selecting the first piece of fiction that was between 2,000 and 6,000 words long. We defined *classic* short stories as those stories written in the first quarter of the century that have sometimes been referred to as "psychological" or "epiphany" short stories. The five classic stories were chosen from those widely reprinted in texts for introductory English courses and considered classic exemplars of this story type. The five *postmodern* short stories included in the sample were chosen for their deliberate violation of the traditional conventions of plot, characterizations, and mimesis (cf. Stevick 1971).[2]

Each story was divided into five roughly equal parts, and at the end of each segment there were five seven-point affect rating scales. The scales were designed to measure suspense, surprise, curiosity about the past, curiosity about the future, and irony. At the end of each story was a questionnaire containing thirteen seven-point scales designed to measure liking, interest, outcome satisfaction, completeness, arrangement, character identification, comprehension, literary quality, story typicality, story point, violence, eroticism, and romanticism. In addition, the participants were asked if the text was a story, and if they had ever read the story before.

The participants in this experiment were 150 undergraduates at the University of Illinois who participated in the experiment in order to fulfill a course requirement. Ten different participants read each of the sixteen short stories. They were asked to read at their own pace and to fill out the scales as they came to them in their booklets.

Figure 17.2 shows the average suspense curves for each of the three story types. The individual stories in each sample have unique characteristics and corresponding unique affect curves, so it is interesting to find that there are nevertheless some general differences in the affect curves across the three story types. The postmodern stories show a low flat suspense curve. The classic stories show a somewhat higher curve with a modest rise and resolution. The popular stories show the highest overall level of suspense and a relatively strong rise and resolution.

Figure 17.2
Suspense Ratings for Five Popular, Five Classic, and Five Postmodern Short Stories

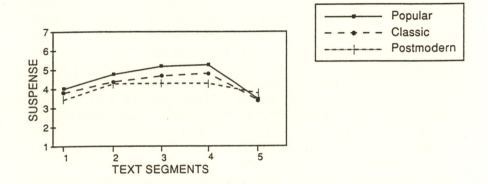

Some of the individual affect curves show even more dramatic differences in rated affect. Figure 17.3 shows the suspense curves for the least liked story in the experiment ("The Beach" by A. Robbe-Grillet) and the best liked story in the experiment ("Tough" by J. Lutz). The suspense curve for "The Beach" is extremely low and relatively flat. The suspense curve for "Tough" is extremely high.

Figure 17.3
Suspense Rating for A. Robbe-Grillet's "The Beach" and J. Lutz's "Tough"

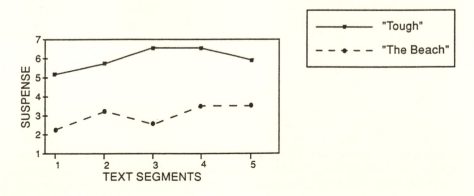

The table below gives the average scores for each story type for overall liking and for story completeness. It also gives the percent of the undergraduates who thought each text was a "story."

<u>Overall Rating for Popular, Classic, and Postmodern Short Stories</u>

Type	Liking	Completeness	Percent Story
Popular	5.3	5.6	94%
Classic	4.2	3.5	56%
Postmodern	3.5	2.5	30%

In general, the undergraduates thought the postmodern stories were incomplete, that the popular stories were complete, and that the classic stories were intermediate. Only 30 percent of the undergraduates thought the postmodern texts were stories, whereas 94 percent of the undergraduates thought the popular texts were stories. Again, the classic texts fell in between (56 percent). When rating how much they "enjoyed" reading the stories, the undergraduates' mean scores indicated that they did not like the postmodern stories, they liked the popular stories, and the classic stories fell in between.

The data show that the structural-affect theory gives a reasonable account of the responses of undergraduate students reading three types of twentieth-century short stories. In particular, they appear to like stories that produce suspense and resolution. The differences across the three story types may be of some interest to those who teach the short story to undergraduates. It appears that undergraduates' story liking is strongly determined by plot as described in the structural-affect framework, and that short stories that remove these plot elements (e.g., most postmodern short stories) or reduce them (e.g., most classic short stories) are not liked by undergraduate readers. This suggests that a major problem for undergraduate instruction is to develop an appreciation in these readers for the literary and aesthetic properties of texts.

NOTES

1. All phases of this work were carried out in close collaboration with Edward L. Lichtenstein. This research was partly funded through the National Institute of Education through Contract No. US-NIE-C-400-76-0116 to the Center for the Study of Reading, University of Illinois, Champaign, Illinois.

2. Popular short stories used in this experiment included Colby Rodowsky, "Happy Happy Thanksgiving," *Good Housekeeping* Nov. 1980: 148-49, 234-37; John Lutz "Tough," *Mike Shayne Mystery Magazine* Nov. 1980: 58-67; Anonymous, "The Knock on our Door that Changed our Lives," *Secrets* Nov. 1980: 13-15, 66; Gary Alexander "SAP-3," *Alfred Hitchcock's Mystery Magazine* 27 Oct. 1980: 17-25; R. L. Stevens, "Deduction, 1996," *Ellery Queen's Mystery Magazine* 6 Oct. 1980: 29-40; and Phyllis MacLennan, "A Report from the Snith Digest," *The Magazine of Fantasy & Science Fiction* Nov. 1980: 50-57, 71. Classic short stories included Sherwood Anderson, "Sophistication," *The Best Short Stories of the Modern Age*, ed. D. Angus (Greenwich,

Conn.: Fawcett Premier, 1962) 182-90; Willa Cather, "The Enchanted Bluff," *Five Stories* (New York: Vintage, 1956) 3-15; Anton Chekhov, "Gooseberries," *Introduction to Literature: Stories*, 2nd ed., eds. L. Altenbernd and L. L. Lewis (New York: Macmillan, 1969) 230-36; James Joyce, "Araby," *Introduction to Literature: Stories*, 2nd ed., eds. L. Altenbernd and L. L. Lewis (New York: Macmillan, 1969) 272-75; and Katherine Mansfield, "The Garden-party," *Introduction to Literature: Stories*, 2nd ed., eds. L. Altenbernd and L. L. Lewis (New York: Macmillan, 1969) 315-23. Postmodern short stories included John Barth, "Autobiography: A Self-recorded Fiction," *Innovative Fiction: Stories for the Seventies*, eds. Jerome Klinkowitz and John Somer (New York: Dell, 1972) 220-24; Donald Barthelme, "A City of Churches," *Story to Anti-Story*, ed. Mary Rohrberger (Boston: Houghton Mifflin, 1979) 709-12; Jose Luis Borges "The Garden of Forking Paths," *Ficciones* (New York: Grove Press, 1962) 89-101; Richard Brautigan, "The Cleveland Wrecking Yard," *Innovative Fiction: Stories for the Seventies*, eds. Jerome Klinkowitz and John Somer (New York: Dell, 1972) 41-47; and Alain Robbe-Grillet's "The Beach," *Snapshots and Towards a New Novel*, London: Calder and Boyars, 1965) 23-26.

WORKS CITED

Brewer, W. F. "Good and Bad Story Endings and Story Completeness." *Empirical Approaches to Literature and Aesthetics*. Eds. R. J. Kreuz and M. S. MacNealy. Northwood, N.J.: Ablex, 1996a. 261-71.

—. "Literary Theory, Rhetoric, and Stylistics: Implications for Psychology." *Theoretical Issues in Reading Comprehension*. Eds. R. J. Spiro, B. C. Bruce, and W. F. Brewer. Hilldale, N.J.: Lawrence Erlbaum, 1980. 221-39.

—. "The Nature of Narrative Suspense and the Problem of Rereading." *Suspense: Conceptualizations, Theoretical Analyses, and Empirical Explorations*. Eds. P. Vorderer, H. J. Wulff, and M. Friedrichsen. Mahwah, N.J.: Lawrence Erlbaum, 1996b. 107-27.

—. "Plan Understanding, Narrative Comprehension, and Story Schemas." *Proceedings of the National Conference on Artificial Intelligence*. 1982. 262-64.

—. "The Story Schema: Universal and Culture-specific Properties." *Literacy, Language, and Learning*. Eds. D. R. Olson, N. Torrance, and A. Hildyard. Cambridge: Cambridge UP, 1985. 167-94.

Brewer, W. F., and E. H. Lichtenstein. "Event Schemas, Story Schemas, and Story Grammars." *Attention and Performance* 9. Eds. J. Long and A. Baddeley. Hillsdale, N.J.: Lawrence Erlbaum, 1981. 363-79.

—. "Stories are to Entertain: A Structural-affect Theory of Stories." *Journal of Pragmatics* 6 (1982): 473-86.

Brewer, W. F., and K. Ohtsuka. "Story Structure and Reader Affect in American and Hungarian Short Stories." *Psychological Approaches to the Study of Literary Narratives*. Ed. C. Martindale. Hamburg: Helmut Buske Verlag, 1988a. 133-58.

—. "Story Structure, Characterization, Just World Organization, and Reader Affect in American and Hungarian Short Stories." *Poetics* 17 (1988b): 395-415.

Dorfman, M. H., and W. F. Brewer. "Understanding the Points of Fables." *Discourse Processes* 17 (1994): 105-29.

Jose, P. E., and W. F. Brewer. "Development of Story Liking: Character Identification, Suspense, and Outcome Resolution." *Developmental Psychology* 20 (1984): 911-24.

—. "Early Grade School Children's Liking of Script and Suspense Story Structures."
   Journal of Reading Behavior 22 (1990): 355-72.
Stevick, P., ed.   *Anti-Story: An Anthology of Experimental Fiction.* New York: The
   Free P, 1971.

18

Story Liking
and Moral Resolution

Paul E. Jose

I am a developmental psychologist who studies how children read and understand stories, with a particular emphasis upon story liking. I will describe how children grow to understand and appreciate moral resolution in stories; in other words, how they acquire the ability to judge whether a story ending is morally satisfying. My major point is that appreciation of moral resolution is something that develops over the lifespan: a child, teenager, or adult understands a particular story resolution if he or she possesses the necessary cognitive sophistication combined with experience with texts of similar and different genres. I will focus on children's reactions in this chapter.

In the early 1980s, William Brewer and I were interested in examining how grade-school children identified with story characters in suspense stories. I wrote some short stories that varied a number of dimensions which we felt would affect children's identification and liking for these stories. Among these dimensions were character valence and outcome valence. In our stories, we crossed these two dimensions so that some stories had a good character who received a positive outcome, a good character who received a negative outcome, a bad character who received a positive outcome, and a bad character who received a negative outcome. We predicted that children would like stories in these two cells in the design: good-positive and bad-negative. We predicted they would dislike stories in the other two cells. This prediction derives from what we in psychology refer to as the "belief in a just world." Melvin Lerner, a social psychologist, has explained that the overwhelming majority of people in this culture prefer these outcomes. In other words, if good people get rewarded and bad people get punished, then we live in a satisfying and orderly world. We are upset by disconfirmations of this expectation—for example, when innocent people die in a plane crash, or when a Nazi war criminal remains at large.

How did our data turn out? We found that the older children confirmed the just world prediction. However, the youngest children, the second graders, did not yield this result. They did not like the negative outcomes for the bad characters. These were not subtle stories. In one story I portrayed the bad character as a liar, a bully, a whiner, and a lazy good-for-nothing. At the end of the story, he suffered a negative outcome: being bitten by a spider while he slept. The youngest children, when asked, "How much did you like or dislike the ending of the story, namely that Mike was bitten by a spider?" failed to take into account that Mike in this story was a lying, bullying goof-off. In a cognitively simplistic way, they answered the question by focusing entirely upon the outcome valence, namely that the outcome was negative.

I have argued from these data, and other data, that young children have difficulty in cognitively combining these two sources of information in judgments of moral resolution. In other words, some young children may be confused about the moral implications of certain stories, particularly ones in which negative outcomes occur to characters.

Why might this be? It is possible that these younger children experience difficulty because of a poor memory; in other words, they can not remember all of the pertinent information. However, I tested these children's recall of the story and they clearly had all of the relevant information in their minds. My view is that it simply does not occur to them to put certain bits of information together. Older children make these connections because they learn that certain story characters deserve negative outcomes. They learn this from reading stories about reprehensible characters who get their comeuppance, or from witnessing in real life that if one is "bad," one gets punished.

Another relevant study, designed with Marcy Dorfman with Dr. Brewer's assistance, concerned fables. We were interested in whether children appreciated the basic moral messages of Aesop fables. We expected to find that young children might have trouble figuring out what an appropriate moral resolution for a fable was, and might have trouble providing an appropriate moral for a fable.

Specifically, we wished to argue that the basic plot of Aesop fables relies upon the belief in a just world. Let us look at "The Tortoise and the Hare" and examine its moral structure. Readers typically reason backward from the outcome to determine what the author of the text is trying to say. Thus, since the rabbit lost the race, the reader reads the implication as being, "Don't do whatever rabbit did because it causes a negative outcome." The rabbit's behavior responsible for this outcome is overconfidence. Thus, part of the moral is "Don't be overconfident." The other half of the meaning comes from the positive outcome enjoyed by the turtle. Since the turtle is rewarded, the reader looks for the behavior responsible for this good result. The other half of the moral is something like, "Good things happen to those who keep plugging away."

The essential point of this hypothesis is that positive outcomes are seen to occur to good characters, and negative outcomes to bad characters. The goodness or badness is interpreted by the reader. Another example is "The Boy Who Cried Wolf." The negative outcome, the sheep being eaten by the wolf, is seen as a punishment for the capricious trickery of the shepherd. Most good, memorable Aesop fables conform to this pattern, we believe. Let me describe the study's design before I go on to the results.

Four groups of texts were used. The first were familiar Aesop fables: "The Tortoise and the Hare," "The Boy Who Cried Wolf," "The Golden Goose," and "The Lion and the Mouse." The second group was constructed by giving each of these fables a "reversed outcome." Then, two sets of stories were invented to test "just world" perceptions. One set involved humans and one set involved animals. Each of these sets provided the following variations:

> good character > positive outcome
> good character > negative outcome
> bad character > positive outcome
> bad character > negative outcome

The readers we studied varied widely by age and experience: thirty-nine kindergartners; thirty-seven first and second graders; forty-seven third and fourth graders; forty-eight fifth, sixth, seventh, and eighth graders; and fifty-four college students.

Each subject received four stories in a random order: regular fable, reversed-outcome fable, human story, and animal story. Readers were asked to respond to the following eight questions:

1. Does the story have a lesson or a moral? (yes or no)
2. What is it? (open-ended)
3. How good or bad is the main character? (7-point scale)
4. How much do you like the main character? (7-point scale)
5. How much did you like the outcome of the story? (7-point scale)
6. Why did the outcome occur? (open-ended)
7. How fair was the outcome of the story? (7-point scale)
8. How much did you like the overall story? (7-point scale)

Here is a summary of our findings. In the case of normal and reversed-outcome fables, the data showed that kindergartners do not seem to like one more than the other; in other words, they liked both types equally. However, by first or second grade, most children preferred the "normal" or original endings. In the case of the two just-world stories and the two non-just-world stories, the adults and older children conformed very well to the predicted result. However, the youngest children did not.

We found the same result we had seen before: stories with bad characters who receive negative outcomes are not liked very much, and stories with bad characters who receive positive outcomes are liked too much. When we asked readers to provide morals for the stories, the kindergarten children offered very concrete and elementary morals, compared to the older children. Furthermore, they provided better morals for the two just-world stories than for the two non-just-world stories.

What are the implications of these results for our understanding of how readers react to moral resolutions in short stories? I believe it is virtually impossible to write a story that is devoid of moral implications. Even if one sought to write a story of that type, that then would be the point of the story. We all live in a world that is thoroughly permeated with moral issues. Even buying a hamburger at McDonald's has the moral implication of whether it hastens the destruction of the rainforests in South America. Thus I believe all stories must pay attention to morality, whether it is highlighted in the foreground or relegated to background music.

Furthermore, the cognitive sophistication of the reader (whether young or old, or mentally incapacitated) matters, as does the cultural background of the reader (the television character Murphy Brown was seen by former Vice President Dan Quayle as a morally bankrupt person and by others as a courageous person), and the literary sophistication of the reader (familiarity with different genres, such as tragedy). These factors interrelate, of course. Young children are probably not exposed to many tragic stories; they get "happy ending" stories primarily. But they may not be cognitively competent to make sense of subtle distinctions or grasp complicated story narrative.

Let me end by stating the moral of my story: good writers are those who are best able to tailor their stories to the characteristics of their audience, taking into account the areas I have been describing here, and others. Good writers do this naturally and implicitly. My interest as a psychologist is to try to note these issues explicitly. Perhaps these observations will have consequences for pedagogical materials for children. I certainly hope so. I love a story with a happy ending.

19

Deixis in Short Fiction: The Contribution of Deictic Shift Theory to Reader Experience of Literary Fiction

Erwin M. Segal

This chapter reports on a research program undertaken by my colleagues and me in an attempt to identify some of the cognitive structures and processes that underlie narrative comprehension and interpretation.[1] Our goal is to be able to specify the processes of narrative comprehension well enough, not only to characterize what a reader does as he or she reads a fictional text, but also to be able to simulate as much of it as possible on a computer. This goal forces us to examine details of the text to be read and what readers do when they read that text. The topic is a vast one, and we have far to go, but we have a style of research and an outline of a theory to share.

Our research program began by our trying to understand the psychological processes involved in following spatial and temporal movement in narrative text, and how the text guides these processes. This research has led us to develop the Deictic Shift Theory of narrative comprehension which has shaped much of our ensuing research. This theory seems to have components that support both experiential and computational approaches to understanding narrative. We think that we have an approach to narrative comprehension and interpretation that, even if it fails, will teach us a great deal about narrative and the human response to narrative.

We believe one of the reasons we have made as much progress as we have is that we have a working interdisciplinary Cognitive Science research group. One advantage of working in a research group such as ours is that we have lively interaction among members who regularly interact on a common problem and can bring information sources and methods of various disciplines to bear on it. Each discipline informs the research of the others. In our group we do conceptual and linguistic analyses of narrative and other texts; study production and comprehension of children and language-disturbed adults; run psychological experiments evaluating comprehension and production in normal adults;

and write computer programs that receive as input natural language text and output structural representations of its content.

One highly rewarding aspect of our shared methodology is the requirement that we pay close attention to the text. We all agree that we need to analyze many "real" narratives sentence by sentence. We consider for each sentence:

- What exactly is the sentence conveying to the reader?
- How is the information conveyed by the sentence expressed?
- What does the reader have to know in order to understand the sentence appropriately?
- How is the sentence's interpretation constrained by its linguistic and non-linguistic context?

Using this cognitive approach, we have looked at several different texts and several different languages. We have examined texts by O. Henry, Steinbeck, McMurty, Keillor, five-year-old children, and retellings by "normal" and handicapped people; the languages have included English, Chinese, Korean, and Japanese. We have begun to develop a theory of narrative comprehension and experience that is consistent with some aspects of current theories, and inconsistent with others. Interestingly, we have found that our interdisciplinary study of narrative enriches our understanding of some basic concepts in core areas of our respective disciplines. In this chapter I will examine some examples of the basic kinds of data we have considered and describe some of the issues that these data suggest. I will conclude with an abbreviated outline of our theory.

Deixis usually refers to linguistic or paralinguistic components of a discourse that gain their specific meaning from the discourse situation rather than, or in addition to, the linguistic meaning of those components. Deictic terms thus generally point to some specific thing (time, place, person, object) purportedly known or discoverable by the hearer using the nonlingistic context as a guide. Such terms might include:

Time: now, then, yesterday, today, tomorrow, last week, next year, recently, soon, at two o'clock
Place: here, there
Person: I, you, she, he, Mother, Uncle Bob
Object: this, that, the book on the table

If a speaker seriously says, "I am talking to you. Come here!"— *I* refers to the speaker, *you* refers to the addressee, *here* refers to a place near the speaker, and *come* refers to a potential physical movement from the location of the addressee to the location of the speaker. *I, you, here,* and *come* thus all gain their particular significance from the details of the physical situation and the context of their expression. When deictic terms are used to express them, someone who is not privy to the situation does not know the references: who, what, when, or where. Linguistically, deixis may be represented through verb tense and by syntax as well as lexically.

Deixis is seen to be very important in linguistic theory and the philosophy of language. One highly regarded new approach to formal linguistics gives it the highest priority in semantic interpretation. Jan Barwise and John Perry, who introduced the theory of "situation semantics," have argued that:

[o]ne of the simplest facts about human language [is the fact that] an utterance must be made by someone, someplace, and sometime. That is, an utterance always takes place in a discourse situation, and so the facts about the discourse situation can always be exploited to get from the meaning of the expression used to whatever information is to be conveyed. (1983, 32-33)

Investigations of the use of deictic terms in narrative fiction have played a primary role in developing our theory. One very interesting characteristic of fictional narrative, however, is that deictic terms almost never refer as a function of the "standard" discourse situation, even though they do refer as a function of some situation. Narrative theory derives in great part from an investigation of the role of deixis and deictic terms in narrative text.

I will develop our approach by considering several examples and some of the problems of interpretation they pose. The first is the first sentence of Ernest Hemingway's short story "The Killers": "The door of Henry's lunchroom opened and two men came in" (1987, 215). Who opened the door? How do you know? Where are the two men when you are first aware of them? From where are you interpreting the sentence? From where is the story being told? Who is telling the story? Who is the narrator addressing?

Clearly, Hemingway contextualized the scene from inside the lunchroom. The reader is first aware of the door opening, not of someone opening it. Only then does the reader see the men, as they "come" toward the reader in the lunchroom. The deictic term "come" can be used only from inside the lunchroom (cf. Fillmore). The narrator would have to be telling the story from inside the lunchroom at the time the event is occurring. At no other location or time would this expression be used. If the sentences were told from outside the lunchroom the expression might have been something like: "Two men opened the door to Henry's lunchroom and went in." Here the men are seen before they open the door and "go" in. If the sentence were told by a narrator at a different time, the time would need to be marked: "Once, when I was in Henry's lunchroom, the door opened and two men came in." Of course, if the narrator and the reader were actually in Henry's lunchroom at the time the men entered, there would be no reason for the text at all. Hemingway *represents* the event of the men entering the lunchroom from the perspective of someone inside it at that time. In order to understand the sentence appropriately, the reader must have some way to interpret the scene from the same perspective. The reader does so by imagining himself or herself there.

Let me now consider the following sentences from Iris Murdoch: "Ten more glorious days without horses! So thought Second Lieutenant Andrew Chase-White recently commissioned in the distinguished regiment of King Edwards Horse, as he pottered contentedly in a garden on the outskirts of Dublin on a sunny Sunday afternoon in April nineteen-sixteen" (1965, 1). How, we might ask, is the exclamation understood? From where is this being told? By whom? When was Lieutenant Chase-White commissioned? Why was the commissioning referred to as recent? To what was it recent? Where is the narrator of this passage?

Note that the first sentence is not formally a sentence at all. Rather, it is an unuttered expression of a pleasurable subjective experience enjoyed by Second-Lieutenant Andrew Chase-White, a fictional character. It is not an assertion by the author, nor a narrator (cf. Banfield 1982). The only one who could have expressed it in a semantically coherent way is Lieutenant Chase-White. We, the readers, become aware of Lieutenant Chase-White's subjective experience by having it presented directly to us. We can observe his thoughts from up close. As Dorrit Cohn has observed, fiction allows for transparent minds.

When was Lieutenant Chase-White commissioned? Obviously sometime in the spring of 1916. But the text was written in 1965. Murdoch does not mean to imply that Chase-White was recently commissioned when she wrote the passage, even though she uses the deictic term *recently*. Instead of recent to her, the commissioning is recent to the time Chase-White is pottering in the garden. The text is contextualized from that time and place. There is no evidence that a narrator is present at the scene. This excerpt does not have the form of a narrated text. It is presented from the subjective perspective of a character. The author and the reader are nearby sensing his experience.

John Searle argues that the words in this excerpt all have the same meaning in the fiction that they would have in any other language use, with the possible exception of *pottered*, and that the sentences are no different from those one might find in a history. He identifies this excerpt as a set of assertions by Murdoch which she pretends to be true. Obviously, however, something about the use of language in this fiction is different from a history—even if the words carry their literal meaning. If Murdoch (or even a fictional narrator) had witnessed Lieutenant Chase-White in his garden in 1916, she would not have described the observation in the language used in the story. My attempt at a historical description generates the tepid: "One sunny Sunday afternoon in April 1916, Second Lieutenant Andrew Chase-White was pottering in a garden on the outskirts of Dublin. He had recently been commissioned in the distinguished regiment of King Edward Horse." Without an interview, I could not mention his excitement at not having to put up with horses, nor could I easily report that he was content to mess around in the garden. The language and the knowledge of the historian is not the same as that of the fiction writer. In non-narrated fiction, the "facts" do not have to be justified or even justifiable by any empirical method (Galbraith 1989; Cohn 1990).

My next example shows that even the author's choice of words is often shaped to represent those of the particular fictional character, if the character's subjectivity is being displayed: "He felt good and thought to himself he was damn lucky to get away from the Twin Cities and Emiscah and that sonofabitchin' foreman" (Dos Passos 1930, 392). There are many examples in fictional texts in which the selection of vocabulary or the selection of function terms represents the emotional or knowledge states of the characters. These are often represented directly rather than filtered through the consciousness of the author or the narrator (Banfield 1982).

Four women now emerged from behind the screens and seated themselves in a group in the space at the front. Each held an instrument of varnished wood of a similar shape, but was not easily describable. The instruments were chiefly different in size.
     One was quite small, two somewhat larger, and the fourth considerably larger. Each woman also held a long rod in the other hand. (Asimov 1986, 418)

When did the women emerge from behind the screens? What are the women holding in their hands? Why did Asimov not use the standard English terms to label the instruments they are holding? This passage illustrates nicely how the author can contextualize a scene from the perspective of the fictional characters and their culture. The event purportedly takes place some time in the distant future, yet Asimov uses the past tense. He uses it in conjunction with the deictic now. The reader interprets the passage from a position in the audience as the women emerge from behind screens into our view. We share the culture of not knowing about Western music traditions. We, the reading audience, may know that Asimov is describing a string quartet, but we would know it more directly if Asimov had called the women a string quartet, or at least used the basic terms for the instruments the women are holding. (Interestingly, we understand even though Asimov made a mistake by giving the quartet two violas instead of two violins.) This description, however, informs us indirectly that the observers from the culture represented in the fiction do not know about our musical instruments. We gain that information by the fact that the text uses more general descriptors rather than basic level terms (Peters and Rapaport 1990).

THE DEICTIC SHIFT THEORY (SEGAL VERSION)

1. A reader constructs a fictional world from a narrative text. We can consider such a world a mental model in that its existence is in the domain of ideas and concepts (cf. Johnson-Laird 1983). These worlds have properties which are generated from our interpretation of the sentences in the text as they interact with our general and specific knowledge about the places and events depicted. The fictional world modeled contains representations of times, places, characters, and events. It also has a set of rules by which it

operates which is inferred by the reader from the text in conjunction with his or her knowledge of both the real world and other fiction.

2. The conceptual substitute for the discourse situation within the fictional world is the *deictic center*. The "here and now" for conversation is the time and place of the discourse. This serves to anchor the deictic referents. When reading fiction we shift the anchor for deictic referents to a movable time and place within the story world. We call the locus of this anchor the deictic center. The deictic terms refer to times, places, persons, and objects within the fictional world. Psychologically, we imagine ourselves, or an image or representation of ourselves, in the story world at the deitic center (Segal 1990). This stance allows us to understand the full meaning of textual deixis without changing the meaning of deictic terms.

3. Many sentences in narrative texts are presented to be directly interpreted from a particular deictic stance without going through the intermediary of a narrator. Deictic shift theory accounts for the generation of fictional text without the need for a narrator. The author contextualizes the scenes from a position in the story world and can describe or represent the local scene without invoking a consciousness to interpret it. In order to have a fictional narrator, the author has to contextualize the events from the perspective of a person's epistemology. This is obviously a possibility, since the author has control of the text, but it is not necessary; the events can be directly represented.

4. The deictic center can be located almost anywhere. At times the text is interpreted from the subjective point of view of a character within the fiction. In these cases we think of the Deictic Center as either being inside that character, or observing the workings of the character's conscious or unconcious mind.

Many narratologists seem to require that all sentences of fiction be justified by being presented through the assertions of a consciousness, often a fictional narrator (cf. Genette 1980). The Deictic Shift Theory, however, argues that is unnecessary. The author can contextualize almost any event from its location or a location near it. Like Superman, language can be used to see the invisible or to pierce impregnable fortresses. One can represent or describe anything from any perspective. One can witness an atomic explosion from within, or one can see the subjective states of characters.

The fact that the Deictic Shift Theory does not require a narrator does not mean that it cannot support narrated text. In narrated text the deictic shift is often into the consciousness of a fictitious character. The fictional world can be described through that consciousness. Interestingly, the theory allows for the potentiality of having any event being presented from the perspective of characters, whether or not they are deemed the narrator. Thus whereas any event can be presented as "objectively true" in the fiction, even subjective states, physical events can be made doubtful if they are contextualized through the consciousness of an unreliable character (cf. Wiebe 1990).

NOTE

1. I share this work with the Narrative Research Group of the Center for Cognitive Science at the State University of New York at Buffalo. We are an interdisciplinary group consisting of linguists, psychologists, computer scientists, and child language and language disability professionals (with an occasional geographer, classicist, narratologist, fiction writer, or philosopher sharing insights with us).

WORKS CITED

Asimov, Isaac. *Foundation and Earth*. Garden City, N.Y.: Doubleday, 1986.

Banfield, Ann. *Unspeakable Sentences: Narration and Representation in the Language of Fiction*. Boston: Routledge and Kegan Paul, 1982.

Barwise, Jon, and John Perry. *Situations and Attitudes*. Cambridge: MIT P, 1983.

Cohn, Dorrit. "Fictional versus Historical Lives: Borderlines and Borderline Cases." *Journal of Narrative Technique* 1 (1990): 3-24.

—. *Transparent Minds*. Princeton: Princeton UP, 1978.

Dos Passos, John. *The 42nd Parallel*. New York: Harper and Brothers, 1930.

Fillmore, Charles J. "Pragmatics and the Description of Discourse." *Radical Pragmatics*. Ed. P. Cole. New York: Academic P: 1981. 143-66.

—. *Santa Cruz Lectures on Deixis*. Bloomington: Universisty of Indiana Linguistics Club, 1975.

Galbraith, Mary. "Subjectivity in the Novel: A Phenomenological and Linguistic Approach to the Narration of Childhood Self." Diss. State U. of New York at Buffalo, 1989.

Genette, Gerard. *Narrative Discourse: An Essay on Method*. Trans. J. E. Lewin. Ithaca, N.Y.: Cornell UP, 1980.

Hemingway, Ernest. "The Killers." *The Complete Short Stories of Ernest Hemingway*. Finca Vigía Ed. New York: Charles Scribner's Sons, 1987. 215-22.

Johnson-Laird, Phillip N. *Mental Models: Toward a Cognitive Science of Language, Inference, and Consciousness*. Cambridge: Cambridge UP, 1983.

Murdoch, Iris. *The Red and the Green*. New York: Viking, 1965.

Peters, Sandra L., and William J. Rapaport. "Superordinate and Basic Level Categories in Discourse: Memory and Context." *Twelfth Annual Conference of the Cognitive Science Society*. Hillsdale, N.J.: Lawrence Erlbaum, 1990. 157-65.

Searle, John. "The Logical Status of Fictional Discourse." *New Literary History* 6 (1975): 319-32.

Segal, Erwin M. "Fictional Narrative Comprehension: Structuring the Deictic Center." *Twelfth Annual Conference of the Cognitive Science Society*. Hillsdale, N.J.: Lawrence Erlbaum, 1990. 526-33.

Wiebe, Janyce M. *Recognizing Subjective Sentences: A Computational Investigation of Narrative Text*. Technical Report 90-03. Department of Computer Science, State University of New York at Buffalo, 1990.

Telling It Again:
"Stories into Novels"

W. P. Kinsella

I think the only difference between novels and short stories is that a novel is a collection of short stories where you don't necessarily have to have a climax at the end of each one. That's been my experience. *Shoeless Joe* (1982) is five stories woven together. I think my novel, *Box Socials* (1991), is about six stories. Both of these novels started out as short stories. I wrote a story called "Shoeless Joe Jackson Comes to Iowa" in 1978, just as I was leaving Iowa City. The story was published in an anthology. The anthology was reviewed in *Publisher's Weekly*, which is the Bible of the book trade. A young editor at Houghton Mifflin in Boston saw the review of the anthology, which had a two-line mention of my story. He was right out of editors' school; he didn't know that editors really don't want to hear from writers. Editors certainly don't want to go looking for writers; they get more stuff in over the transom than they can handle in a lifetime. He hadn't realized this yet, so he wrote me a letter and said, "Gee, we're all baseball fans here at Houghton-Mifflin. I haven't seen your story yet, but the idea of this person building a baseball diamond in his cornfield is so wonderful that if this is a novel, we really would want to see it, and if it isn't, it should be."

Well, it wasn't, and I decided that it should be.

So I started thinking novel, and I knew that I always wanted to write something about J. D. Salinger because he makes himself conspicuous by hiding. Who else do you know who hasn't published in thirty-five years and still manages to stay on the front pages? He put himself through college working as an actor on a cruise ship, so he knows how to hold an audience, and he has held his audience forever.

The name Ray Kinsella came about because I went back and reread all of Salinger's collected and uncollected work and discovered that he had used two characters named Kinsella in his fiction—Richard in *The Catcher in the Rye*

(1951), and Ray in an uncollected story called "A Young Girl in 1941 with No Waist at All," published in *Mademoiselle* in, I think, July 1947. I said, "There's the connection. I can now name my character Ray Kinsella, and he can go and turn up on Salinger's doorstep and say, 'Hey, I'm one of your fictional characters come to life and come to see you'." Interestingly enough, I got a letter about two years ago from a Jack Kinsella in, I think it was, Ohio. He had been Salinger's college roommate. So that was how Salinger came to use the name because it is, of course, an uncommon name.

I also knew that I wanted to write about Moonlight Graham. I had discovered his name in the *Baseball Encyclopedia* and I thought, "What was this Southerner doing up in the coldest place on earth?" I was curious about him. I knew, too, I wanted to write about Eddie Scissons, the name I gave to the old man I met on the streets of Iowa City. One day I was standing on the corner of Burlington and Dubuque streets waiting to cross the street and this old man came up to me and sort of poked his white cane in my navel and said, "Can you tell me what time it is?" It was cold and miserable, and I reluctantly pushed up my cuff and said, "It's five after two," and he said, "Good. I've got ten minutes to catch my bus." He said, "Did you know I'm eighty-seven years old and I used to play for the Chicago Cubs?" I said, "Well, no. I didn't know that."

And so my mind started racing at this point. I thought, "This old dude has got to be the oldest living Chicago Cub." Ernie Banks was then the public relations man for the Cubs. I thought, I'll just phone Ernie Banks, and surely he'll want this fellow to throw out the first pitch. I'll get a free trip up there with him, get to sit in a box seat. I can surely do something for the trip, maybe a little piece for *Sports Illustrated*. I was already counting the cash because I was a graduate student at the time, and so I made arrangements to go and interview this fellow the next night and I dropped what I was doing, walked across the street to the Iowa City Public Library, got the *Baseball Encyclopedia*, opened it up, and . . . nothing. He was a storyteller just like I am. When you get to be eighty-seven years old, you can claim to have played major league baseball for anybody you damn please, and a lot of old guys do. There are a lot of baseball imposters around. I've turned up a number of them over the years.

The film people transformed J. D. Salinger into "Terrence Mann" when they made the movie *Field of Dreams* from *Shoeless Joe* for two reasons. They knew that Salinger really couldn't do anything, but they were afraid that he would launch a nuisance lawsuit just at the moment they were preparing to spend $10 million to publicize the movie and release it. It would take six to eight weeks to get rid of the lawsuit; then they would have to spend another $10 million to publicize the movie, so he could hurt them without ever accomplishing anything. That was the main reason they decided to rewrite the character and make him large and black and cantankerous so Salinger couldn't say, "Well, this is just a thinly disguised me." The other reason was that there were perhaps half a million copies of the book in circulation. If the movie was successful, twenty million people would see it in a matter of days, so only a very small percentage would know that the book had been changed anyway.

What happened originally was that I had to spend a couple of days with my publisher's libel lawyers. They made me make a couple of changes in the manuscript, but then they said, "Look, essentially the only thing Salinger can sue us for is about the sixth definition of libel which is called false light. In order to do that, he would have to go to court himself, which he won't want to do, and he'd have to say, 'Look, I've been portrayed in this novel as a kindly, loving, humorous individual. In reality, I am a surly son-of-a-bitch who sits in a bunker on the side of a hill and shoots at tourists when they drive by my house. Therefore, I've been portrayed in a false light.'" They said it was unlikely that he'd do that.

I did not write the filmscript of *Field of Dreams*. I had nothing to do with it. I have done a couple of television scripts which I've been paid well for, but which have died in preproduction. I don't like the medium myself. I love watching television. I go to hundreds of movies a year, but I don't like writing filmscripts. Short stories and filmscripts are totally, totally different. It's like the difference between being a plumber and a carpenter. Each one has a general idea of what the other one does, but they don't know the fine points. Screenplays are a medium unto themselves, and I think that is one reason that most books that are adapted to the screen by their authors fail very badly.

I would not have had the heart to make the cuts in *Shoeless Joe* necessary to make it a commercially viable project. I was lucky that Phil Robinson loved the book so much he wanted to do something good to it. He said, "Look, there is no way we can get a three-hundred-page novel into an hour-and-forty-minute movie. We have to cut all sorts of characters. We have to cut scenes. We have to telescope time. We have to change dates." I think he captured the essence of the book, while at the same time making the changes I would never have had the heart to make. The characters were as I would have liked them to be, and I can't imagine anyone better than Kevin Costner and Amy Madigan playing Ray and Annie. I didn't care much for the little girl. I thought they could have gotten someone who at least looked like she might have been Kevin and Amy's daughter, but other than that, I thought the casting was great. In bad hands, *Field of Dreams* could have been another car chase movie.

My novel *Box Socials* is, I think, about six different story lines mixed together, and it too started out as a short story. I was going to write a story called "Truckbox Al's Big Break" about an awkward farm kid who almost gets a tryout with the St. Louis Cardinals, and I thought about twenty pages was what it would take. So I started writing, and the story grew and it grew until it was about forty pages, and there was nowhere to market a forty-page short story. I noticed there was a novella contest coming along with a minimum of eighty pages, so I said, "Well, if I embellish this and put in another story line, I can get it up to eighty pages." So I did that, and I sent it to the novella contest, and it came in second.

Unfortunately, only the first prize got money, so I was then stuck with an eighty-page novella, and there is nothing you can do with an eighty-page novella. You can't even put it in a short story collection, because it's too long to go in a story collection. It's too short for a novel. Nobody wants to publish eighty pages, so you're stuck. So I looked at it again, and I thought, "Well, now if I came up with a couple more plot lines, I could make this into a novel." So that is what I did, and I liked the voice so much that *Box Socials* is now the first book of a trilogy, and the other two books are finished, and I'm working on a fourth book that is not related to them, but uses the same voice.

Box Socials is autobiographical in the sense that I used the setting and the situation where I grew up. My Dad was an American who had played some minor league ball in Florida and California, and settled down late in life in rural Canada. When the Depression came along, he was too proud to take welfare and ended up buying a stony and worthless quarter section of farmland a hundred miles from anywhere where I spent the first eleven years of my life. Now I always wanted to write something about growing up in these unusual circumstances. I was an only child; the nearest neighbors were miles away. Where the nearest neighbors with children were I never knew because I never saw any children while I was growing up. I moved to the city when I was eleven, and I have been suffering culture shock ever since. When I came to write about this situation I discovered, of course, that nothing interesting had ever happened to me. There would be a lot fewer bad autobiographical novels if more writers would realize that.

Occasionally, however, I have written short stories about other real people. Salinger was interesting because he's mysterious. Elvis Presley is one of the most interesting people in the world. The premise of my short story "Elvis Bound" is: what would happen if a young woman was so infatuated with Elvis Presley that the only way she could make love was to have a poster of him beside the bed with a pink light shining on it? Many years ago, I also wrote a short story about Janis Joplin. I wanted to write something about Janis, and I carried the notes around with me for years. The idea I had was: what would happen if someone responsible had come along and managed to keep Janis alive for another fifteen years? That was the premise that I worked with in the story. The story is quite fantastical in that you can never quite tell for sure whether this really happened or not.

Fact and fiction writing are in no way related. You can use facts any way you want, and it doesn't matter if insiders know the difference. You may know the San Francisco music scene, so you can say, "He really doesn't know what he's talking about in this story." But ninety-nine percent of the readers won't know that, and if I do a good enough job, they'll say, "Yes, I believe that's the way it is." I don't know any baseball players. I know virtually no Indian people. It is not necessary to commit suicide in order to write about it. Imagination is what fiction writers work with, and I play fast and loose with facts all the time because I don't feel that it matters at all.

This Janis Joplin story is the only story where I have been surprised by a critical interpretation. I find it frightening that there are tens of thousands of people out there who make a living dreaming up strange and ludicrous interpretations of writers' work. I'm generally amused by critical writing on my work. Sometimes it's fairly astute, but I'm generally never surprised. Someone did an interpretation of the Janis story, however, that came up with something that is obviously there. In the last lines of the story, there is obviously something there that I didn't see when I wrote it, and the critic was able to point it out. This is the only time I've ever been surprised critically.

Part V

The Future of the Short Story

20

The Way We Write Now:
The Reality of AIDS
in Contemporary Short Fiction

Sharon Oard Warner

> She knew as much about this disease as she could know.
> Alan Barnett, "Philostorgy, Now Obscure"

The line above comes from a short story by Allen Barnett, who died of AIDS in 1992. The "disease" the line refers to is, in fact, AIDS, and the "she" is a woman named Roxy, who asks her friend Preston whether he intends to go on DHPG. (To invoke the acronym AIDS is to call forth a whole legion of acronyms: HIV, ARC, PCP, AZT, KS, FDA, CDC.) Roxy knows DHPG is a drug used to treat CMV (cytomegalovirus), and that it requires "a catheter inserted directly into an atrium of his heart" (1990, 36). Roxy has done her homework. In her room, Preston finds "a photocopy of an article from the *New England Journal of Medicine*," as well as "a book on the immune system and one on the crisis published by the National Academy of Sciences, and a list of gay doctors" (43). Roxy has read extensively and cares deeply, but there is still much she cannot know.

I identify with Roxy: I have read extensively (though not as much as she has), written some, and care deeply, but like her, there is much I cannot know. What I do know, however, I have learned not so much from television documentaries, though I have watched them, and not from articles and reports, though I have read them. What I know about AIDS—about living with it and dying from it—I have learned from literature, from novels and poems and essays, and most of all, from short stories.

Most of us knew little about AIDS when Susan Sontag's story "The Way We Live Now" was published in 1986 in *The New Yorker*. "The Way We Live Now" was one of the first stories about AIDS to appear in a mainstream periodical, and it is still—by far—the best-known story on the subject. Not only was Sontag's story included in *Best American Short Stories of 1987*, it was also chosen for the volume *Best American Short Stories of the Eighties*. To raise funds for AIDS charities in 1992, the story was released once again, this time as a small and expensive volume, complete with illustrations by British artist Howard Hodgkin. In *The New York Times Book Review*, Gardner McFall proclaimed this newest incarnation of the story "an allegory for our times" (20).

Presumably, the allegorical elements of the story are in what is left out: the name of the main character—the man who is ill—and the name of the disease. These two subjects, person and illness, we learn about through hearsay, second and third hand in a variety of voices:

I've never spent so many hours at a time on the phone, Stephen said to Kate, and when I'm exhausted after the two or three calls made to me, giving me the latest, instead of switching off the phone to give myself a respite I tap out the number of another friend or acquaintance, to pass on the news. (Sontag 1988, 2)

Surely, one of Sontag's intentions was "to pass on the news" to the reader. However, the message may not be getting across, at least not to everyone, and perhaps not to those most in need of hearing it. When I first taught "The Way We Live Now" in the fall of 1991—five years after its appearance in *The New Yorker*, a period of time during which approximately 120,000 Americans died of AIDS—several students in my class insisted that the disease in question might not be AIDS at all. One young man was adamant; no amount of argument would serve to convince him. He simply preferred to believe that Sontag intended some other disease—any other disease. The meaning of the allegory, if indeed "The Way We Live Now" is an allegory, was certainly lost on this student.

While Sontag's story may have well have been the first story to avoid the name of the illness, it certainly was not the last. The first volume of stories on AIDS, *A Darker Proof: Stories From a Crisis* (1988), by Edmund White and Adam Mars-Jones, mentions the acronym only once in 233 pages. In the foreword to his newest collection of stories, *Monopolies of Loss* (1993), Mars-Jones comments that the "suppression" (4) of the term in the earlier book was intentional.[1] My own experience with writing about AIDS is similar. In writing a story about a foster mother to a baby with AIDS, I deliberately sidestepped the term until page six, and thereafter used it only twice. My concern was that editors and readers would be turned off by the subject, so I made sure my audience was well into the story before I divulged the truth. Even in fiction, it seems, we are invested in keeping AIDS a secret.

But more problematic than avoiding the name of the illness is the practice of evading the person with AIDS. In Sontag's story we never learn the man's name or much else about him for that matter, except that he has a large number of devoted and talkative friends. In a very real sense, Sontag's story has no main character. What it has instead is, at best, a subject of conversation; at worst, grist for the gossip mill. As several of my students pointed out, "The Way We Live Now" is reminiscent of the children's game, "Telephone," in which players sit in a circle and whisper a message in turn:

At first he was just losing weight, he felt only a little ill, Max said to Ellen, and he didn't call for an appointment with his doctor, according to Greg, because he was managing to keep on working at more or less the same rhythm, but he did stop smoking, Tanya pointed out, which suggests he was frightened, but also that he wanted, even more than he knew, to be healthy, or healthier, or maybe just to gain back a few pounds, said Orson. (1988, 1)

This technique is catchy, but it may well cast suspicion on the veracity of what is at hand. After all, the charm of the children's game comes from the inevitable distortion of the message. (If everyone reported correctly, what fun would it be?) Were it only one of many stories on AIDS, the issues of technique and omitted names might be simply matters to be hashed out among literary critics; but in fact, "The Way We Live Now" continues to be the best-known story on the topic and one of the few to have been published in a commercial periodical.

By and large, the stories about AIDS that have followed Sontag's have also kept their distance from the subject. (Here, I am speaking of stories that have been published in mainstream literary and commercial publications.) As good as these stories are, and some are excellent, most are not stories about people with AIDS; they are stories about people who know other people with AIDS. Once again, the disease and those who suffer from it are kept at a distance.

The main characters of these stories tend to be siblings or friends of people living with AIDS. Three good examples are "Close" by Lucia Nevai, which appeared in *The New Yorker* in 1988; "A Sister's Story," by Virginia DeLuca, which appeared in *The Iowa Review* in 1991; and "Nothing to Ask For," by Dennis McFarland, which appeared in *The New Yorker* in 1989 and was later included in *The Best American Short Stories 1990* (1991). Guilt plays a major role in all three stories. While a friend or a sibling struggles with AIDS, the main characters of these stories struggle with their own feelings.

In Nevai's story, a social worker named Jorie is flying home for the funeral of her brother Jan, "who had contracted AIDS seven months earlier and had not let anyone in the family know" (1988, 36). Jan's lover Hank cared for him, "made sure he never lacked for visitors," "made sure he had painkillers," "helped him write a will" (37). The pain of knowing that she was intentionally excluded from the last months of Jan's life is hard for Jorie to bear, but by the end of the story she realizes that "pain was stronger, pain was hungrier. Pain would win this one" (39).

DeLuca's story also concerns a sister whose brother dies. Much of "A Sister's Story" is told through journal entries, and the effect of this technique is the same sort of distance one feels in Sontag's story. As in Nevai's story, the sister feels a great deal of guilt, partly because her husband is afraid of AIDS and therefore afraid of her brother, Mike. At one point, the sister confesses her husband's fears to Mike. His response is rage:

July 16, 1986
Nancy tells me that I've hurt him beyond repair. That he will never recover from this.
That he'll die faster, now. I believe her. (DeLuca 1991, 172)

Of the stories about people who know people with AIDS, "Nothing to Ask
For" gets closest to both the illness and those who suffer from it. In the Con-
tributor's Notes to *Best American Short Stories 1990*, Dennis McFarland explains that "Nothing to Ask For" is based on a visit he paid to a close friend
just weeks before the friend died of AIDS. He admits that he had trouble with
the narrator: "It was hard to let the story be his, while never allowing his concerns to upstage those of the characters who were dying" (1991, 351). Perhaps
because upstaging was a concern for him, McFarland's story succeeds in allowing "the horror of the disease to speak for itself" (1991, 351). The result is a
story full of reverence for life and for those in the midst of leaving it.

The main character of "Nothing to Ask For" is a man named Dan who is
spending the day with his friend Mack, who is close to death, and with Mack's
lover, Lester, who is also sick with AIDS. Guilt is an issue in this story as well.
At one point, Lester finds Dan in the bathroom sprinkling Ajax around the rim
of the toilet bowl:

"Oh, Dan, really," he [Lester] says. "You go too far. Down on your knees now, scrub-
bing our toilet."
    "Lester, leave me alone," I say.
    "Well, it's true," he says. "You really do."
    "Maybe I'm working on my survivor's guilt," I say, "if you don't mind."
    "You mean because your best buddy's dying and you're not?"
    "Yes," I say. "It's very common."
    He parks one hip on the sink, and after a moment he says this: "Danny boy, if you
feel guilty about surviving . . . that's not irreversible, you know. I could fix that."
    We are both stunned. He looks at me. In another moment, there are tears in his eyes.
(1991, 146)

McFarland takes pains to develop both Lester and Mack as characters in their
own right. To do so, he pulls us directly into their lives, bypassing gossip,
memories, and journal entries. In order to prepare Dan for the sight of him
naked in the bath, Mack calls out, "Are you ready for my Auschwitz look?"
(1991, 144). As Dan bathes him, Mack muses on his fate: "You know, Dan,
it's only logical that they've all given up on me. And I've accepted it mostly.
But I still have days when I think I should at least be given a chance" (1991,
145). A chance is what McFarland gives this character—a chance to express
himself, to enter our psyches, to change us in a way hearsay can never do.

As one might predict, most of the writing about AIDS is being done by gay
writers, but readers may not realize that most of this writing is published in
collections marketed primarily for gay readers. Not until I began searching out
stories dealing with AIDS did I begin to realize how segregated that market is.
A number of the stories I wanted to read were unavailable in local bookstores—

even in the bigger and better ones—and the books had to be special ordered. Others were available in a special section set aside for gay readers. So I was not surprised to find that, of the twenty entries under the subject heading AIDS in the Short Story Index for 1990, eight were published in an anthology called *Men on Men 3: Best New Gay Fiction* (1990), and four were published in a collection by Allen Barnett called *The Body and Its Dangers* (1990), which I could not find in libraries or bookstores, despite the fact that the book won a PEN/Hemingway award. The eight remaining were either reprints (McFarland's and Sontag's) or stories appearing in individual collections. Not one of the stories in the 1990 listing appeared in a periodical of any kind. Because few people outside the gay community are exposed to these stories, few are reading them. And we all need to be reading them. These are the stories that go to the heart of the matter, stories by writers who are either HIV-positive themselves or who know enough to risk writing from the point of view of someone with AIDS.

The Darker Proof: Stories From a Crisis (1988) was the first collection of fiction dealing with AIDS.[2] It includes four stories by the British writer Adam Mars-Jones and three long stories by American novelist Edmund White. These stories plunge right in, no intermediaries or second-hand information. For instance, Mars-Jones's story "Slim" begins this way:

I don't use that word. I've heard it enough. So I've taken it out of circulation, just here, just at home. I say slim instead, and Buddy understands. I have Slim. When Buddy pays a visit, I have to remind myself not to offer him a cushion. Most people don't need cushions; they're just naturally covered. So I keep all the cushions to myself, now that I've lost my upholstery. Slim is what they call it in Uganda, and it's a perfectly sensible name. You lose more weight than you thought was possible. You lose more weight than you could carry. Not that you feel like carrying anything. (1988, 1)

Of the twenty stories included in *Men on Men 3*, eight are concerned with AIDS. All are well worth reading, but by far the best is "Part One: Halfway Home" by Paul Monette. Though actually an excerpt from a novel, Monette's piece works remarkably well as a piece of short fiction. Monette was a versatile man—a poet, essayist, screenwriter, and novelist—and one of the finest writers I have read in years. His book *Borrowed Time: An AIDS Memoir* was nominated for the National Book Critics Circle Award in 1988. It is the intensely moving account of the life and death of Roger Horwitz. In *Borrowed Time*, Monette remarks that "families do not always come together neatly in a tragedy" (1988, 293), and his story "Part One: Halfway Home" is a poignant illustration of this sad truth.[3]

Tom Shaheen, who is in his early thirties, has not seen his brother Brian in nine years, not since their father's funeral. He fully expects to die without seeing his brother again, and he fully expects to die soon. Until then, he is living in a bungalow by the sea, rent-free courtesy of a gentle and unassuming man named Gray Baldwin. Every day Tom makes his way slowly down the eighty rickety steps—"my daily encounter with what I've lost in stamina"—to the entrance to a cave by the surf (Monette 1990, 12-13). There, he broods over "missed chances," and "failures of nerve" (12). He does not, however, probe the painful tooth of his childhood—his "scumbag drunk" of a father (30), his "whimpering" mother (33). In particular, he avoids thinking about his older brother Brian—beautiful as a Greek god, ruthless as a terrorist. Monette prepares the reader carefully for an unexpected visit, but he is such a skillful writer that Brian's abrupt entrance still takes us by surprise. The encounter is brutal. Monette does not spare Tommy or Brian or the reader. Guilt is an issue here, too, but now we see it from the other side. When Brian tries to say he is sorry, Tommy feels not forgiveness but the added burden of his brother's regret:

Suddenly I feel drained, almost weepy, but not for Brian's sake. . . . The whole drama of coming out—the wrongheaded yammer, the hard acceptance—seems quaint and irrelevant now. Perhaps I'd prefer my brother to stay a pig, because it's simpler. And even though he's not the Greek god he used to be, fleshier now and slightly ruined, I feel more sick and frail in his presence. Not just because of AIDS, but like I'm the nerd from before too. "You can't understand," I say, almost a whisper. "All my friends have died." (27)

"Part One: Halfway Home" cannot be neatly summed up. It is not simply about a confrontation between two brothers, a story about AIDS, or self-pity, or a growing acceptance of death. It is about all these issues—and more. As George Stambolian explains in the Introduction to *Men on Men 3*, "The epidemic . . . challenges and tests our beliefs, makes time directly perceptible to our hearts and minds." He goes on to quote Robert Gluck: "Now death is where gay men . . . learn about love" (4). And love is a subject Monette knows more about than any other contemporary writer I can think of. Near the end of the story, Tommy steals into the bedroom where his brother is sleeping. Looking down at Brian, Tommy feels intense hate—"I'm like a bad witch, rotten with curses, casting a spell even I can't see the end of"—and bitter love:

I take a last long look at Brian, and on impulse I lean above him, hover over his face and brush my lips against his cheek. . . . I've never kissed my brother before. He doesn't flinch, he doesn't notice. Then I turn and stumble back to my room, pleading the gods to be rid of him. (36)

When I was working on my own story about AIDS, a writer friend advised me to change the disease. "I really like this story," she told me, "but why does the baby have to have AIDS?" I had no answer for that question. Why does anyone have to have AIDS? The impetus for my story was something I overheard about a single woman in Chicago who nurses babies with AIDS. When one child dies, she simply turns to caring for another. After hearing about that brave woman, I wanted to get to know her, and because I am a fiction writer, that meant writing a story. While I could change many things about "A Simple

Matter of Hunger," I could not change the disease. Of that much, at least, I am sure.[4]

The tragedy is that babies do have AIDS, that an estimated one million people in the United States are infected with the HIV virus. It is not something we can avoid as writers, as readers, or as human beings. "But I was taught not to write about social issues," my friend explained to me. "They just don't last. In a hundred years, it is possible that AIDS may be completely forgotten." We can hope for that, I suppose, but it does not change the present. Right now, we need to know as much about this disease as we can know.

Sontag ends "The Way We Live Now" this way: "I was thinking, Ursala said to Quentin, that the difference between a story and a painting or a photograph is that in a story you can write, He's still alive. But in a painting or a photo you can't show 'still.' You can just show him being alive. He's still alive, Stephen said" (1988, 19). Ironically, in this most famous story about AIDS, "he," whoever he might be, is not *shown* still alive. For that, we have to take Stephen's word. And while his word might have been enough to begin with, now and in the future we will need something more. We will need stories like Monette's, stories whose main characters speak to us directly: "I've been at this thing for a year and a half, three if you count all the fevers and rashes. I operate on the casual assumption that I've still got a couple of years, give or take a galloping lymphoma. Day to day, I'm not a dying man, honestly' (1990, 14). See there, Tom Shaheen is still alive. Take it from Monette, someone who knows.[5]

NOTES

1. *Monopolies of Loss* includes all four stories from *The Darker Proof: Stories From a Crisis* (1988) plus four new stories dealing with AIDS.

2. Allen Barnett's collection *The Body and Its Dangers* (1990) also deals extensively with AIDS. In 1993, two new collections on the subject appeared: Adam Mars-Jones's *Monopolies of Lies* and Jameson Currier's *Dancing on the Moon: Short Stories about AIDS*. The first story in Currier's collection, "What They Carried," borrows much in terms of structure and technique from Tim O'Brien's "The Things They Carried," and from Susan Sontag's "The Way We Live Now." It is also worth noting that only one story in *Dancing on the Moon* is written from the viewpoint of a character with AIDS. The main characters in the other stories are lovers, relatives, and friends, some of whom may be HIV-positive.

3. Paul Monette received the 1992 National Book Award in nonfiction for *Becoming a Man: Half a Life Story*.

4. Since writing this story, I have edited an anthology of stories on AIDS, *The Way We Write Now: Short Stories from the AIDS Crisis* (Seacaucus, N.J.: Citidel, 1996).

5. Paul Monette died of complications from AIDS in 1995.

WORKS CITED

A version of this article appeared in *Studies in Short Fiction* 30 (1993): 491-500.

Attinello, Paul. "Ave." *bloodWhispers: L.A. Writers on AIDS*. Ed. Terry Wolverton. Los Angeles: Silverton Books, 1991. 63-66.

Barnett, Allen. *The Body and Its Dangers*. New York: St. Martin's, 1990.

—. "Philostorgy, Now Obscure." *The New Yorker* 4 June 1990: 36-46.

Cashorall, Peter. "The Ride Home." *Men on Men 3: Best New Gay Fiction*. Ed. George Stambolian. New York: Plume, 1990. 298-317.

Cave, Tracy. "Coco." *bloodWhispers: L.A. Writers on AIDS*. Ed. Terry Wolverton. Los Angeles: Silverton Books, 1991. 91-95.

Currier, Jameson. *Dancing on the Moon: Short Stories About AIDS*. New York: Viking, 1993.

Davis, Christopher. "The Boys in the Bars." *Men on Men 2: Best New Gay Fiction*. Ed. George Stambolian. New York: Plume, 1988. 322-37.

Davis, Susanne. "Segue." Unpublished manuscript.

Decker, Paul. "Excerpts From 'Things To Do.'" *bloodwhispers: L.A. Writers on AIDS*. Ed. Terry Wolverton. Los Angeles: Silverton Books, 1991. 84-88.

DeLuca, Virginia. "A Sister's Story." *Iowa Review* 21.2 (1991): 161-84.

Gutierrez, Eric. "The Go-Go Prince." *bloodWhispers: L.A. Writers on AIDS*. Ed. Terry Wolverton. Los Angeles: Silverton Books, 1991. 35-40.

Haile, Mark. "Estate Sale." *bloodWhispers: L.A. Writers on AIDS*. Ed. Terry Wolverton. Los Angeles: Silverton Books, 1991. 89-90.

Haule, Robert. "Blond a Dog." *Men on Men 3: Best New Gay Fiction*. Ed. George Stambolian. New York: Plume, 1990. 48-70.

Homes, A. M. "The I of It." *The Safety of Objects*. New York: Norton, 1990. 145-50.

Innaurato, Albert. "Solidarity." *Men on Men 2: Best New Gay Fiction*. Ed. George Stambolian. New York: Plume, 1988. 87-118.

Jeffers, Alex. "My Face in a Mirror." *Men on Men 3: Best New Gay Fiction*. Ed. George Stambolian. New York: Plume, 1990. 275-81.

Johnson, Greg. "Intensive Care." *A Friendly Deceit*. Baltimore: Johns Hopkins UP, 1992. 122-31.

Leavitt, David. "Gravity." *A Place I've Never Been*. New York: Viking, 1990. 76-80.

—. "A Place I've Never Been." *A Place I've Never Been*. New York: Viking, 1990. 1-17.

Mars-Jones, Adam. "Bears in Mourning." *Granta* 38 (Winter 1991): 225-35.

—. "An Executor." *The Darker Proof: Stories From a Crisis*. New York: New American Library, 1988. 11-55.

—. *Monopololies of Loss*. New York: Knopf, 1993.

—. "Remission." *The Darker Proof: Stories From a Crisis*. New York: New American Library, 1988. 106-29.

—. "Slim." *The Darker Proof: Stories From a Crisis*. New York: New American Library, 1988. 1-10.

—. "A Small Spade." *The Darker Proof: Stories From a Crisis*. New York: New American Library, 1988. 56-105.

McFall, Gardner. Rev. of *The Way We Live Now*, by Susan Sontag. *The New York Times Book Review* 1 Mar. 1992: 20.

McFarland, Dennis. "Nothing to Ask For." *The Best American Short Stories 1990*. Eds. Richard Ford and Shannon Ravenel. New York: Houghton Mifflin, 1991. 133-48, 351.

Monette, Paul. *Borrowed Time: An AIDS Memoir*. New York: Avon, 1988.

—. "Part One: Halfway Home." *Men on Men 3: Best New Gay Fiction*. Ed. George

Stambolian. New York: Plume, 1990. 11-36.

Moores, David. "Excerpt from Dead Cat: Do Not Open." *bloodWhispers: L.A. Writers on AIDS*. Ed. Terry Wolverton. Los Angeles: Silverton Books, 1991. 41-47.

Mordden, Ethan.' "The Dinner Party." *Everybody Loves You: Further Adventures in Gay Manhattan*. New York: St. Martin's Press, 1988. 205-34.

Nevai, Lucia. "Close." *The New Yorker* 7 Nov. 1988: 36-39.

Palmer, Martin. "Journey." *Men on Men 3: Best New Gay Fiction*. Ed. George Stambolian. New York: Plume, 1990. 220-36.

Rosas, Crespin. "The Waiting Room." *bloodwhispers: L.A. Writers on AIDS*. Ed. Terry Wolverton. Los Angeles: Silverton Books, 1991. 67-70.

Searle, Elizabeth. "My Body to You." *My Body to You*. Iowa City: U of Iowa P, 1993. 1-16.

Sontag, Susan. "The Way We Live Now." *The Best American Short Stories of the Eighties*. New York: Houghton Mifflin, 1988. 1-19.

Spinrad, Norman. "Journals of the Plague Years." *Full Spectrum*. Eds. Lou Aronica and Shawna McCarthy. New York: Bantam, 1988. 409-83.

Stambolian, George, ed. *Men on Men 2: Best New Gay Fiction*. New York: Plume, 1988.

—. *Men on Men 3: Best New Gay Fiction*. New York: Plume, 1990.

Verghese, Abraham. "Lilacs." *The New Yorker* 14 Oct. 1991: 53-58.

Vernon, David. "How Not to Get Attached to a Fish." *bloodWhispers: L.A. Writers on AIDS*. Ed. Terry Wolverton. Los Angeles: Silverton Books, 1991. 96-99.

Viegener, Matias. "Twilight of the Gods." *Men on Men 3: Best New Gay Fiction*. Ed. George Stambolian. New York: Plume, 1990. 237-47.

Warner, Sharon Oard. "A Simple Matter of Hunger." *Learning to Dance and Other Stories*. Minneapolis: New Rivers Press, 1992. 129-42.

—. *The Way We Write Now: Short Stories from the AIDS Crisis*. Seacaucus, N.J.: Citadel, 1996.

White, Edmund. "An Oracle." *The Darker Proof: Stories From a Crisis*. New York: New American Library, 1988. 168-209.

—. "Palace Days." *The Darker Proof: Stories From a Crisis*. New York: New American Library, 1988. 130-67.

—. "Running on Empty." *The Darker Proof: Stories From a Crisis*. New York: New American Library, 1988. 210-33.

Wolverton, Terry, ed. *bloodWhispers: L.A. Writers on AIDS*. Los Angeles: Silverton Books, 1991.

21

The Future of the Short Story: A Tentative Approach

Claire Larriere

Foretelling the future of the short story is a risky task. Former predictions incite one to wariness. H. E. Bates, who predicted that World War II would prove a great source of inspiration for short story writers, had to admit his mistake: "When I prophesied in *The Modern Short Story* in 1941 that the inevitable distrust and dislocation of war's aftermath would lead new writers to find in the short story the essential medium for what they had to say, I felt certain I was right: time has proven me wrong" (Beachcroft 1968, 213).

Is the future of the short story, in fact, predictable? In considering it, we implicitly assume that the term short story applies to a particular literary genre; but does it still correspond to a short prose narrative in English which is not fairy tale, detective story, or science fiction, as it did about a century ago? Already critics such as Clare Hanson have decried the inappropriateness of the term short story. Anyone can claim its reconsideration in terms of postmodernism and deconstruction.

However, for Europeans (and more precisely for the French), the short story, even translated as *la nouvelle de langue anglaise*, is a typical product, which is in full expansion. It has several times happened to me, when asking French publishers if they would accept *des nouvelles*, that the publishers would query, "*Sont-elles traduites de l'anglais?*" ("Are they translations from English?"— meaning English or American). If they were not, the publishers would decline publication without even looking. Short stories in English, untranslated, whether from Great Britain, the United States, or any other part of the world, enjoy at present a growing fame in France. This is confirmed by the Parisian booksellers whom I recently contacted: *NQL International, FNAC Interna-*

tional, Village Voice, and others. People ask more and more for collections of stories in English. Each time I consider the future of the short story, its present, if not its past, comes to my mind and takes precedence over its prospects, for perhaps more than any other genre, the short story's future is illuminated by its development. We must examine its themes (or its subject matter), its "manner" or form, and its readers. Great short story writers from various parts of the world—including Guy de Maupassant, Anton Chekhov, Katherine Mansfield, Eudora Welty, and others—claim to draw inspiration from their own experience, and advise young writers to do likewise. Our contemporaries do so, but their scope of experience has been enlarged in a spectacular way owing to obvious causes: greater access to and ease of travel; the instantaneous worldwide diffusion of information and thus the common knowledge of circumstances formerly unknown; and, therefore, the extended contacts of all. This enlarging of scene and circumstances can, by itself, be a source of inspiration for short story writers. This theme or subject matter appears clearly in Canadian short stories: the confrontation of various populations. The clash of different ways of life and different allegiances has inspired such stories as Clark Blaise's famous "A Class of New Canadians" or Bharati Mukherjee's equally famous "The Lady from Lucknow." Such clashes become inspiring forces in stories by Americans who live on other continents. A prominent example is Frank B. Wilderson's "Soweto."

This leads me to assert that the short story has always been, and will always be, a voice of rebellion. Extended literacy and the widening of publications have allowed minorities—oppressed women and homosexuals, people of color all over the world—to express themselves. The success of collections of stories by women, like *The Secret Self* (1952), or about homosexuals carrying AIDS, like Adam Mars-Jones and Edmund White's *The Darker Proof* (1988), testify to the breach in taboos and conformism that the short story has opened. There is little chance of these minorities disappearing from the earth. Were they to be granted due rights and recognition, others would take their place. They already do so: submerged white people in colored majorities, men harassed by women, fathers deprived of their fatherly rights. The very nature of the short story, as defined in the 1960s by Frank O'Connor in *The Lonely Voice* (1963), is not likely to change.

Neither is it likely that political commitment will ever be the essential motivation of short story writers. Over and again writers affirm (as William Sansom, V. S. Pritchett, and Eudora Welty have done) that they do not write to defend great causes but to tell stories. Short story writing, like story telling, is primarily an art, not a demonstration. Nor is it akin to reportage, however close to the news of the day and however realistic short stories may be. For in the short story, as in other forms of art, reality is transmuted. It seems to me that in this world of mounting violence, where our senses and our brains are constantly assaulted, the short story can reflect this violence only by transcending it, by transcending the sensational as Joyce Carol Oates does in her superb story "Heat." Stories dealing with horror, such as Ian McEwan's "First Love, Last Rites," require particular talent: our horror, even more than our taste, will be shocked by exaggerated mawkishness.

Violence, however, is not a subject in itself. What stories will be about in the future shows little prospect of drastic change because some subjects are particularly suited to the genre and have been so since the short story's birth in the nineteenth century. One of the most common of these subjects is children's experiences and, more specifically, the process of children's initiation. The successive stages of a child's initiation are such staple elements of short stories that my students detect them with great rapidity. Various forms of initiation stand a good chance of remaining popular subjects of short story writers faced with the widening scenes of life, scope of experience, and subtlety of implication.

Violence, morbidity, and the problems of childhood. Bernard Bergonzi indicted the short story for these themes in 1970. Bergonzi declared that the short story's

tendency to write about life's victims also shows itself in a concern with forms of consciousness that are exceedingly limited: children, imbeciles and persons in a low state of cultural development. . . . the short story, in its present condition, seems to be unhealthily limited, both in the range of literary experience it offers and its capacity to deepen our understanding of the world, or of one another. (1970, 216, 218)

This was perhaps true in the 1970s, but I do not think it applies to the short story in the 1990s. On the contrary, the short story today is dynamic; its plots are enriched by encounters, coincidences, exoticism. It is, in countless cases, brightened by fantasy and poetry. In respect to deepening our understanding of the world, it seems to me that the short story underlines the great evil of our contemporary Western civilization, which is (ironically) the lack of communication between individuals. There seems little chance that the distresses of solitude and misunderstanding will disappear from the short story in the future, but this only confirms that the short story is a seismograph of our world and that it ignores complacency.

Is this the reason why love is so rarely the subject of short stories? Instead, they abound in couples in conflict, triangular (and unhappy) relationships, deserted wives, marriages that turn out badly. I was immensely happy to read Adam Schwartz's story "The Grammar of Love" in *The New Yorker* a few years ago. The narrator, a young white instructor, falls in love against all odds with one of his black students whose grammar he spends his day time and his night dreams correcting. Isn't it revealing that to experience love he has to lend himself to the influence of his illiterate students—a young mother—and her inarticulate baby, and practically deny the grammar he has always used? It requires H. E. Bates' imprudence and a certain impudence to predict a renewal of romance in the short story. If the genre reverts to this tendency, at least it will be enriched by the implicitness, subtlety, and economy the short story has gained in the course of this century.

Foreseeing that the short story's form will be different from what it is at present, or from its shape in the past, is even more adventurous. However, even though no writer has ever written quite like Henry James or Joseph Conrad, or even Somerset Maugham, there is at present, and there promises to be, more varieties of story writing than ever before. What a publisher or an author may call a collection of short stories often actually includes fantastic stories, animal stories, and fables. One thinks of the beautiful stories of Angela Carter who deserved much more fame than she got and is getting now—after her untimely death. I believe that the short story, while keeping its denomination, will enlarge its scope, its subjects, its manner.

The looseness of terms applied to the genre appears in French where a short story writer is called *un nouvellier* by some critics and *un nouvelliste* by others. What is important for the future of the short story is the intense interrogation of the genre by critics and authors. Since the 1970s, critics, theorists, and writers have endeavored to analyze the short story's nature and circumscribe its territory. *Superfiction or The American Story Transformed*, a 1975 anthology which is really a collection of short stories, reflects this questioning. The stories are classified as Fantasy-Fabulation-Irrealism, Neo-Gothic, Myth-Parable, Metafiction-Technique as Subject, Parody & Put-On. It seems to me that the short story, which has never been an innocent genre, can be even less so than ever. Questionings about technique and genre have filtered through creation. This is more important than the influences of particular writers upon others, even though great short story writers' teaching has been the breeding ground for new writers. There will be ever more spontaneous and individual experiments, particularly with rhythm, and they will be encouraged by greater pressures for economy of language.

Indeed transitions in a piece of writing are less and less necessary. Short story readers are intelligent and quick-minded consumers used to the rapid movements of the camera and the extension of its angle. They also know and implicitly accept the codes of the genre. But whether the story is presented as personal experience by the author (or one of his or her characters) or reported as personal experience by an anonymous, invisible narrator, the short story reader recognizes the author's voice among all others, even if the author does all he or she can to remain unidentified. The short story writer's predicament has been well expressed by Sean O'Faolain: "the author, sensitive about intruding himself, fully conscious of the personal nature of his work, and just because he is so near at hand, for that very reason sensitive about being discovered prowling among his characters" (1951, 53). Here again there is little chance of a change of rules; if anything, the short story is shorter today than it has been in the past. There are now collections of "short shorts" and "sudden fiction" which scarcely existed fifty years ago. The game of hide-and-seek is bound to be more and more exciting.

If booksellers sell more short stories than formerly, we might be tempted to infer that more and more people read them and that the short story market is prosperous. In fact, the situation is paradoxical. There certainly are more readers of stories, but reviews and magazines that used to publish stories either have disappeared (like *Encounter*), or publish fewer and fewer stories. Alice Adams, in her introduction to *The Best American Stories 1991*, sets forth the problem clearly:

> Where are the stories from the women's magazines, many of which were publishing good short fiction as recently as ten years ago? It is my impression that these magazines, though they continue from time to time to declare great interest in serious fiction, are publishing much less of it (if any), and that their editorial policies, always condescending toward their readership, have gotten considerably worse. (xiv)

Those well-paying magazines which Adams calls the "male slicks" only occasionally publish good stories. If fewer stories appear in magazines, it means more anthologies and collections are read by lovers of stories. Of course, the ideal would be for both sorts of publications to thrive, and perhaps this will occur in the future. But for the present, I think one of the most hopeful signs of new interest in short stories is the growing number of meetings around the world where writers, critics, and editors can share their insights and enthusiasm.

WORKS CITED

Adams, Alice. Introduction. *The Best American Stories 1991*. Eds. Alice Adams and Katrina Kenison. Boston: Houghton Mifflin, 1992. xiii-xvii.

Beachcroft, T. O. *The Modest Art*. Oxford: Oxford UP, 1968.

Bergonzi, Bernard. *The Situation of the Novel*. New York: Macmillan, 1970.

Hanson, Clare. "The Short Story as a Late 20th Century Form." *Visions Critiques* 5 (1988): n.p.

O'Faolain, Sean. *The Short Story*. New York: Devin-Adair, 1951.

22

Where Do We Go from Here?
The Future of the Short Story

Mary Rohrberger

Where do we go from here?

I used to think that if I were prescient enough I could tell by consulting Hawthorne somewhat in the way devoted followers consult the *I Ching*. Some short story theorists establish the early nineteenth century as the beginning of the short story and point to such authors as Hawthorne and Poe and Gogol as forbears of the genre. Such theorists, and I am one, do not deny that stories that are short existed from the time people began to tell stories; what we hold is that something happened to the form of the short story that caused Poe in the early 1840s to offer a new definition of the form on the occasion of his review of Hawthorne's *Twice Told Tales*, and Brander Matthews, another American short story writer and critic some forty years after Poe, to proclaim the birth of a new genre: the short story.

Matthews was clearly influenced by Poe and Poe by Hawthorne; thus, I have looked to Hawthorne's early stories to find prototypes. Indeed, as early as the early 1830s Hawthorne was writing such aesthetically satisfying stories as "My Kinsman, Major Molineaux" and "Roger Malvin's Burial." But even more important for present purposes, he did not commit to the fire stories like "The Wives of the Dead" and "The Hollows of the Three Hills." What is intriguing about all of this is that in the great Hawthorne Renaissance inspired by the New Critics in the 1940s, 1950s, and early 1960s, scholars recognized the narrative coherence of the former but spoke of the latter as merely sketches. In fact, we needed to learn how to read the so-called sketches; and learning how to read them took us through modernism to postmodernism, acquainting us with epiphanic structures and the sometimes plotless, imagistic forms of the post-modern metafictionist or alternate reality stories.

It is true that most of Hawthorne's stories, including "My Kinsman, Major Molineaux" and "Roger Malvin's Burial," seem to fit the traditional frame: rising action to climax and denoument.

Figure 22.1
Traditional Story Structure

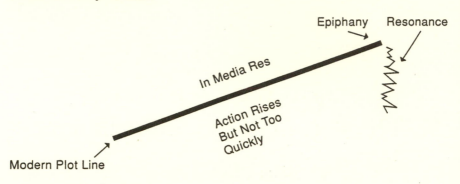

Hawthorne's "sketches," however, fit more recently named plot structures. "The Hollow of the Three Hills" is clearly epiphanic:

Figure 22.2
Epiphanic Story Structure

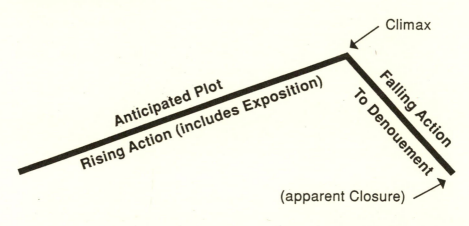

The in medias res beginning presents a woman, young and graceful, but "smitten by untimely blight" and an image of what she may become—another woman, an ancient crone withered and decrepit to whom the young woman has come for help. The young lady's confession echoes in the cursed and sepulchral hollow of the three hills as the old woman becomes simultaneously mother, midwife, confessor; and epiphany reverberates between young and old woman, between confession and absolution, rebirth and absolute damnation, and it resonates in the ghastly confusion of mourning and mirth punctuated by the old woman's demonic cackle.

"The Wives of the Dead" is postmodern in plot structure, presenting alternate realities. One must imagine these stories' lines stacked one upon another:

Figure 22.3
Postmodern Story Structure

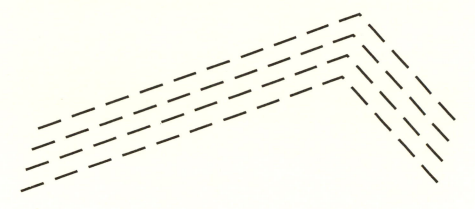

The wives of the dead are Mary and Margaret, recent brides of two brothers who occupy a single house with a parlor separating twin sleeping rooms, yet with a part of each room reciprocally visible one to the other. Previously, sleeping rooms have been occupied by husband and wife, but the wives have been notified almost simultaneously of the deaths of their husbands. Thus twinning wives, husbands, and bedrooms, Hawthorne carefully plots four story lines any of which did or did not happen, could or could not happen. There is no way to tell from the text. Rather, all seem to exist in a ghost world of possibility.

But what is even more intriguing than rereading sketches and finding stories is rereading Hawthorne's so-called traditional stories and finding not simple climax and denouement but "ghost" plot lines intersecting with "real" plot lines where, at the point of intersection the apparent merges with the real providing an analogical base for the story itself.   Let me try to explain. In "My Kinsman, Major Molineaux," Robin confronts his kinsman, a tarred and feathered figure, the object of the townspeople's scorn. At the climax, Robin's laughter joins with the laughter of the crowd signaling the story's probable end when

Robin tells the gentleman who befriends him that he must retreat from the city where he had come to seek his uncle and his fortune. In this outline, the plot of the story seems to take the traditional form—a movement toward and a withdrawal from. But the story does not end here. The friendly gentleman invites Robin to stay in the town in order to seek his fortune with the help of his kinsman. What we have here is a clear reversal that sends us scurrying back along the plotted path to discover where we lost our way. Is the friendly gentleman another father freed from Robin's anger and hostility upon whom Robin will continue to depend? Is Robin mature enough to stand on his own? Well, he will and he will not; he is and he is not. I find no closure in this story.

In "Roger Malvin's Burial," Reuben's fatal quest leads unerringly to a climax, the accidental death of his son and the tears of release that follow. But again, Reuben may be released from a sin he consciously committed, but in killing Cyrus, Reuben also subconsciously admits to the murder of his surrogate father and all that that implies, including the question of necessity. Are all men doomed to Oedipus's fate? Had Cyrus lived to establish his own patriarchal kingdom on earth, would there have been a son to unthrone him? Do the tears of release fall from blinded eyes? Is this the way it was, or that, and in how many other ways? Perhaps a graph of plot and ghost plot would look like this.

Figure 22.4
Plot and Ghost Plot Story Structure

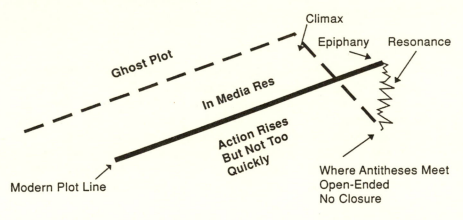

Young Goodman Brown's fears and desires bounce back and forth between lines like this: and Rappaccini and Baglioni debate appearance and reality. Between such intersecting lines a Maypole takes on the trappings of a whipping post and daydream becomes nightmare.

One thing scholars almost uniformly say about Hawthorne is that in his stories the appearance is never the reality. But upon second thought, maybe the appearance is the reality. Quite possibly it both is and is not. Quite possibly this paradox is the mystery that is revealed in the story's epiphany—revealed but not easily explained, thus defying closure. Maybe the paradox is the base of a story's controlling metaphor, the essence that a short story writer like Katherine Mansfield sought and often achieved; the form antithetical to plot that Sherwood Anderson searched for, the truth Hawthorne knew could be revealed only in the darkness and by means of the light of the moon.

How should I conclude? Perhaps by making the point that surface content is of no consequence as an indicator of the short story's future. Short stories are not really about manners, about people interacting in society. Novels take these matters as their own. Short stories question the existential world that the novel demonstrates. Short stories are philosophic at bottom, built on the metaphysical assumption that the ideal and the real merge at a moment of revelation, a moment as profound as epiphany. So it does not really matter what stories appear to be about. They will continue and succeed and be valued as short stories as long as they retain the basic genre characteristics established by Hawthorne and demonstrated by Poe and all major short story writers from Hawthorne to John Barth to Joyce Carol Oates and well beyond.

Speaking of Writing:
"Spies with Music"

Barry Hannah

I have gotten old enough to be a little bit humble about what is going on. One thing I have always realized is that I have written for an audience that knows as much as I do or more, and I am very conscious that there are too many words in the world. I work against the grain of the writer who is the conspicuous consumer of words. Like Ray Carver and some of the others attacked for "minimalism" now, I have always believed in compression and brevity, as I was taught by my wonderful high school teacher.

I do think that what starts the story for me is music. It is a tone. I used to be hilariously impressed by a paragraph I read about a sitar player in India who tuned his instrument by listening to a rock. I thought that was the most laughable damned thing that I had ever heard in my life. I just howled like a good Westerner and Southern American. "Jesus Christ. You do that? Let me tell you." But you get older and you find out, among other shockers, that this is true, that there are tones running through your mind all the time. There is a music that the writer wants to put into words. The writers that interest me always have a music. It is no mystery.

I have never been baffled by the idea of people who say when they are young, as I did, "I really want to write, although I have nothing to say." It is not even a paradox to me because the music comes before the message, and I think you will find a lot of young writers around the nation waiting just simply to get subject matter. They've already got the tune. They've had the tune a long time.

Spies with music. I have just lately discovered the great works of John Le-Carre. I love his language, his attention to his world, and I find myself comforted and awed by his metaphor of the circus, because I feel we have signed away something we have been given as writers: an invitation to the circus. That is, we are spies. And if you make it to forty, fifty, sixty, or seventy years old—much longer than you thought you ever would when you were eighteen, kind of obscenely old—you're living better, you're watching more.

You know you've made a bargain that is going to be hard on your children, on your wife, and on your friends, just as the spy, the CIA man, makes a bargain. You're going to be a watcher. Your self-consciousness is going to be so awesome and your watching others is going to get in the way of your relationship with your wife, your children. You didn't know that when you started, but you find that you're a double agent. It's not that you don't like your wife who says, "You're such a great writer, why don't you write a letter to me, like your momma, you know?" It is that you are terribly interested in the world. You're just sincere about too much. You're a triple, quadruple agent. And I'm a person who knows, having lost three friends to suicide last year, that people disappear in the service. Their points of view are gone. They are unnoted. Their challenges to immortality are not rewarded.

The few awards I have gotten, the little fame, they are undistinguished, and yet they were there, and they were important. And this is the way the deaths go when you get older, as your friends, your acquaintances, die. You actually collect a kind of strength by knowing that you are never going to be rewarded and that it was always hopeless. Gore Vidal said, "It is better to be futile than hopeless." If you get real, you know that the act of writing a story is futile; you are not going to have an immense impression on your century, probably. But you've got messages. You've been watching so long you are haggard. And you "gots dat music." Music does come out of a rock. The Indian man is right. He is not just buffaloing you.

Also you find out, if you work as I do, that your audience knows more than you do. The man in the street knows things that you think you've come on very privately shouting "Eureka!" The same things that work with your day, work with his. So I find the more I write, the less I respect wisdom. I have a kind of lack of regard for the kind of person who reads Shakespeare and writes "How true" in the margins. You've got enough wisdom when you are eighteen to get through, mainly. And if you've survived adolescence, as Flannery O'Connor said, you can write novels the rest of your life.

What you want is some true music and awe and wonder. I don't think there is enough awe and wonder in American writers. I think there's too much return to the pedagogue. I think the reviews and the spirit of the times are so puritanical and pedagogical that it is worse that the 1950s because people are reviewed for their attitudes, their correctness. You would sometimes think a man is reviewing a manual, a how-to manual, or that a *story* doesn't matter. It's *just* a message; the attitude is what matters, and the reviewers are apt to chide you, like your third-grade teacher, into the right attitude.

Well, thank God for the differences. Don't you read for the differences? Don't you read for incorrectness? Don't you read for grave error? Don't you read for wrongness? I personally read for dumbness. I think Samuel Beckett answered very honestly one time. He said, "I want to explore ignorance." And

Beckett got so dead honest that he bored some people because the messages right from sheer honesty are not alive with great music, unless you can put music to the subject—as Beckett did. But the messages "I can't go on. I can't go on. I must go on," happen to us every morning. There's really no point in dragging it out. The world doesn't need you. The queen of the world is not going to fall in love with you at five this afternoon. You are not going to get the prom queen to jump in your car at midnight like you thought you were when you were seventeen cruising in your Impala. These things are probably not going to happen.

I am awed by the presence of the great Gay Talese because he knows what a spy is and is still one of the classiest men around, the most dapper and dashing. I've tried enough journalism to be humiliated by my own presence. *Rolling Stone* sent me on the road with a band one time, and I was so full of self-hatred for just hanging around that I forgot the story. Indeed, with my little fame somebody from a big magazine once sent a guy to my house to write about me, and do you know how awful that is to have some looming thing around you looking on? Well, that was back in my drinking days. It was all right for *me* to write about others, but this guy. . . . After about four days I got angry and drunk one night and I said, "What the fuck are you looking at?" Now this blew possible fame in a big way. He got on a plane and got out, as I would have.

But that's the true question of the writer: "What the fuck are you looking at? Get out of my face." Your children ask you that, not profanely, but, "Daddy, what's on your mind? Why aren't you here?" Your wife says, "Why don't I get a note? You've been celebrated by the academy, where are the love messages you used to send? Where are the nice letters?" My mother says the same thing. My dad, who wanted me to be James Michener, wanted me to write more often, showing him my literary skills and my devotion to him. You do tend to leave your loved ones behind. You need very tough loved ones who understand you.

But the music out of the rock. The tone you hear is essential to those of us who love the writing. You do hear music, all your life. William Faulkner professed never to like jazz, or music from the outside. He said he had too much orchestra going on inside himself. He was a tyrant at home. He wouldn't let his daughter play the phonograph in her room. He abjured places where jazz and loud dance music were played, although he wrote about them beautifully. But that music in Faulkner's head is no surprise to us. It's Faulkner's music. He's got the tune already written, and he delivers it in one way. The complaint about him is that the music often starts before there's a subject. My townsman Faulkner. I worship the idea of Faulkner, but nowadays I have some complaints with myself and other writers who start the music before they have anything to say. You're going to say it your way before you hear the music of others, of life.

Other people do have music. That's why Gay Talese is so good. He captures others' music. He can do the negative capability; he can make himself a spot on the wall, deny his own arrogance, catch the music of DiMaggio and Sinatra and others we want to hear about. I admire that terrifically. I have not got that talent, that unselfishness, but more and more I am willing to be silent and listen, and to gather others' music. Quite frankly, you get to be fifty years old and you start boring yourself with the same tune. You write to get out of yourself. The others are divine; the others are interesting. That face in the mirror is an old, old movie with a bad score.

If you write like I do, you write for people who get the joke. John Ruskin back in the nineteenth century expressed it very well. If you look deeply enough at the heart of things, you are going to see something you are not inclined to laugh at. But good ol' boys in Iowa and Mississippi, they knew that a long time ago. That's why they laugh; that's why they like to laugh. The common man knows that at the deep, dark heart of things there's something unsmiling; the grave never smiles. My father passed away last year. I was just amazed at the conventional feelings I had. How appropriate that tune "Amazing Grace" was for his life; how deeply I missed and admired him, because now he was a pioneer in death. He had a full life at eighty-six. I admired him—the man who wanted me to be James Michener—for his diligent life insurance sales, and for his banking, and for his real estate.

The very people I despised when I was a hippie, I adored when I lost them. But the common man has known that life is grim just as surely as Samuel Beckett has. He has a sense of the absurd. Do you think that you're the only one conscious of the bleak and stupid and pointless games that life consists of? No. You are not. So I don't think you ought to count on—unless you are a Christ or a Mohammed—delivering real wisdom, final wisdom. I think your trek should be a little humbler, that you should bring wonder and awe to people. I think that we have always had the wrong questions about God. If he is there, the questions are not relevant. There are no answers. Some things just *are*. All the questions are wrong. Things simply *are*.

The music just simply *is*. You don't know who built the music in your head. You don't know why you have to write. You can make more money doing other things. If you really want to get rich, give yourself a year and I'll bet you can. But what you can't do is get lucky. And that's what writers do. They work long and hard and practice long enough so that they start making their own luck. I sincerely believe in that; the music has been with them long enough that when the happenstance gets them, they hear the music out of the rock. They hear a song that nobody else heard. The best thing you can say about a writer is that this thing cannot be changed, although it is imperfect, because nobody can do it that way again.

I wrote a little story about twelve years ago. It was written honestly about certain real feelings joined to a beloved place in my past, a river lake, an overflow lake. They call it oxbow down in Mississippi where people fish and the old gather on this rail to lie to each other. The story is called "Water Liars." I once found the music of lies going on around me and it became a quite beautiful thing. I remember this in relation to a problem of perception I had a long time time ago during a divorce. Some things in life are so low and mean and desolate that there's no music. Those of you who have gone through divorce or the loss of a child—there's absolutely no consolation. There's no music and it's a great horror. There was more music at my dad's funeral than there is in a divorce. There's a bleak lack of anything consoling in divorce; it's one of the most awful things that you do—a death without a death, if you care.

And so these were the feelings I had when I wrote this story. I was just desperately searching for music. People were advising yoga—and poems. There is nothing more stupid than a poem which is relevant to your situation. Homer, you can't touch this. You just can't touch it, Shakespeare; you ain't been there, baby. Nobody can touch it. George Jones can't touch it; he doesn't sing sad enough. You're not down there, George, at that personal hurt. And fully, the music finally came to me.

Selected Bibliography

Achebe, Chinua. "English and the African Writer." *Transition* 18 (1965): 27-30.

Achebe, Chinua, and C. L. Innes, eds. *African Short Stories*. London: Heinemann, 1985.

Adams, Alice. Introduction. *The Best American Stories 1991*. Eds. Alice Adams and Katrina Kenison. Boston. Houghton Mifflin, 1992. xiii-xvii.

Ahmad, Aijaz. "Jameson's Rhetoric of Otherness and the 'National Allegory'." *Social Text*. 17 (Fall 1987): 3-25.

Aldridge, John. *Talents and Technicians: Literary Chic and the New Assembly-Line Fiction*. New York: Scribners, 1992.

Anderson, R. C., and P. D. Pearson. "A Schema-theoretic View of Basic Processes in Reading Comprehension." *Handbook of Reading Research*. Vol. 1. Eds. R. C. Pearson, et al. White Plains, N.Y.: Longman, 1984. 255-91.

Ashcroft, Bill, Helen Triffin, and Garth Griffiths. *The Empire Writes Back: Theory and Practice in Post-Colonial Literatures*. London: Routledge, 1989.

Asher, S. R. "Topic Interest and Children's Reading Comprehension." *Theoretical Issues in Reading Comprehension*. Eds. R. J. Spiro, B. C. Bruce, and W. F. Brewer. Hillsdale, N.J.: Lawrence Erlbaum, 1980. 525-34.

Balogun, F. Odun. *Tradition and Modernity in the African Short Story: An Introduction to a Literature in Search of Critics*. New York: Greenwood Press, 1991.

Banfield, Ann. *Unspeakable Sentences: Narration and Representation in the Language of Fiction*. Boston: Routledge and Kegan Paul, 1982.

Bell, Madison Smartt. "Less Is Less: The Dwindling American Short Story." *Harper's* (Apr. 1986): 64-69.

Benson, Margaret S. "The Structure of Four- and Five-year-olds' Narrative in Pretend Play and Storytelling." *First Language* 13 (1993): 203-23.

Black, J. B., and G. H. Bower. "Story Understanding as Problem Solving." *Poetics* 9 (1980): 223-50.

Bower, G. H., J. B. Black, and T. J. Turner. "Scripts in Memory for Text." *Cognitive*

Psychology 11 (1979): 177-220.

Bower, G. H., and D. G. Morrow. "Mental Models in Narrative Comprehension." *Science* 247 (1990): 44-48.

Bradshaw, Michael. *Regions and Regionalism in the United States.* Jackson: UP of Mississippi, 1988.

Brewer. W. F. "Literary Theory, Rhetoric, and Stylistics: Implications for Psychology." *Theoretical Issues in Reading Comprehension.* Eds. R. J. Spiro, B. C. Bruce, and W. F. Brewer. Hillside, N.J.: Lawrence Erlbaum, 1980. 221-39.

—. "Plan Understanding, Narrative Comprehension, and Story Schemas." *Proceedings of the National Conference on Artificial Intelligence.* 1982. 262-64.

—. "The Story Schema: Universal and Culture-specific Properties." *Literacy, Language, and Learning.* Eds. D. R. Olson, N. Torrance, and A. Hildyard. Cambridge: Cambridge UP, 1985. 167-94.

Brewer, W. F., and E. H. Lichtenstein. "Event Schemas, Story Schemas, and Story Grammars." *Attention and Performance.* Vol. 9. Eds. J. Long and A. Baddeley. Hillsdale, N.J.: Lawrence Earlbaum, 1981. 363-79.

—. "Stories are to Entertain: A Structural-Affect Theory of Stories." *Journal of Pragmatics* 6 (1982): 473-86.

Brewer, W. F., and K. Ohtsuka. "Story Structure and Reader Affect in American and Hungarian Short Stories." *Psychological Approaches to the Study of Literary Narratives.* Hamburg: Helmut Buske Verlag, 1988a. 133-58.

—. "Story Structure, Characterization, Just World Organization, and Reader Affect in American and Hungarian Short Stories." *Poetics* 17 (1988b): 395-415.

Busnell, David I. *Drawings by A. De Batz in Louisiana, 1732-1735.* Washington D.C.: Smithsonian Institution, 1927.

Cameron, Donald. *Faces of Leacock.* Toronto: Ryerson, 1967.

Carver, Raymond. "On Writing." *Fires: Essays, Poems, Stories.* New York: Vintage, 1989. 22-27.

Castro, Joy. "To Practice the Thing." *Short Story.* 2:2 (Winter/Spring 1992): 1-4.

Chinweizu, Onwuchekwa Jemie, and Ihechukwu Madubuike. *Toward the Decolonization of African Literature.* Washington, D.C.: Howard UP, 1983.

Chopin, Kate, "Ma'am Pelagie." *The Complete Works of Kate Chopin.* Ed. Per Seyersted. Baton Rouge: Louisiana State UP, 1970. 232-39.

Cohn, Dorrit. "Fictional versus Historical Lives: Borderlines and Borderline Cases." *Journal of Narrative Technique* 1 (1990): 3-24.

Columb, Gregory G. "Cultural Literacy and the Theory of Meaning." *New Literary History* 20 (1987): 411-50.

Cothern, Nancy B., Bonnie C. Konopak, and Elizabeth L. Willis. "Using Readers' Imagery of Literary Characters to Study Text Meaning Construction." *Reading Research and Instruction* 30 (1990): 15-29.

DeFalco, Joseph. *The Hero in Hemingway's Short Stories.* Pittsburgh: Pittsburgh UP, 1963.

de Gransaigne, Jean, ed. *African Short Stories in English.* New York: St. Martin's Press, 1985.

de Gransaigne, Jean, and Gary Spackey. "The African Short Story Written in English: A Survey." *Ariel* (Apr. 1984): 73-85.

Dorfman, Marcy H., and William Brewer. "Understanding the Points of Fables." *Discourse Processes* 17 (1994): 105-29.

Ferguson, Suzanne. "The Rise of the Short Story in the Hierarchy of Genres." *Short*

Story Theory at a Crossroads. Eds. Susan Lohafer and Jo Ellyn Clarey. Baton Rouge: Louisiana State UP, 1989. 176-92.

Feuser, Willfred F. "French-English-Portuguese: The Trilingual Approach: 2. Aspects of the Short Story." *European-Language Writing in Sub-Saharan Africa.* Ed. Albert S. Gerard. Vol. 2. Budapest: Akademai Kiado, 1986. 1106-20.

Fillmore, Charles J. "Pragmatics and the Description of Discourse." *Radical Pragmatics.* Ed. P. Cole. New York: Academic P: 1981. 143-66.

___. *Santa Cruz Lectures on Deixis.* Bloomington: University of Indiana Linguistics Club, 1975.

Fisher, Philip. *Hard Facts: Setting and From in the American Novel.* New York: Oxford UP, 1985.

Flora, Joseph M. *Hemingway's Nick Adams.* Baton Rouge: Louisiana State UP, 1982.

Fox-Genovese, Elizabeth. "Between Individualism and Community: Autobiographies of Southern Women." *Located Lives: Place and Idea in Southern Autobiography.* Ed. J. Bill Berry. Athens: U of Georgia P, 1990. 20-38.

Gass, William H. "Finding a Form." *Finding a Form: Essays.* New York: Knopf, 1996. 31-52.

Genette, Gerard. *Narrative Discourse: An Essay on Method.* Trans. J. E. Lewin. Ithaca, N.Y.: Cornell UP, 1980.

Gentry, Marshall Bruce, and William L. Stull, eds. *Conversations with Raymond Carver.* Jackson: UP of Mississippi, 1990.

Gilles, Christina Marsden. "'Where Are You Going, Where Have You Been?': Seduction, Space and a Fictional Mode." *Studies in Short Fiction* 18 (1981): 65-70.

Gray, Richard. *Writing the South: Ideas of an American Region.* Cambridge: Cambridge UP, 1986.

Gray, Stephen. "The Politics of Anthologies." *Staffrider* 9.3 (1991): 43-50.

___. "A Sense of Place in the New Literatures in English, particularly South African." In *A Sense of Place in the New Literatures in English.* Ed. Peggy Nightingale. St. Lucia: U of Queensland P, 1986. 5-12.

Gretlund, Jan Nordby. "An Interview with Eudora Welty." *Conversations with Eudora Welty.* Ed. Peggy Whitman Prenshaw. Jackson: UP of Mississippi, 1984. 211-29.

Hanson, Clare. "The Short Story as a Late 20th Century Form." *Visions Critiques* 5 (1988): n.p.

Hibbard, Allen. "Crossing to Abbassiya." *Cimarron Review.* 99 (Apr. 1992): 17-19.

Hicks, Deborah. "Narrative Skills and Genre Knowledge: Ways of Telling in the Primary School Grades." *Applied Psycholoinguistics* 11 (1990): 83-104.

Hobson, Fred. Prologue. *Tell About the South: The Southern Rage to Explain.* Baton Rouge: Louisiana State UP, 1983: 3-16.

Holland, Norman. *5 Readers Reading.* New Haven: Yale UP, 1975.

Ingram, Forrest L. *Representative Short Story Cycles of the Twentieth Century: Studies in a Literary Genre.* Paris: Mouton, 1971.

Jameson, Fredric. "Third-World Literature in the Era of Multinational Capitalism." *Social Text* 15 (Fall 1986): 65-88.

Johnson-Laird, Phillip N. *Mental Models: Toward a Cognitive Science of Language, Inference, and Consciousness.* Cambridge: Cambridge UP, 1983.

Jose, Paul, and W. F. Brewer. "Development of Story Liking: Character Identification, Suspense, and Outcome Resolution." *Developmental Psychology* 20 (1984): 911-24.

___. "Early Grade School Children's Liking of Script and Suspense Story Structures." *Journal of Reading Behavior* 22 (1990): 355-72.

Julien, Eileen. "Of Traditional Tales and Short Stories in African Literature." *Presence Africaine* 125 (1983): 146-65.

Kintsch, W. "On Comprehending Stories." *Cognitive Processes in Comprehension.* Eds. Marcel Adam Just and Patricia A. Carpenter. Hillsdale, N.J.: Lawrence Erlbaum, 1977.

Knister, Raymond. Introduction. *Canadian Short Stories.* Freeport, N.Y.: Books for Libraries P, 1928.

Komey, Ellis Ayitey, and Ezekiel Mphahlele, eds. *Modern African Stories.* London: Faber and Faber, 1964.

Kroetsch, Robert. "No Name Is My Name." *The Lovely Treachery of Words: Essays Selected and New.* Toronto: Oxford UP, 1989. 41-52.

Larson, Charles, ed. *Opaque Shadows and Other Stories from Contemporary Africa.* Washington, D.C.: Inscape, 1975.

Lohafer, Susan. "A Cognitive Approach to Storyness." *Short Story* 1 (Spring 1990): 60-71.

—. *Coming to Terms with the Short Story.* Baton Rouge: Louisisana State UP, 1983.

—. "Stops on the Way o 'Shiloh': A Special Case for Literary Empiricism." *Style* 27 (Fall 1993): 395-406.

Lohafer, Susan, and Jo Ellyn Clarey, eds. *Short Story Theory at a Crossroads.* Baton Rouge: Louisiana State UP, 1989.

Lo Liyong, Taban. *Fixions and Other Stories.* London: Heinemann, 1969.

Lynch, Gerald. *Stephen Leacock: Humour and Humanity.* Montreal-Kingston: McGill-Queen's UP, 1988.

Mandler, Jean M. "On the Psychological Reality of Story Structure." *Discourse Processes* 10 (1987): 1-29.

—. *Stories, Scripts, and Scenes: Aspects of Schema Theory.* Hillsdale, N.J.: Lawrence Erlbaum, 1984.

Mansfield, Katherine. *Undiscovered Country: The New Zealand Stories of Katherine Mansfield.* Ed. Ian A. Gordon. London: Longman, 1974.

Mars-Jones, Adam, and Edmund White. *The Darker Proof: Stories From a Crisis.* New York: New American Library, 1988.

May, Charles. *Fiction's Many Worlds.* Washington: D. C. Heath, 1993.

Miller, Christopher L. *Blank Darkness: Africanist Discourse in French.* Chicago: U of Chicago P, 1985.

Nelson, K. E. "How Children Represent Knowledge of their World in and out of Language." *Children's Thinking: What Develops?* Hillsdale, N.J.: Lawrence Erlbaum, 1977.

New, W. H. *Dreams of Speech and Violence: The Art of the Short Story in Canada and New Zealand.* Toronto: U of Toronto P, 1987.

Ngugi wa Thiong'o. *Decolonising the Mind.* London: James Currey, 1986.

Oates, Joyce Carol. "When Characters on the Page are Made Flesh on the Screen." *The New York Times* Sunday 23 Mar. 1986: 1, 22.

O'Connor, Frank. *The Lonely Voice: A Study of the Short Story.* New York: Harper and Row, 1963.

O'Faolain, Sean. *The Short Story.* New York: Devin-Adair, 1951.

Penner, Dick. "The First Nick Adams Story." *Fitzgerald/Hemingway Annual* (1975): 195-202.

Peters, Sandra L., and William J. Rapaport. "Superordinate and Basic Level Categories in Discourse: Memory and Context." *Twelfth Annual Conference of the Cognitive*

Science Society. Hillsdale, N.J.: Lawrence Erlbaum, 1990. 157-65.

Poe, Edgar Allan. "The Cask of Amontillado." *Collected Works of Edgar Allan Poe*. Ed. Thomas Olive Mabbott. Cambridge, MA: The Belknap Press of Harvard UP, 1978. 1256-66.

Porter, Carolyn. "The Art of the Missing." *Contemporary American Women Writers: Narrative Strategies*. Eds. Catherine Rainwater and Will J. Scheick. Lexington: UP of Kentucky, 1985. 9-28.

Prenshaw, Peggy Whitman, ed. *Conversations with Eudora Welty*. Jackson: UP of Mississippi, 1984.

Rumelhard, D. E. "Notes on a Schema for Stories." *Representation and Understanding Studies in Cognitive Science*. Eds. Daniel G. Bobrow and Allan Collins. New York: Academic Press, 1975. 211-36.

Saltzman, Arthur M. *Understanding Raymond Carver*. Columbia: U of South Carolina P, 1988.

Sarbin, Theodore R., ed. *Narrative Psychology: The Storied Nature of Human Conduct*. New York: Praeger, 1986.

Schank, R. C. E., and R. Abelson. *Scripts, Plans, and Goals*. Hillsdale, N.J.: Lawrence Erlbaum, 1977.

Schmidt, Peter. *The Heart of the Story: Eudora Welty's Short Fiction*. Jackson: UP of Mississippi, 1991.

Searle, John. "The Logical Status of Fictional Discourse." *New Literary History* 6 (1975): 319-32.

Segal, Erwin M. "Fictional Narrative Comprehension: Structuring the Deictic Center." *Twelfth Annual Conference of the Cognitive Science Society*. Hillsdale, N.J.: Lawrence Erlbaum, 1990. 526-33.

Segal, Erwin M., Judith F. Duoan, and Paula Scott. "The Role of Interclausal Connectives in Narrative Structuring: Evidence from Adults' Interpretations of Simple Stories." *Discourse Processes* 14 (1991): 249-75.

Shaw, Valerie. *The Short Story: A Critical Introduction*. London: Longman, 1983.

Slemon, Stephen, and Helen Tiffin, eds. *After Europe: Critical Theory and Post-Colonial Writing*. Sydney, Australia: Dangaroo Press, 1989.

Smith, Paul. *A Reader's Guide to the Short Stories of Ernest Hemingway*. Boston: G. K. Hall, 1989.

Stein, N. L., and C. G. Glenn. "An Analysis of Story Comprehension in Elementary School Children." *New Directions in Discourse Processing*. Ed. R. O. Freedle. Hillsdale, N.J.: Lawrence Erlbaum, 1979.

Stein, N. L., and T. Trabasso. "What's in a Story?: An Approach to Comprehension and Instruction." *Advances in Instructional Psychology*. Ed. R. Glaser. Vol. 1. Hillsdale, N. J.: Lawrence Erlbaum, 1982. 213-68.

Stein, N. L., T. Trabasso, and M. D. Liwag. "The Rashomon Phenomenon: Personal Frames and Future-Oriented Appraisals in Memory for Emotional Events." *The Development of Future-Oriented Processes*. Eds. M. Harth, et al. Chicago: U of Chicago, 1994.

Tanselle, G. Thomas. "Hemingway's 'Indian Camp'," *Explicator* 10 (Feb. 1962), Item 53.

Taylor, Jacqueline. *Grace Paley: Illuminating the Dark Lives*. Austin: U of Texas P, 1990.

Thorndyke, P. W. "Cognitive Structures in Comprehension and Memory of Narrative Discourse." *Cognitive Psychology* 9 (1977): 77-110.

Trabasso, T., T. Secco, and P. Van den Broek. "Causal Cohesion and Story Coherence." *Learning and Comprehension of Text.* Eds. H. Mandl, N. L. Stein, and T.
Trabasso. Hillsdale, N.J.: Lawrence Erlbaum, 1984. 83-111.

Trabasso, T., and P. Van den Broek. "Causal Thinking and the Representation of Narrative Events." *Journal of Memory and Language* 24 (1985): 612-30.

Urbanski, Marie Mitchell Olesen. "Existential Allegory: Joyce Carol Oates's 'Where
Are You Going, Where Have You Been?'" *Studies in Short Fiction* 15.3 (Spring
1978): 200-203.

Van den Broek, P. "Causal Reasoning and Inference Making in Judging the Importance
of Story Statements." *Child Development* 60 (1989): 286-97.

—. "The Effects of Causal Relations and Hierarchical Position on the Importance of
Story Statements." *Journal of Memory and Language* 27 (1988): 1-22.

Waldhorn, Arthur. *A Reader's Guide to Ernest Hemingway.* New York: Farrar, Straus
and Giroux, 1972.

Wali, Obi. "The Dead End of African Literature?" *Transition* 10 (Sept. 1963): 13-16.

Welty, Eudora. "Place in Fiction." *The Eye of the Story.* New York: Random House,
1978: 116-33.

Wiebe, Janyce M. *Recognizing Subjective Sentences: A Computational Investigation
of Narrative Text.* Technical Report 90-03. Dept. of Computer Science, State University of New York at Buffalo, 1990.

Yussen, S. R., S. Mathews, T. Huang, and R. Evans. "The Robustness and Temporal
Course of the Story Schema's Influence on Recall." *Journal of Experimental Psychology: Learning, Memory and Cognition* 14 (1988): 171-79.

Yussen, S. R., and N. Ozcan. "The Development of Knowledge about Narratives."
Issues in Education: Contributions From Educational Psychology. Greenwich,
Conn.: JAI Press, in press.

Yussen, S. R., A. D. Stright, R. L. Glysch, C. E. Bonk, I. Lu, and I. Al-Sabaty.
"Learning and Forgetting of Narratives Following Good and Poor Text Organization."
Contemporary Educational Psychology 16 (1991): 346-74.

Zwaan, Rolf A., Joseph F. Magliano, and Arthur C. Graesser. "Dimensions of Situation
Model Construction in Narrative Comprehension." *Journal of Experimental Psychology: Learning, Memory, and Cognition* 21 (1995): 386-97.

Index

About the Contributors

JOHN BARTH is the author of one of the most influential volumes of metafictional short stories: *Lost in the Funhouse: Fiction for print, tape, live voice* (1968). *On with the Story: Stories* (1996) is his most recent collection of short fiction. His three linked novellas are titled *Chimera* (1972), and his novels include *Giles Goat Boy* (1966), *The Sot-Weed Factor* (1967), *Letters: A Novel* (1979), *Sabbatical: A Romance* (1982), *The Tidewater Tales: A Novel* (1987), and *The Last Voyage of Somebody the Sailor* (1991). Although he has retired from teaching writing seminars at Johns Hopkins University, Barth continues to live and write in the tidewater country of Maryland.

ROGER BERGER is an Associate Professor of English at The Wichita State University. His doctoral dissertation, "Telling Stories: Transformation of the Twentieth-Century American Short Story," examines the changes in the modern short story between modernism and postmodernism. Berger has published essays on contemporary American, African, and postcolonial literatures, and on anthropology. He is currently completing a book titled *Black Comedy: The Comic Imagination in Sub-Saharan African Literatures*.

WILLIAM F. BREWER is a cognitive psychologist currently carrying out research in five broad areas: knowledge acquisition, knowledge representation, human memory, the structure of discourse, and the psychology of science. A Professor of Psychology at the University of Illinois at Urbana-Champaign, he has developed a theory of stories for researchers in the cognitive sciences that attempts to capture many of the insights of work carried out in the humanities. Brewer and his colleagues have used this structural-affect theory to study American and Hungarian short stories, fables, artificially constructed texts, children's responses to texts, and cross-cultural characteristics of texts. He is a fellow of the American Psychological Association, the American Psychology Society, and the American Association for the Advancement of Science.

EWING CAMPBELL is a Professor of English at Texas A & M University at College Station. He is the author of *Raymond Carver: A Study of the Short Fiction* (1992), and his most recent work of fiction is *Madonna, Maleva*. He spent the first part of 1997 in southern Spain at work on new fiction; then he lectured in Tenerife on late twentieth-century American narrative.

ANN CHARTERS is the editor of three volumes: *The Story and Its Writers: An Introduction to Short Fiction* (1994, 4th ed.), *Major Writers of Short Fiction: Stories & Commentaries* ((1993); and *Literature and Its Writers* (1997). She is currently a Professor of English at the University of Connecticut.

ROBERT COOVER is the author of "The Babysitter," one of the most famous and widely anthologized American short stories of the twentieth century. A Professor of English at Brown University in Providence, Rhode Island, he is the author of the short story collections *Pricksongs & Descants* (1969), *In Bed One Night & Other Brief Encounters* (1983), and *A Night at the Movies, or, You Must Remember This* (1987). In 1973, Coover edited with Kent Dixon *The Stone Wall Book of Short Fictions*. His novels include *The Origins of the Brunists* (1961), *The Universal Baseball Association* (1968), *The Public Burning* (1977), *Spanking the Maid* (1982), *Gerald's Party* (1985), *Pinocchio in Venice* (1991), and *John's Wife* (1996).

BRENDA O. DALY is an Associate Professor of English and Women's Studies at Iowa State University. She has published numerous essays on Joyce Carol Oates, and her book *Lavish Self-Divisions: The Novels of Joyce Carol Oates* (1996) contains discussion of Oates's short fiction as well. Daly is currently completing two books: *Radical Revisions of the Wor(l)d: Father-Daughter Incest in Contemporary Novels by Women*, and *Authoring a Life: An Autobiographical Analysis of a Woman's Survival in Literary Studies*.

BARBARA C. EWELL is a Professor of English at City College of Loyola University in New Orleans. Her chapter in this volume grew from a National Endowment for the Humanities Summer Seminar for Teachers titled "Linking Region, Gender, and Genre in the Short Fiction of Kate Chopin, Flannery O'Connor, Alice Walker, and Eudora Welty," which she directed several times. Ewell's publications include *Kate Chopin* (1986) and the co-edited volume *Louisiana Women Writers: New Essays and a Comprehensive Bibliography* (1992).

BARRY HANNAH currently serves as the Writer in Residence at the University of Mississippi at Oxford. His short stories are collected in *Two Stories*

(1982), *Captain Maximus: Stories* (1985), *Bats Out of Hell* (1993), and *High Lonesome* (1996). He has also written *Power and Light: A Novella for the Screen from an Idea by Robert Altman* (1983), and his novels include *Geronimo Rex* (1972), *Nightwatchmen* (1973), *Airships* (1978), *Ray* (1980), *A Tennis Handsome* (1983), and *Hey Jack!* (1987).

PAUL E. JOSE teaches and conducts research in developmental psychology at Loyola University in Chicago. His interest in children's understanding and appreciation of stories dates back to work he began in a postdoctoral position at the Center for the Study of Reading at the University of Illinois at Urbana-Champaign in 1982. Since then, Jose has studied how children make sense out of short stories. His most recent work focuses on children's memory, comprehension, and appreciation of short moral stories and on adolescents' appreciation for "tragedy stories." Jose is also interested in cross-cultural comparisons of children's understanding and appreciation of fables.

W. P. KINSELLA lives and writes in Canada. He earned his Master of Fine Arts degree from the University of Iowa Writer's Workshop and has written a number of short stories set in Iowa, including those collected in *The Iowa Baseball Confederacy* (1986). He expanded an earlier short story, "Shoeless Joe Jackson Comes to Iowa" (1980), into the novel *Shoeless Joe* (1982), which became the film *Field of Dreams*. A humorist in the tradition of Mark Twain, Kinsella's short story collections also include *Scars: Stories* (1978), *The Alligator Report: Stories* (1985), *The Fencepost Chronicles* (1986), *The Further Adventures of Slugger McBatt* (19888), and *The Dixon Cornbell League, and Other Baseball Stories* (1995). His other novels are *Red Wolf, Red Wolf* (1990), and *Box Socials: A Novel* (1991).

CLAIRE LARRIERE has devoted her academic and creative life to the short story in English. Her 1981 doctoral dissertation at the Sorbonne was titled "The English Short Story (1945-1965)," and she organized the First International Conference of the Short Story in English, held in Paris in 1988. Larriere was the chief editor of *Visions critiques*, a yearly collection of articles on the short story, published from 1984 through 1991, and she currently edits *Paris Transcontinental*, a biyearly magazine of short stories in English from around the world. Larriere writes short stories herself as well as short story criticism, and she edited the 1991 collection *Victorian Short Stories.*

SUSAN LOHAFER has worked in the area of short fiction theory for most of her career at The University of Iowa, where she currently serves as a Professor of English. Her books in short fiction theory include *Coming to Terms with the Short Story* (1983), and the coedited collection *Short Story Theory at a Crossroads* (1989). Her articles have appeared in *Short Story, Style,* and *Visions critiques,* and she has published short stories in *The Southern Review, The An-*

tioch Review, Story Quarterly, and the *South Carolina Review.* Lohafer continues to be active in planning international short story conferences, and she was the first elected president of the Society for the Study of the Short Story.

GERALD LYNCH is the author of *Stephen Leacock: Humour and Humanity* (1988) and two short story cycles of his own, *Kisbey* (1992) and *Troutstream* (1995). He also has authored individual short stories which have been collected in the volume *One's Company* (1989). He currently teaches in the Department of English at the University of Ottawa in Canada.

CHARLES MAY is a Professor of English at California State University at Long Beach. His books include *Short Story Theories* (1976), *Twentieth Century European Short Story: An Annotated Bibliography* (1989), *Edgar Allan Poe: A Study of the Short Fiction* (1991), *Fiction's Many Worlds* (1993), *New Short Story Theories* (1994), and *The Short Story: The Reality of Artifice* (1995). Most recently, May has taught and conducted research in Ireland as a Fulbright Fellow.

SUSAN JARET MCKINSTRY is a Professor of English and Media Studies at Carlton College in Northfield, Minnesota, where she teaches courses in the contemporary American short story. She writes both short fiction and poetry, and she has published articles on Ann Beattie, Margaret Atwood, and Fay Weldon, as well as on film adaptations of fiction.

JOYCE CAROL OATES, who was born in Canada, is an associate editor of *The Ontario Review.* She currently teaches at Princeton University in New Jersey. A prolific writer of both short and long fiction (as well as essays and reviews), her short story collections include *By the North Gate* (1963), *Upon the Sweeping Flood, and Other Stories* (1966), *The Wheel of Love, and Other Stories* (1970), *Marriage & Infidelities: Short Stories* (1972), *The Goddess & Other Women* (1974), *Where Are You Going, Where Have You Been? Stories of Young America* (1974), *The Hungry Ghosts: Seven Allusive Comedies* (1974), *The Poisoned Kiss, and Other Stories from the Portuguese* (1975); *The Seduction & Other Stories* (1975), *Crossing the Border: Fifteen Tales* (1976); *Nightside: Eighteen Tales* (1977), *All The Good People I've Left Behind* (1978), *A Sentimental Education: Stories* (1980), *Last Days: Stories* (1984), *Raven's Wing* (1986), *The Assignation: Stories* (1988), *Heat* (1991), *Where is Here?: Stories* (1992), *Haunted: Tales of the Grotesque* (1994), and *Will You Always Love Me?, and Other Stories* (1996). She has also coedited the anthologies *Scenes from American Life: Contemporary Short Fiction* (1973) and *Story,* and she selected the stories and wrote the Introduction for the 1992 *Oxford Book of American Short Stories.*

IAN REID is the author of *The Short Story*, which has been in print since its publication two decades ago and has been translated into European and Asian languages. His more recent books include *Narrative Exchanges* (1992), *Framing and Interpretation* (1994, with Gale MacLachlan), and *Higher Education or Education for Hire?* (1996). He is currently a Deputy Vice-Chancellor at Curtin University of Technology in Perth, Western Australia.

MARY ROHRBERGER is the author or editor of a dozen books, seven chapters in books, and more than 350 articles and reviews. Almost all of her work has been in the area of prose fiction, the bulk of it in the short story. She is the founder and editor of the journal *Short Story*, founder and executive director of the biannual International Conference on the Short Story in English, and fiction editor of *The Journal of Caribbean Literatures*. She is currently Visiting Scholar in English at Tulane University.

BARRY SANDERS holds a joint appointment in medieval literature and the history of ideas at Pitzer College of the Claremont Colleges in California. His short stories have appeared in *The North American Review*, and his books include *The Sacred Paw: The Bear in Nature, Myth and Literature* (1985, with Paul Shepard), *ABC: The Alphabetization of the Popular Mind* (1988, with Ivan Illich), *A is for Ox: Violence, Electronic Media, and the Silencing of the Written Word* (1994), *Sudden Glory: Laughter as Subversive History* (1995), *A Complex Fate: Gustav Stickley and the Craftsman Movement* (1996), *Johnny Got His Book* (1997), and *The Private Death of Public Discourse* (1998).

ERWIN M. SEGAL is an Associate Professor in the Department of Psychology and the Center for Cognitive Science at the State University of New York at Buffalo. His research group has explored the cognitive bases of narrative comprehension and interpretation from historical, developmental, linguistic, literary, analytic, computational, educational, and experimental perspectives. The group has produced at least ten Ph.D.s in six disciplines based on this research and has published some of its findings in *Deixis in Narrative: A Cognitive Science Perspective* (1995). (Segal has two theoretical chapters in this volume.) Segal is currently working on a series of experiments in narrative interpretation examining the effect of modifying story tense and narrative persona. He and his students have also begun studies attempting to teach readers about some of the different ways in which to read fiction, particularly reading from a deictic shift perspective.

HILARY SIEBERT teaches courses in oral and written storytelling traditions at Radford University in Virginia. He currently serves as the criticism editor for the journal *Short Story*, and has essays forthcoming on "Raymond Carver" and on "Lyrical Knowledge in the Discourse of the Short Story."

LESLIE MARMON SILKO lives and writes outside of Tuscon, Arizona, which has long been the home of her Laguna Pueblo family. *Storyteller* (1981), her first volume of stories, has been widely celebrated, as has her subsequent collection of short fiction and essays, *Yellow Woman* (1997). Silko's novels include *Ceremony* (1977) and *Almanac of the Dead* (1991).

H. R. STONEBACK is a Professor of English and Director of Graduate Studies at the State University of New York at New Platz. He has published scores of essays on Ernest Hemingway's fiction and is currently at work on a critical guide to Hemingway's novel *The Sun Also Rises*. Besides publishing his own fiction, poetry, and songs, Stoneback has published many articles on American, British, French, and Chinese literature.

MARY SWANDER has published short stories, essays, articles, and poems in *The New Yorker, The Nation, The New Republic, The New York Times Magazine, National Gardening Magazine,* and *Poetry*. She is the author of three books of poetry: *Succession* (1979), *Driving the Body Back: Poems* (1986), and *Heaven-and-Earth House* (1994). Her artful nonfiction includes *Parsnips in the Snow*, a book of literary interviews named by *Publisher's Weekly* one of the best books of 1990; a coedited collection of nonfiction and artwork on Iowa's Loess Hills, *Land of the Fragile Giants* (1994); and a memoir, *Out of this World* (1995). A Professor of English at Iowa State University in Ames, Swander's most recent work includes two anthologies published in 1997: an anthology of garden writing, *Bloom and Blossom*, and an anthology on recovery from illness, *The Long Way Home*.

GAY TALESE has written his "stories with real names" first for his college newspaper at the University of Alabama in the early 1950s, and then for *The New York Times, Esquire,* and other publications. His works of narrative nonfiction include *New York: A Serendipiter's Journey* (1961); *The Bridge* (1964); *The Overreachers* (1965); and four consecutive bestsellers, *The Kingdom and the Power* (1969), *Honor Thy Father* (1971), *Thy Neighbor's Wife* (1980), and *Unto the Sons* (1992).

SHARON OARD WARNER is the author of a book of short stories, *Learning to Dance and Other Stories* (1992), and is the editor of the anthology *The Way We Write Now: Short Stories from the AIDS Crisis* (1995). Her first novel will be published by Dial Press in 1998. Warner teaches creative writing and literature at the University of New Mexico at Albuquerque.

STEVEN R. YUSSEN has been Dean of the College of Education at the University of Iowa since 1991, where he is also a Professor in the Department of Psychology and a Professor in the Program in Educational Psychology. Yussen is widely known for his research on children's learning and cognitive development, and for his work on metacognitive and cognitive aspects of reading. He is the coauthor of a leading textbook on child development and has served as Associate Editor of the journal *Child Development*. Yussen has been the recipient of numerous awards in recognition of his scholarship, including a Guggenheim Fellowship for his work on metacognitive development and a Fulbright Lectureship to teach at the Hebrew University.

ISBN 0-313-30396-7

90000>

EAN

9 780313 303968

HARDCOVER BAR CODE